Letters from an Actor

Letters from an Actor

ANNIVERSARY EDITION

William Redfield

APPLAUSE
THEATRE & CINEMA BOOKS
Essex, Connecticut

APPLAUSE
THEATRE & CINEMA BOOKS

An imprint of Globe Pequot, the trade division of
The Rowman & Littlefield Publishing Group, Inc.
4501 Forbes Blvd., Ste. 200
Lanham, MD 20706
www.rowman.com

Distributed by NATIONAL BOOK NETWORK

Originally published as a hardcover in 1967 by The Viking Press in the United
States and Cassell and Company in the United Kingdom. Subsequently
published in paperback in 1969 by Viking Compass, and again in 1984 by
Limelight Editions.

Library of Congress Cataloging-in-Publication Data Available

ISBN 978-1-4930-8460-9 (pbk.: alk. paper)
ISBN 978-1-4930-8461-6 (electronic)

♾️™ The paper used in this publication meets the minimum requirements of
American National Standard for Information Sciences—Permanence of Paper
for Printed Library Materials, ANSI/NISO Z39.48-1992.

To the only begetters:
M.R., B.R., L.R., and A.R.

Contents

Foreword

SAM MENDES

The fact that there were two books written about a single production of *Hamlet* in 1964 might give you some idea of its cultural significance at the time. I found this particular book (long out of print) at the legendary Strand Bookstore while living in New York twenty years ago. *Letters from an Actor* is a rare thing—a detailed account of a production and all its flaws by someone who was in it. But the book also manages a more difficult feat. Somehow, through the cracks, it provides a fleeting glimpse of the life of a supporting actor: the hotel rooms, the shotgun friendships, the late-night carousing, the desperate last-minute recalibration of performance, the delicate dance around the star, the endless frustrations with the director. More than all of that, it creates a dialogue with a long-dead author who seduces you with his genius, but then frustrates you with endless possibility.

The production itself was a perfect storm: the world's biggest male movie star, Richard Burton, recently married to its biggest female star, Elizabeth Taylor, electing to spend their honeymoon in freezing Toronto, while Burton stumbled and raged through a lightning-fast rehearsal period for a Broadway-bound production of *Hamlet*. This production would be directed by Sir John Gielgud, once the greatest Hamlet of his generation, but now in danger of becoming a kind of theatrical relic, a forgotten man. The two men—who had happily worked together before—imagined peaceful concord, but the reality was entirely more combative. The modernist versus the classicist. Sensibility versus sense.

So much talent here, so much experience, so many laudable motives, so many excellent ideas. Redfield leads you through the various ways in which they all fall short. The maze he describes is, in many ways, the anatomy of most classical theatre productions: compromises are made, ideas abandoned, misunderstandings ensue, tempers are frayed, missteps abound. And yet . . . something happens. Amidst it all, if you watch the production (thank you, YouTube) there are moments of magic, of lightning caught in a whisky bottle. It is all so long ago, and yet feels so deliciously familiar. Because, in the end, most of us who have worked on Shakespeare are part of a long and noble tradition of *partial* success. We might find moments which sing, images that endure—but ultimately the best we can hope for is to stand on each other's shoulders, trying to reach the text. We might get close, but these plays remain, for most of us mortals, tantalizingly out of reach.

There are also, of course, the wonderful particularities of the time and personalities involved: martinis, cigarettes, attempted passes, late lunches, paparazzi, crazy press speculation, and some hilarious Gielgud-isms. But beyond all that, there seems to be a search for something simply assumed to be important: to make a great and transformative production of *Hamlet*—the most famous play ever written.

Beyond everything, this wonderful book seems to say, the *search* is the thing. The destination might be elusive, but the journey is often thrilling.

To the Reader:

These letters were written before and during the rehearsals and engagement of the Gielgud-Burton *Hamlet*. They were rewritten during the making of three motion pictures (*Morituri, Fantastic Voyage,* and *Duel at Diablo*). They have since been expanded, contracted, edited, beaten with a stick, and told to behave. Whatever may have been in my mind at the moment of composition, the letters eventually developed a life of their own.

At any rate, they were originally posted to Mr. Robert Mills between January and August of 1964. Mr. Mills is a literary man who is curious about the inner workings of the theatre. For several years he has been after me to set down some of the thoughts and stories I have bandied about in conversation. The Gielgud-Burton *Hamlet* supplied the framework I wanted and I chose to write the letters to Robert Mills himself.

But—as you will quickly discover—the letters are not written to Robert Mills alone. Bob serves as a target. He is the "Dear Reader" who sounds so old-fashioned today. I wished to avoid the cramped and solitary tone of a diary, log, or journal, and that is the nitty-gritty of the matter. Besides, there may be a lot of Robert Millses in the world.

Although the letters are fundamentally concerned with a singular production of *Hamlet*, they also permit a number of side trips, excursions, and fantasies. The personalities of the theatre intrigue me quite as much as the technical details of production and I have allowed myself to continue talking long after leaving the stage door.

I have written extensively of John Gielgud because he is a great man of the theatre who found himself holding a bagful of worms. I have examined the brilliant Richard Burton in detail because he elected to play Hamlet at a time in his career when many a comparable fellow would have decided to take things easy. I have intruded Marlon Brando into my speculations not only because he is the most significant of American actors, but because he is just such a comparable fellow. In other words, Brando could have been a contender. And probably the Champ.

Most important, I have endeavored to describe the theatrical situation from the standpoint of the working actor. In the course of so tricky an effort, I have told stories from three decades as well as a few which travel some of the miles back to the original performances of *Everyman* and *Piers Plowman*.

What would please me most, of course, would be to hear a fellow actor say: *That's the way it is. That's the way it really is.*

But, if a non-actor were to ask: *Is that the way it really is?* I should be quite content.

—WILLIAM REDFIELD

The Cast

Bernardo	Robert Burr
Francisco	Michael Ebert
Marcellus	Barnard Hughes
Horatio	Robert Milli
Claudius	Alfred Drake
Voltimand	Philip Coolidge
Cornelius	Hugh Alexander
Laertes	John Cullum
Polonius	Hume Cronyn
Hamlet	Richard Burton
Gertrude	Eileen Herlie
Ophelia	Linda Marsh
Ghost	The voice of John Gielgud
Reynaldo	Dillon Evans
Rosencrantz	Clement Fowler
Guildenstern	William Redfield
Player King	George Voskovec
Player Prologue	John Hetherington
Player Queen	Christopher Culkin
Lucianus	Geoff Garland

Fortinbras	Michael Ebert
A Gentleman	Richard Sterne
First Gravedigger	George Rose
Second Gravedigger	Hugh Alexander
Priest	Barnard Hughes
Osric	Dillon Evans
English Ambassador	Hugh Alexander

Lords, Ladies, Officers, Sailors, Messengers, and other attendants:
Robert Burr, Alex Giannini, Frederick Young, Claude Harz,
John Hetherington, Gerome Ragni, Linda Seff, Carol Teitel

Prologue

Dear Bob . . .

If a man—in fury—hacking at a piece of wood, constructs thereby the image of a cow, is that beautiful? If not, why not? This ancient riddle, which attempts to define art through chicanery, first came to my attention some fifteen years ago. Was it in James Joyce or E. M. Forster? I cannot remember. But I remember the riddle because the answer is important. So important that I continue to stalk the question. My initial reaction (or answer) was: if the result is beautiful, the process of creation does not matter. The unconscious works in mysterious ways, the more mysterious the better. Still true, I believe, but accidents in art do not add up to careers in art. Sooner or later, a fellow must find out how to do what he wants to do and why he wants to do it. That piece of wood will not always yield a cow or anything else worth keeping. A work of art must be worth keeping. The riddle can be answered, but only on one level. What the riddle impishly implies cannot be answered with finality, which is why I still take pleasure in it after all these years. A riddle readily answered is no damned fun at all. As for these letters, perhaps I too am hacking at a piece of wood—with or without fury.

The first hack took place over three months ago when I auditioned for John Gielgud on the naked stage of the Golden Theatre. It all happened by accident but appropriately perhaps, since I believe theatre art to be the most elusive art of all and acting its most accidental factor. A hearing had been arranged for me but I saw no purpose in keeping my appointment, since I was already discussing salary with another management. Moreover, I'd been told that all the really good roles in *Hamlet* had been filled. Alfred Drake was set for Claudius, Hume Cronyn for Polonius; Richard Basehart and Rip Torn had been named for Horatio and Laertes (though these two were not finally engaged); and what was left? What especially that could interest me more than a leading role in a musical comedy? *Hamlet* could not possibly pay as well as the musical—although it surprisingly did—and the respective parts were simply not comparable. "But," said my agent, "go anyway. What have you got to lose? Gielgud should know you."

So, I went, feeling more than a little disgruntled and fully aware that a half-hearted showing might damage my future relations with Gielgud, should there be any. When I arrived backstage, a young and courteous stage manager showed me upstairs to a dressing room where two fellow actors were already nervously waiting. This was the #2 dressing room of the Golden. I had occupied it seven years before as the leading man of a disastrous venture entitled *Double in Hearts*. Another coincidence—or accident—which did not improve my spirits. I was handed a playscript as well as a list of available parts. The list was an onion-skin copy which bent immediately double when held by less than two hands. Typewritten upon this mockery of paper were the following characters: Rosencrantz, Guildenstern, Osric, Marcellus, Bernardo, the Player King, the 2nd Grave-digger—and on into oblivion. I leafed impatiently through the Rosencrantz-Guildenstern scenes, grumbling and murmuring to myself about wasting time and energy on silly, colorless parts. There is, you see, a profound weariness, a deep inner revulsion which proceeds from the playing of unrewarding roles. Note I do not say "small"; I say unrewarding. Since I have been active in the theatrical business for twenty-seven years and have endured every sort of degradation in every medium, I have gone understandably cranky. Well, perhaps not understandably, but definitely cranky. I did not want to play Rosencrantz and certainly not Guildenstern. I even found myself saying it half-aloud. "I do not want to play Rosencrantz," I whispered, but became aware again of the two actors seated close by. They both looked baffled and embarrassed. They deserved to. *What were they doing in my dressing room? Did they call themselves actors? I didn't know them. Not by sight, at any rate, and an actor I didn't know by sight was not yet a functioning actor. In fact, he simply did not exist.* Such wicked, uncharitable thoughts bobbed about in my mind as I waited. I looked at my watch and saw that I had been waiting for twenty minutes. Again, my thoughts turned fancy: *I don't like waiting. No one keeps me waiting. Not even John Gielgud. If I am kept waiting, I leave.*

Indeed, I was about to leave when my name was sounded. "Mr. Redfield," the same young stage manager whispered, appearing suddenly (like the elder Hamlet's Ghost) in the doorway. I had to appreciate and even admire his discreet manner. He seemed perhaps aware of my explosiveness and reluctance. Surely he was determined to keep me calm and orderly at all costs. Perhaps he even knew that I would not be such a potentially difficult customer were I to read for Laertes. And, too, what explanation could there be for his tact and *politesse* other than my reputation? Obviously, Gielgud knew of me and genuinely wanted to see me. Obviously I was being granted precedence over the two actors who had been waiting longer than myself. My impatience was being assuaged. Sir John considered me of some importance. Very well, then. I would unbend myself. But lest you begin seeing these grandiose thoughts as merely fatuous, allow me to suggest that they are also part of a subtle preparation which has been learned most expensively in the arena of the theatre. It is more like a bullfight arena than some people imagine. The danger to the body is slight, but the danger to the ego is mortal, and to be psychologically prepared is half the battle. I descended the metal staircase to the stage in a reasonable state of grace.

John Gielgud greets auditioning actors in a manner which other directors could well emulate. The house lights are half lit, thereby eliminating one of the actor's pet peeves: seeing merely a vast black void out front from which parental voices instruct him. An audience should be a void, no doubt, but a director never should. Moreover, there is no "wrecking crew" sitting silent and blank-faced in the fourth and fifth rows, waiting grimly to be shown what cannot and should not be shown at an audition: a performance. Most actors have learned to "perform" at auditions in order to reassure producers, directors, and authors who are normally more terrified than the actor himself, if the actor could only so realize. But such "performances" are parodies, and the director who does not invite them will be given a great deal more. Gielgud is looking for that great deal more. He stands alone, just below the footlights. Well in the back of the house sits one assistant who possesses a genius for protective coloration, thereby remaining invisible until the auditioner is almost done. Her name is Jessica Levy, and of her more later.

On stage there are two young actors to assist whoever auditions. This is unusual. Normally one reads with a stage manager who cannot read at all but is alarmingly addicted to upstaging *you*. Why, I will never know, since he already has *his* job and there are no critics in front to review him, more's the pity. While he upstages you, he reads in a meaningless monotone and manages to look as though he thinks you the worst actor he has ever encountered. Those of us who are experienced in the theatre have learned to ignore such fellows entirely, but it is not possible to ignore Gielgud's young men. They stand at either side of you and "feed." They are well trained. But before I knew this, I was introduced to Gielgud. He shook hands cordially, popped a mint into his mouth, and then asked a surprising question: "Now, then —which part would you like to play in *Hamlet*?"

I stopped myself from saying "Hamlet" and said "Laertes." He shook his head and said (in his strangely touching, reed-flute voice): "You see, we are doing the play in rehearsal clothes and without a formal set. I must force myself to cast according to type. I want a rather modern, delinquent quality from Laertes. Frightfully young. Altogether shifty—untrustworthy."

I argued a bit, but not for long. Gielgud's head-shaking was polite but definite. "Would you," he asked, "consider reading Guildenstern for me? Do you think you could make him rather a booby? Rather eager to please? Perhaps a bit of comedy from him at last. I've already chosen a rather sinister, Italianate Rosencrantz and would like something of contrast to him. Also, I must not have boys or fops in these roles. Hamlet must be played as thirty-five, because of Richard Burton, and you must be contemporaries of his. Do you see?"

I said I did, and so I read. Some five lines later, Gielgud turned his back and strolled up the center aisle. Momentarily disconcerted, I continued reading. Three lines later, he turned round and returned to the footlights with a smile. He stopped my reading and offered me the part. I realize now that his seeming discourtesy was nothing of the kind. He wanted to hear me for a moment without watching me and also from a distance. But I was astonished by his offer, and therefore said nothing remotely intelligent during the remainder of the interview. My confusion was, in one sense, unwarranted since precisely the same thing had happened to me once before. But it had been twenty-two years before, when Moss Hart hired me to play in *Junior Miss*. I could not help remarking to myself how seldom, during the intervening years, I had been in the presence of a man who knew exactly what he wanted.

Gielgud then made a speech not easily matched for charm in my experience. "I know," he said, "that you have another offer. I also know that the part I offer you is small. I do hope, however, that you can see your way to doing it. You would be a great asset to us even if we cannot be so great an asset to you. Will you consider it?" I said I would, but Sir John's good graces were not yet exhausted. "Since, as I mentioned, the production is in rehearsal clothes, with few props and little furniture, I must have the most vivid personalities even in the small roles—and correctly cast, too, as to type and quality."

"Do you think," I asked, "that I have a vivid personality?"

He smiled at me with, I believe, a full understanding of what was in my mind. "Ah, well," he said, "you most certainly do."

The negotiations began the following morning and were quickly concluded. Alexander Cohen is not an overly near producer and Gielgud, within very broad limits, gets what he wants. In the intervening time, I performed in a project at the Actors' Studio, stepped up my singing lessons, took a few speech classes, and read every well-thought-of interpretation and text of *Hamlet* I could find. Since there is not much in Guildenstern to think about and since final decisions about him would have to be reserved for the rehearsal period anyway, I packed my mind instead with the play and what history grants us of its previous productions. I met several times with the actor playing Rosencrantz, an intelligent chap named Clem Fowler, and we picked each other's brains to a point of exhaustion. My preparations are done. All that remains is the production itself.

But two days ago—exactly one week before the commencement of *Hamlet*'s rehearsals—I heard from an old friend and one-time co-worker, Marlon Brando. He was on his way to New York for a few days' visit. Would I meet him in his Plaza Hotel suite at 6:30 on Saturday evening? Drinks to be followed by dinner? The message came not personally but through channels, as becomes a super-star, but I intend no irony. Film stars are busier than you may imagine. As I hung up the phone, I found myself licking again at the edges of my riddle—like a tasty cake which might be poisoned. Brando, whom I regard as a truly great actor, is one who now hacks at a piece of wood to no visible purpose whatever. Friendship aside, it seemed appropriate and even valuable to see him again just before rehearsing *Hamlet*, since it is a role I believe he should have played: at least ten years ago, if not before. Tyrone Guthrie stoutly maintains that an important actor should play Hamlet, Benedick, Romeo—even Bassanio—during his early years if he is to grow properly, and I agree. Better a poor Hamlet at twenty-five than a bad Lear at fifty. Or even a bad Willy Loman. The actor is stretched by the verse roles, his muscles grow strong from heroic assignments. They cannot be fudged as naturalistic parts or film assignments can be fudged. More important, the borders of the individual talent are finally defined, and Brando—as a young actor—seemed bounded by no borders at all.

Since he was not only the most unusual actor of the postwar period but also the God Priapus of modern American playing (we see Brando in the performances of nearly every young actor who achieved notoriety during the 1950s and 1960s), it seems worthwhile to consider his alternatives as well as his talent. They compare surprisingly with Richard Burton's.

Though he has not appeared in the New York theatre since 1949, Brando remains the only American actor to be seriously thought of as Hamlet during the last three decades. Before him, there was only Burgess Meredith, circa 1935. Meredith never played the part either, until a quarter century later in a production which could not, for some reason, get out of Texas. But even more than Meredith, Brando was the American challenge to the English-speaking tradition in the classic roles. We who saw him in his first, shocking days believed in him not only as an actor, but also as an artistic, spiritual, and specifically American leader. Since he was not only truthful but passionate—not only Greek-handsome but unconventional—we flung him at the English as though we owned him and we all but shouted, "He does it without your damned elocution lessons, your fruity voices, your artificial changings of pitch and stress, your bleeding love of words, words, words, and your high-toned, fustian, *bombace* technique. He throws away your books and he burns your academies. He does it from within. And he is better than all of you!"

Unreasonable and overheated it may sound, but it was true. His

Kowalski on stage (forget the film) generated true mystery and overwhelming excitement. Surely there had never been such a person! But he was standing before us and we believed him as one believes an eccentric encountered in a subway. Uncomfortable and dangerous, perhaps, but *there*. Such behavior seemed hardly possible in a living room, let alone on stage, but it took place before one's eyes and could not be denied. It was a fire within him. Even Laurence Olivier, hugely accomplished though he was, could not produce such incendiary effects. Technically, Olivier drew rings around him, but Brando's heartbeat was stronger. Olivier could not match him, with all his voice and knowledge, any more than Edith Evans (great) could challenge Laurette Taylor (greater). As Richard Burton has said of Brando, "He surprises me. He's the only one who does." That he should say it of his film work leaves me dismayed, but on stage it was certainly true.

At any rate, in 1947 many of us felt that Brando promised a vindication of the American conviction and style. Perhaps we now realize that what we wanted all along was Olivier's training, will power, and intellectual application grafted onto Brando's muscles, sensibility, and passion. For passion, in Brando's dish-shattering hands, was a thrilling sight indeed. He has not matched it since. And on film he surely never will, for film cannot hold a great actor. Theatrically speaking, Brando was our candidate in the late forties (much like Kennedy, Roosevelt, or even Eisenhower)—he was American; he had brawn; he was beautiful; his head was shaped like a bullet; and he had guts. He would show those damned superior Englishmen with their rhetorical nonsense what acting could really be. If speaking was so almighty necessary, he would learn to speak. He was good in *Julius Caesar*, after all, except that it was a movie and few things can be learned from a movie, least of all by an actor, but it surely demonstrated that he could speak with clarity when clarity was required. He would take singing lessons if he had to (he didn't) and dancing lessons (he did) and fencing lessons (he did), but perhaps these things were not quite so necessary as the academicians maintained. Perhaps acting really did come from the soul and the English

were even more fraudulent than we suspected. Perhaps even
Talma was mistaken when he defined acting as "Voice! Voice!
And *more* voice!"

True, Brando didn't have much voice. It was pretty, in a
feminine way, but lightweight and mushy. As for his speech, it
was disconcerting even when his more spectacular faculties were
at their highest. During the run of "Streetcar," some dissenters
cried that he couldn't even be *heard*. His inaudibility has been
much exaggerated and was, in fact, more a conscious selection
than his detractors could concede, but it is true that a number of
words were woolly. No amount of rationalizing can get around
his love of mumble, but he had a way, in those days, of making
meanings clear without the help of words. He was like a prize
fighter: brutal, but strangely graceful; illiterate, but unaccount-
ably sophisticated. Hamlet would be a preparation, but the real
parts for him would be Macbeth and Othello. As for *Liliom*, he
would knock it down with one hand. He was born for it. Goddammit! He was *better* than those Englishmen!

But he wasn't. Because he would not or could not accept any
of the challenges an English actor accepts every season. He would
not study, nor would he attempt important roles. His final stage
appearance was in *Arms and the Man* on the straw-hat circuit in
1953. He played Sergius (by choice) and your correspondent
played Bluntschli. He was brilliant once or twice a week, usually
when nervous or otherwise disturbed. The remainder of the
performances he threw away. When I occasionally complained,
he would say gently, "Man, don't you get it? This is *summer
stock!*"

After one matinee in Framingham, Massachusetts, a delegation
of angry housewives accosted me at the stage door to inquire
whether or not he would emerge. I told them he would not.
"Well, look here, Mr. Redfield," their spokeswoman said, "we'd
like you to tell him that we're not a bunch of yokels. Does he
think we can't see that he's laughing at us while we sit out there?
Does he think we're deaf and dumb?"

I told them I would convey the message, but I knew it would
make no difference. By that time he was indifferent to the audi-

ence unless it contained Adlai Stevenson or Pandit Nehru. Originally he had been hostile to the audience, and when he was young his fury constituted a major part of his strength. Too many young actors are intimidated by the crowd in front. Truthfully, I think the young Brando was afraid of them, too (some young actors consciously cultivate hatred of the audience in order to counterbalance their fears), but being afraid only angered him, and so he came on stage to defy his tormentors—to pound the wits and wise guys into submission.

But by 1953 he no longer cared—which is the last stop on the streetcar. To try may be to die but not to care is never to be born. Indifference may fascinate an audience for more than a minute, but beware the Second Act. A number of critics worship boredom in an actor (they confuse it with relaxation), but the audience despises it on balance, and Brando can no longer fool a *theatre* audience for five minutes. And he knows it. And that is what is sad. Unhappily for the American conviction, Scofield, Finney, Burton, Richardson, Guinness, and Olivier are the remaining first-rank actors who continue to play major roles. Brando is nothing of the kind. He is a movie star. A little more than kind (Rock Hudson) and less than kin (Spencer Tracy).

But what will Richard Burton's future be? Is there a similar disillusion or even disaster ahead—since, after all, Burton faces precisely the choice Brando faced ten years ago? Will Burton confine himself to film and deteriorate as all actors who so confine themselves inevitably must? For the moment, the answer is obviously no. If only from Burton's impending appearance in *Hamlet,* we see that he is not yet afraid and far from indifferent. Some flame of ambition still licks at his innards—some sublime cognizance that there is something he can do which neither Spencer Tracy nor Cary Grant (surely the best of the film stars) can any longer consider—that "something" is called acting. Whether Burton wins or loses as Hamlet, he remains an actor: too big for films, really, and not merely a commodity, a product on a shelf—which is all a movie star can ever be, since nothing more is required and nothing else sells tickets.

Brando knows this, I believe. He knows it all. He is no one's fool. I believe he even knew it ten years ago, but it was too difficult for him and too expensive, and so he temporized. Brando is not to be blamed, merely regretted. The money he commands is irresistible, while important roles alarm him. As an actor, Brando must be either forgotten or fondly remembered.

But those of us who—for good reasons or bad—still cling to the theatre and who are unhappily not possessed of Brando's genius must, if we are to attempt important roles, compromise our intensities with the English methods of rhetorical playing. We must speak as well, move as well, fence as well, and sing as well. The last is not hard. An American actor (after ten proper lessons) will normally outsing an Englishman who has studied ten years (please exempt the Irish); but perhaps we can also bring some of Brando's early passion, spontaneity, and immediacy, which the English so often sorely lack. If Brando no longer functions as an actor, he can still do proper service as a spook. Memories of his theatre performances spook me even now, and should an especially gifted American actor one day combine a bit of his shifty and graceful boxing with Olivier's vocal preparations and overwhelming knowledge, such a dream chap could throw about some heavy, exciting weight. The English are not basically stronger than we, or even more talented. They *work* harder. They are hacking at that piece of wood with a purpose and they know what they are doing. Moreover, they are respectful of their audience's affections, and there is something to be said for that.

Our rehearsals begin on January 30 in Toronto. I shall write to you next from there.

Best wishes . . .
William

PART I

The Toronto Rehearsals

JANUARY 30–FEBRUARY 25

Dear Bob . . .

The *Hamlet* rehearsals are now nearly two weeks old. Fully realizing that I promised you (and myself) that I would write to you daily during the rehearsal period, I must now wring my hands, beat my breast, and finally eat crow, humble pie, and other disappealing dishes. All I can say in my defense (did you attack?) is that I write to you every night but I write on paper napkins in cocktail lounges and cannot very well stuff such stuff into envelopes and apply postage. Notes, notes, notes—stuffing up and down again—and there's no discharge from the war.

Do believe that I am coordinating all printable information and that you will finally be told every story I can remember, going back to Br'er Rabbit Meets Othello. In the meantime, I am too busy trying to figure out who Guildenstern is and why he thinks so little of me.

You will hear from me before the Toronto opening (February 26th). In the meantime, keep the faith because I seem to have left mine on the plane.

Best wishes . . .
William

Sunday, 23 February 1964—Toronto

Dear Bob . . .

Perhaps I am no good at short letters. To say nothing of daily dispatches. We are now standing, somewhat uncertainly, with three and a half weeks of rehearsal behind us. I have jotted down many notes and will doubtless integrate them into the letters which follow. This slapdash, catch-as-can technique I use, which combines notes scribbled on cocktail napkins (the bureau drawers of my hotel room are jammed full with paper napkins and I have no room left for my underwear), along with occasional sentences banged into my typewriter as I hastily ingest a continental breakfast—all this, you see, sends me into a panic and thence into a toil. Nevertheless, it seems best at the moment to set down a total impression of the month just past without resorting to napkins.

We will have our official opening on Wednesday night but face our first audience the night before. Some sort of gala preview benefit for blind Nazi Generals. Anyway, we're ready (mm-hm), except that we have had no appreciable access to the O'Keefe stage during the period of our rehearsals. *Little Me* (Sid Caesar) has been playing here since we arrived and ended its engagement only last night. Except for a brief Sunday afternoon, none of us have had any experience with this enormous and unusual theatre. Worse than that, we have been rehearsing in a practice hall—an arrangement which tends to deceive a director. From the very beginning, Gielgud has been no further than two feet from us—which makes things which are too interior seem manifest, along with much other confusion.

At the moment I write, our set is being erected. We are allowed to see it tomorrow but forbidden to pad about until tomorrow evening at 7:30, when we essay a dress rehearsal: surely a euphemism, since no lighting has been done, nor have any stagehands been briefed on the needs of our production. That we have been unable to rehearse in a proper theatre (*any* theatre) strikes me as a severe handicap. The next week or so will either bear me out or crush my argument. Never before have I wanted so much to be crushed.

As for the rehearsals themselves, there is much of interest to report. Highlights? It is all one great highlight. This over-glamorized, sun-drenched production faces a super-challenge. The stars? Gielgud, Burton, Elizabeth Taylor in the wings, and (one hopes) William Shakespeare.

But what is specific? What really takes place? Try a tape-recorder. What *I* can tell you is what reaches *me*, and that becomes downright personal. Still—that's the idea. Isn't it?

There have been many special moments. At the first reading of the play (more than thirty actors deployed around an endless rectangular table) Mr. Richard Burton read through the role of Hamlet as though fire were consuming the theatre and he had bloody well to get out of the building in order to save his hide. At the completion of our reading, John Gielgud asked for a total timing, since he is much concerned that the audience not leave the playhouse before Hamlet dies. "The rest is silence" (Hamlet's final line) is one which many theatregoers have never heard. And I mean many who have seen *Hamlet*. Understandably, too. Commutation is a problem for us all. Communication (sufficiently intense) may conceivably surmount commuting, and that is Gielgud's hope. Nevertheless, he began from the first day to keep a weather eye on the text, the text (emphasis deliberate); on its *length*, above all, without risking an emasculation of Shakespeare's intent. Once given the timing (three and a half hours), Gielgud ordered an eight-o'clock curtain and hoped aloud that we would not have to cut the play further. As much text as possible, as little bowdlerizing of Shakespeare's wishes, but get those poor commuters to their midnight trains.

Richard Burton said of his reading, "I have banged along so quickly because I am so nervous. In the recent production with Peter O'Toole at the Old Vic, they played the full four-hour text. Since there are no cabs outside the Vic in the late evening, a Londoner without a private car has to catch the 11:20 underground or he'll spend the night with friends. According to O'Toole, the final scenes were played not in terms of Shakespeare but the subway. Actors simply used their lines to plead with the audience to remain. 'Good night, sweet Prince' was not a farewell to dying Hamlet but a sad good-by to departing patrons. As for Fortinbras, the people who saw the O'Toole production wouldn't know him from the Second Gravedigger."

A joke? Yes. But I don't think Burton's rapid reading was without a hidden purpose. Nor was it due merely to fear. He is determined to give the modern audience a rapid, active Hamlet —gentle, yes, but not at all passive; instead, a throbbing inner rhythm which will last throughout his performance. The day of pallid, withdrawn Danes is past us now. All of us know too much, and Burton knows how much we know down to his marrow. He is not an explainer—nor any sort of pedant—but he is a deeply educated and remarkably unself-conscious man. He combines education with intuition to an unusual degree. He is a brilliant actor (in fact, he is *all* actor), but he is also an enemy to vulgarity and a man at war with boredom. He does not believe in a social elite nor will he take lodging in an ivory tower. He is a worker with a mind, but the worker remains. Happily, he is not snobbish in any direction. The kind of common background from which he springs sometimes produces, after success, a snobbism in reverse which is quite as pervasive as that of the Racquet Club: All rich men are lice. All middle-class men are the servants of lice consuming crumbs from the tables of lice. In other words, there are no good bosses and no bad workers. No such nonsense-inside-out from Burton. He sincerely likes all manner of humanity, and I envy the characteristic. He is sophisticated without being cynical. He is generous without aggrandizing himself. He is a first-class acting companion, and I admire his personality without reservation.

But what is most interesting of all is that he is, in many respects, wrong for this particular part. He is far too strong and far too well put together. His hope, in this production, is that Gielgud will soften him sufficiently so that a reasonable equation evolves. Then, too, the sheer beauty of Burton's verse speaking, added to his physical agility—the trick of "stopping dead" when surprised—and, more than anything, his absolutely tremendous stamina will all combine, I hope, in a performance so attractive, honest, and thrilling that a sufficient majority of observers will forget that it is not Hamlet they are seeing but, instead, an acting artist so bedazzling that he can pull off any interpretation whatever. One hard truth: the very notion of Richard Burton not killing a man who stands in his way strains credulity. Since this particular killing has been ordered by the earth-haunting ghost of his *father*, any hesitation at all causes the mind to boggle.

Burton is direct. As a tank is direct. Throw what mortar you will, a tank keeps coming until it is annihilated. So does Burton. I can imagine him fighting with a severe head wound. I can picture him with an arm chopped off fighting fiercely with what remains. If the other arm be chopped off, he would use his feet quite a lot and do much butting with his head. He is a fighter. He will survive. But to imagine him hesitating to punish an incestuous fratricide is to imagine Beowulf bursting into tears because he misplaced his poleax.

Yet Hamlet (in fact) is a bitch of a part. Almighty rewarding, but there are times when the game seems not worth the candle. This is especially true under the conditions of the modern American theatre, where one must play night in, night out with no alternating repertoire. Such an assignment would tax the energies of any actor—even a fraud. Actors like Burton are all honesty and inner force; they give a lump of themselves to each moment of stage life. Burton has played Hamlet on three different occasions, each time vowing earnestly never to do so again. I believe he returns to it not because it is an absolutely correct or even satisfying assignment for him but because heroic actors are rare in this particular era and some part of Burton's ego is at stake. As Samuel Johnson said of lady preachers, it is not that they do it well but that they can do it at all. Burton may not be able to play Hamlet, but he *can* play Shakespeare—and brilliantly. Moreover, who else could draw in the box-office gelt to make such a production feasible? Brando? Of course—but we have discussed his reluctance. As for whatever new, young people a John Gielgud would be willing to direct in so great a role —no such animal on this side of the Atlantic. The Actors' Studio endeavors to fill this universally acknowledged gap, but what has the Studio really produced? In the main, a rather casual cote of film stars—hardly the purpose for which it was created.

And so our theatre managers and theatregoing public must rely upon and return to Richard Burton: an actor fully trained for the theatre who, although now emerging as a film star for a variety of damp reasons, is hardly a casual one.

———•••———

Our rehearsals were curious from the start. Out-of-town rehearsals are unusual to begin with, but to rehearse in a hall attached to a theatre in which the production will open is positively eldritch. I have already told you that our stage was occupied by another show throughout our rehearsals; nor can I overemphasize my fear that this factor alone will cost us dear, but let me now go back to the beginning, where a good correspondent belongs: January 30th, 1964. A Thursday.

All Thursdays are dangerous. Astrologists and wise men have known this since Monday. Various mythologies describe Thursday as treacherous, and the actress Joan Hackett (who reads palms) will not read a friend's palm on a Thursday. A Thursday recollected in tranquillity will probably conjure up Macbeth's witches and cost the recollector his tranquillity. Thursday means agony; Thursday means pox. But I dare damnation even though I myself always think of Thursday as Prussian and full of *Sturm und Drang*. This is unfair and subjective, but if you choose a will-o'-the-wisp to guide your flight, you must not take things too precisely. Anyway, our rehearsals began on a Thursday.

With the exception of Richard Burton and Elizabeth Taylor, both of whom proceeded to Toronto by train from California, and Mr. Hume Cronyn, who is a native Canadian and arrived a few days early to set his mansions in order, the body of the *Hamlet* company traveled from New York to Toronto by plane and arrived in Canada well before noon. We were settled in our respective hotels before the lunch hour, some of us electing to stay at the King Edward Hotel, a stone's throw from the theatre, while others who can make their own breakfasts and tire easily of restaurants chose a charming apartment hotel entitled the Waldorf-Astoria, and grandly enough. Since I had personally notified our press agent (Mr. David Rothenberg) that I was willing to pay more than Mills Hotel rates for a sizable suite and fully equipped kitchen, I ended up with digs large enough to accommodate the Castro Brothers and their retinue. Unhappily, I also ended up a fifteen-minute taxi ride from the theatre; and, even though the Toronto subway was conveniently located and surprisingly rapid, my choice turned out to be impractical. But that is another and less-than-hilarious story, and so I must tell it to you when you are disgustingly drunk and not listening.

I had never imagined that we would actually rehearse on our arrival day, feeling positive that no sophisticated man would begin rehearsals on a Thursday, but when we got in, Mr. Seymour Herscher (Alex Cohen's business manager) told me there would be a press conference at 3 p.m. in the mezzanine lobby of the O'Keefe Centre.

He was right.

But I *still* did not believe we would *rehearse.* What I did believe was this: We would meet for the press conference. Once the press had been dispersed, Richard Burton would cry out to the entire cast, "Come to my rooms, all ye wearers of sock and buskin! Meet my woman and make wassail!"

This Elizabethan fantasy of mine turned out to be woefully unrealistic. In fact, we adjourned to the rehearsal hall immediately after sucking up to the press. But first, the press conference itself.

Detail #1: The O'Keefe Centre. Brendan Behan described it irreverently as a "sanctified garage," but I must demur. The

O'Keefe could easily remind one of a garage, but it is far from being sanctified or even blessed. Not one accredited saint stalks its vast corridors. There hasn't been time. What the O'Keefe *is*, in fact, is the most beautifully decorated aeroplane hangar in the world. And it reminds me of Old Man Rockefeller's Center Theatre. Young fellows such as yourself will not recall the Center Theatre, but I am within three years of being forty (which makes me old) and my memory is compulsive (which makes me tiresome) and I remember two things about Old Man Rockefeller: he gave away dimes to strangers and he gave away millions to the Center Theatre.

I shook hands with John D. Senior when I was ten years old, and he gave me a dime. He loved the Center Theatre, which was built as a twin to the Music Hall. The Center, however, housed legitimate attractions and lost quite a lot of money, while the Music Hall played films and made a fortune. Old Man Rockefeller put his money where his mouth was for many years and caused many an extravagant turkey to continue running at the Center regardless of the cost. *White Horse Inn*, *The Great Waltz*, *The American Way*, and quite a few other productions were kept alive far beyond their ability to pay, only because of the elder Rockefeller's slogan, "The Center shall not stand dark in the winter." To most young fellows of ten, battlecries such as "Don't give up the ship," "I have not yet begun to fight," and "Pass the ketchup" are stirring, but to me "The Center shall not stand dark" was not only a thrill, it was bread and butter with honey on the side. After the death of John D. Senior, John D. Junior tried ice shows and other such *kitsch* at the Center, but nothing could make a go of it, so he sold the site to U.S. Rubber, and all that is left of what was once a 3500-seat monument to theatrical art are the memories which bobble about in the heads of old-young actors like me.

I played the Center Theatre in 1937 when I was ten years old (that's how I got my dime); the show was called *Virginia* and featured a cast of two hundred and fifty. Quite a few paychecks to hand about in those still depressed days. Mr. Arthur Schwartz, who wrote the score, refers to me to this day as a nice little boy, which drives his wife crazy because she can easily see that I am losing my hair. Besides being taught to tap-dance backstage by John Bubbles, I performed several minor functions in front of the scenery. I hawked newspapers on the Norfolk dock; I began Act Two by rolling a hoop across the Center's infinite stage; I appeared as an upper-class British boy, all got out in blue velvet like something from Gainsborough; and I was literally "the kid with the drum" in the Spirit of '76. The latter trio was an integral part of the show's Grand Finale, which celebrated the American Revolution in song, dance, and chorus. The Spirit of '76 (myself included) marched along thrillingly on a treadmill; an enormous chorus of Negroes chanted thrillingly about freedom; the 100-piece orchestra throbbed Arthur Schwartz's title tune quite thrillingly; and finally the actor who played George Washington rode thrillingly onto the stage astride an enormous white horse. I tell you, it brought a tear to one's eyes and not a little dampness elsewhere, too. But on the night of our final preview, this stirring Grand Finale came a Grand Crapper. The gloriously maned white horse misbehaved. Now, many an animal has caused an accident in the theatre, but hardly while the Father of Our Country was in saddle and the Spirit of '76 danced attendance. And all those chorus members, too! That was an embarrassed horse if ever I saw one.

The following night was our official opening, with Hope Hampton and half of Broadway in front. I arrived at the stage door a bit early and saw the white horse all the way across the other side of the stage. It looked uncommonly still to me. I crossed the backstage area to get a closer look. Once I got within fifty feet of the horse, I saw that it stood not on hoofs but on wheels. Leon Leonidoff was taking no further chances. *Virginia* opened with George Washington astride a wooden horse. Ars longa; vita brevis.

This and like memories shuffled about in my over-active head as I was ushered through the glamorous lobbies, escalators, and offices of the O'Keefe Centre. How similar it all was! Even the decor, the carpeting, the murals! Was this a theatre in which to play *Hamlet?* Artistically speaking, would *Hamlet's* white horse misbehave and have to be exchanged for a wooden one—a safe but dead thing? Was all this chrome glamour appropriate to so timeless a work?

Detail #2: The press conference. David Rothenberg escorted me up the escalator to the enormous mezzanine lobby. Already I could see the vast corps of press photographers and newsreel cameramen clustered combatively around what was obviously Richard Burton.

He perspired profusely throughout an hour of flash bulb and question. He was also polite, charming, and articulate—greeting high and low with grace. Miss Taylor was not present for the occasion, which seemed to me a wise decision on someone's part. I greeted my old friend and ex-boss, Hume Cronyn. Several of us who were billed as stars were asked to congregate around Mr. Burton and chat casually while both television and still cameras ground out fifty times the film they would ever actually use. In my own case, I was aware that no photo involving me would be printed or published and that Mr. Burton's "supporting cast," so far as Toronto was concerned, included no more than Hume, Alfred Drake, John Gielgud, and Eileen Herlie.

Detail #3: I was partly wrong. Several pictures were printed of Linda Marsh, who would play Ophelia. One caption read: "A threat to Liz?"

Enough details and photos. The reporters were dismissed and we adjourned to our rehearsal hall for a read-through of the play. I have already told you of this, but something more should be added. After Gielgud requested the total timing and expressed pleased surprise that we were able to read so full a text in three and a half hours (we are almost uncut), he delivered himself of an interesting explication of what he intends by calling our production a "rehearsal run-through." I shall quote his remarks as accurately as possible:

Much fumbling with a fresh cigarette, a bit of squinting, and some polishing of his spectacles. Then, he twists his ring—a large one—which he wears on the third finger of his left hand. A short cough, a blush, and a brief, gentle smile. "Some of you may well ask: why a 'rehearsal' production? Why not merely modern dress? I think this: Like all of you, I have so often seen a final run-through, before the costumes and sets arrive, which had a drive and simplicity and . . . oh, an ease, somehow . . . which the actors never got back once the stone columns and marble tables came on and all the yards and yards of red velvet and blue silk and ruffs and farthingales were tossed about their simple bodies. So much for traditional productions. Very well, then, why not contemporary clothing and drawing-room sets? Because it's even *more* depressing really, and I've seen so much of it. I'm sure you have, too. Claudius drinks a martini and Rosencrantz and Guildenstern enter with frightfully tight umbrellas, to say nothing of their trousers, and Laertes offers Ophelia a Lucky Strike from a gold cigarette case and they both puff away while Polonius talks of the French. . . . It makes the audience uneasy when they've come to see Shakespeare. What I'd like to do is to *free* the verse from all its fustian trappings, but I see no point in obscuring it some other way merely to be modern. Edwardian productions and Victorian productions are perfectly fine, but they've been done to death in the last ten years and the novelty's gone.

"Richard and I have discussed this endlessly, and finally wondered if it wouldn't be a neat trick to do a run-through. As few props and gimmicks as possible. A pre-dress rehearsal run-through of a traditional production put on just before the sets have been erected and the costumes fitted. We will all have to be careful of what we wear, but I have so often been fascinated by what actors wear to rehearsals. Have you noticed that what an actor wears on the first day usually indicates how he feels about his part? One even gets a hint of how he feels about *himself*. Weeks later, we see the actors wearing things entirely different, and we all know why, don't we? It's a form of evolution in the shortest possible time. The actor changes his mind about his role so many times, and whenever he does he changes his clothes. I would like to keep this production lively and quick and still in rehearsal. Granville-Barker used to say that *Hamlet* was a permanent rehearsal, and I believe that. I would like you to wear what you would normally wear to rehearsals, and sooner or later we'll all hit upon something. I think it could work out quite well. Don't you?"

The company showed its approval by applauding and so did I, but I have a reservation. Not about the fundamental idea, which I think is bold and beautiful, but about the way it is being handled. The theatre is not a place so magical that wishing will make things so. To imagine thirty separate actors independently choosing not only the right sort of "casual" clothes for themselves but then being able to vary colors and styles properly with their twenty-nine colleagues is wishful thinking in the extreme, and I told Jessica Levy so over five weeks ago. To pull off such a feat in *Toronto*—with each actor four hundred miles from a tailor he trusts—is next door to impossible. The hardest costume design conceivable is what we call "rehearsal clothes"—more difficult by far than suits of mail, Elizabethan-Tudor, or Louis Sixteen. One man's notion of rehearsal clothing conflicts with another's, and it takes but *one* contradiction to throw the scheme off center. I am also told that our costume coordinator (note that she is not called a designer) does not go on salary for ten days to two weeks—a mortally false economy. We should all have been discussing these "rehearsal clothes" for months. Oh, get thee behind me, Cassandra.

Immediately after Gielgud's short speech, he showed us a detailed model of our set. It is a beautiful job by Ben Edwards, but it is a *set*, which surprises me hugely. It is designed to *look* like the backstage of a theatre, but it is demonstrably *not* the backstage of a theatre. We have wooden platforms and staircases to run about on, which is perfectly all right, and Ben has designed them ingeniously. God willing, they will suggest the sort of hasty structures a generous management puts up during rehearsals in order to get the actors accustomed to what is coming later on. So far, so good. But why not a black cyclorama behind it all? Or a plain brick wall with the steampipes showing? To have two loading doors at the rear is simply confusing, and to see sandbags hanging down in full view of the audience carries us back at least twenty years. Though there are sometimes sandbags in the wings these days, nothing would show *inside* the proscenium arch except counterweights. The model is lovely to look at, but will the full-sized set be delightful to know? Doubtless it will be impressive, but I have the feeling the audience will be confused. Further, if we have a set such as this, will there be lighting? If so—why? There would never be any but the most minimal lighting during a run-through.

It is my uneasy guess that Sir John's production idea, though marvelously intriguing and *young*, has not been completely thought through. Since we are rehearsing away from home base, those parts of the notion which are but half-baked will be all the more insoluble later on. I sincerely hope I am wrong.

But there was one element in Gielgud's words and demeanor which excited me, and I mean turned me on. Here is a theatrical gentleman in possession of a conviction. And that conviction is the Actor. First and foremost, eternally and always, when it comes to the theatre, the actor. For without the actor and without assuring the final supremacy of the actor, there is no truly great theatre. Oh, I can imagine affrighted scholars crying, "The *play's* the thing!" Indeed it is, if one refers to the modern, expensive and sophisticated show-business situation, but the playwright (with all due respect) is not the *sine qua non* of the theatre. He is not an integer. The center of the theatre is the actor, and every word Sir John said proved to me that he knows it. For example, if a group of primitive men sit around in a cave, can a playwright entertain them? Not unless he's an actor, he can't. Not unless he's a singer, juggler, tight-rope walker, dancer . . . some form of *actor*. Which means, of course, a performing artist. Someone who can put on a show single-handed. A playwright cannot do so completely, a director can only coordinate, and a producer is a man who raises money.

For this reason alone, actors should be handled not as employees (even though they are) but in much the same way a prize fighter is handled or a bullfighter. They are the creatures (finally) who must appear before the crowd and hold the attention of the crowd. Experience counts, intelligence counts, and courage counts most of all, but the final performance depends on a number of factors that have to do with temperament and security. The actor must not only "do his job" in a conscientious manner, which is what anyone must do; he must also trap his unconscious (a neat trick) and he must trap it *on cue* (a neater trick).

Other artists must trap the unconscious, too, but if things don't work out tonight, they can take another crack tomorrow. Or, at least, revise what they have done. But an actor? He is stuck on stage eight times a week and must put the play across whether he's got his stuff or not. A baseball pitcher (comparable fellow) remains in the game when his curve breaks sharply and his fast ball has a hop. In other words, when he can keep opposing batters from hitting. If he has an off day, the manager takes him out. But not an actor. If the audience begins to "hit" the actor, he must stand out there anyway—spewing out his words like a ventriloquist's dummy, knowing that he's having a perfectly frightful night, pretending to the world that everything is A-okay, and feeling those triples and home runs whizzing past his shoulders like enormous white wasps. A favorite reminder of mine is: eleven o'clock always comes. Actors must invent axioms for themselves, must embrace the most philosophic, Buddhistic sort of thinking if they are to survive their professional pressures. They are the gladiators of the arts. Those producers, directors, and playwrights who hold them in contempt or condescension are themselves beneath contempt. Still, a playwright contemptuous of actors is a rarity indeed. I have never met one. The play's the thing, all right, but there is no play at all without the actor.

As for Gielgud, I infer that it is this fundamental actor's power, this integral quality, he wishes to unleash and put to Shakespeare's use. He aims for swiftness, lucidity, and a clean, sharp line. Since he is dealing with a great play and an electric star, he gambles that the rest of us can be efficient enough to meet our challenges without the help of fur and flugelhorns; that we can be kings without crowns, soldiers without epaulets. Tasks such as these separate ambitious boys from men who want to act. The job of the actor is not to "make a hit" or steal the scene or show off his devastating charm. The actor's contribution is a marriage between himself and his material. It is a commitment to the *rightness* of what a playwright intends and implies. No matter whether the playwright knows what he has written; the actor must. This is the *real* contribution and, if the subject is any sort of actor at all (many stars are not), he must make such contribution even while knowing that a different approach might well secure him greater success. Personal notices and bravos must not dog the creative midnights of the actor. He must make his contribution fully aware that his own personality (important) could be better reflected in some other way. Some theatre people say, "Oh, just *do* it, will you?" (Eli Wallach says, "Do *what?*") or "Stop thinking so much. Just *act!*" or, "Acting is a simple thing—just say the words!"

Though it is sometimes valuable to simplify things and not worry too much, I doubt that acting is a simple thing or that a fellow can merely do it and "say the words."

Perhaps the most cynical actor who ever rattled rafters was the late John Barrymore. He reached a vertex of disenchantment after his opening night of *Hamlet* in London: a performance he claimed to have played ill from alcohol and exhausted from a full day of whoopee. During the famous "O, what a rogue and peasant slave am I" soliloquy, he painfully eased his body onto a three-foot wall, held his dizzy head in his hands, and dangled his legs to keep the blood running. He chose this new piece of staging, he said, not out of a spirit of invention but because he feared that further moments on his feet would make him vomit. Later in the performance, he actually darted off stage to vomit in the wings. On the following morning, he received even better reviews for his performance than he had in New York. Some London reviewers commented on the "brilliant leg-dangling," "the face in the hands," "the sudden running off, only to return immediately—his face ashen," as well as "Mr. Barrymore's sorrowful mien, his pale complexion."

Barrymore concluded that acting was tommyrot if he could go on half drunk, played out from dalliance, and still make the snobbish British critics call him great. He told Leslie Howard,

"My performance as Hamlet was the hammiest thing you ever saw." He told Gene Fowler that to be an actor was to be the garbage man of the arts.

Honi soit qui mal y pense. Barrymore's history of bad boy making good in the theatre is not unique. Just as good boy too often falls flat on his phiz. Let's face it: acting is an art defiant of logic. It comes from the soul and it is a slippery business. There are rules and they should be observed, but the rules alone will never make great acting.

Still, if *drinking* were the secret, alcoholics would be stars and Alfred Lunt (an abstemious man) would not be allowed to carry greasepaint to their whisky-sotted rooms. This is a theory, of course, but the word theory evolves from the same Greek root as the word theatre. Not only is there no theatre without theory, we will not normally see great performances from drunks. As for Barrymore, let us remember that he had played Hamlet for over 100 performances in New York with (I assume) some degree of sobriety. Surely he knew the sinews and strains of the role extremely well by the time he opened in London. More than this, he was overwhelmingly beautiful and richly endowed with talent. He was also, in part, an unpretentious and even diffident man. It offended his sense of justice when hard-working actors he knew could not get arrested on Broadway while he himself thumbed his nose at all the rules and regulations only to climb greater heights after every peccadillo. Because of his curiously egoistic modesty (and humor), Barrymore did not care to evaluate factors other than his drinking and insouciance. Besides— and lest we forget—the combination of drinking, super-sex, and insouciance finally did him in as both actor and man. The rules may not insure fine acting, but guzzling and humping won't either.

Gielgud's directorial approach seems concerned not merely with how good the actor *is* but with how good he might be: how best a particular talent can be used to *create* a part rather than merely describe it. This is no small ambition. What an actor *is* cannot change during a four-week rehearsal. Nor can any director bestow or bless an actor with extra dollops of talent or retrain the kinks in his technique in so short a time. But a director *can*, as it were, memorize the actor. He can "identify" with him sufficiently to bring the best from him in a particular role. Such an approach takes work and sympathy. It also takes *faith*, a willingness not to manipulate players as though they were screw drivers or the dials of a safe.

Gielgud's attitude toward me individually is gratifying but puzzling. He approached me after our first rehearsal to say quietly that he could not be happier with my attack on the role. "You and Fowler," he whispered, "are going to be wonderful. Absolutely first rate." I was taken aback by his praise, for I did not think either of us had done anything notable, other than to avoid interpreting these two evil innocents as fops or fairies. But the actor's psyche responds reflexively to praise, even when he fears it's undeserved. Strangely enough, even unwarranted praise sometimes stimulates an actor to finer achievement while an over-critical "candid" approach might freeze him. One of the trickiest corners any director must negotiate involves how frank to be with his actors. Shall it be the white light of brutal truth or the comforting mist of white lies? The choice depends somewhat upon the temperament, skill, and experience of the actor; but it also depends upon the personality of the director. Many directors have nowhere near the self-control the profession requires.

I later discovered that Sir John had not been just smearing me with butter. When my old friend George Rose arrived (he will play the First Gravedigger), he took me aside and whispered a surprising question: "What sort of production of Hamlet *is* this where Rosencrantz and Guildenstern are all the rage?" I laughed and asked him who said so. "John Gielgud, old sock. I saw him on the train this week end. When I asked him how things were going, he showed me his Gioconda smile and said, *Veddy well. Rosencrantz and Guildenstern are brilliant.* End of conversation. Not a word about Hamlet, Claudius, Gertrude. I mean, old sock, I *ask* you!"

Well, old sock, I don't know why he's so enthusiastic any more than George does. Granted the rehearsals were just over a week old when Rose arrived, I still felt at sea in the part as well as headed in no particular direction. Amazing, this praise from Caesar, for it was George Rose himself who told me (during our lengthy run in *A Man for All Seasons*) how crushing Gielgud could be when displeased with an actor. "If you ever work for him," George had said, "make up your mind to take nothing personally. He forgets how exalted he is and can be awfully sharp and impatient. But anything he tells you—no matter how harsh it sounds—will be true."

Harsh? I found myself longing for a bit of harshness and a definite approach to my role. But Hamlet waits too long in the wings while Guildenstern carries on over trifles.

As I have already suggested, Burton's driving, lickety-split first reading was due not only to nerves, though it was ingratiating of him to say so. He was obeying Gielgud's notion of the play, perhaps unconsciously, but he was also training his reflexes to a rapid, pounding rhythm which he can later—if necessary—spread out, as one might spread a thick jam on bread. But the thickness must be created first; the thickness within: the role must be compressed into Richard's fists and condensed into Richard's heart before he can thin it by knife. One cannot spread thin jam thinner. Burton, I believe, wants to keep the original mixture thick and rich so that he can later spread it tastefully according to the dictates of the audience and his own intelligence. The final result then (let's drop the bread and jam—I'm no longer hungry) . . . the final result may be slow or even measured to the *ear* of the audience, but for the actor it will be fast and ever faster within: a rapid, throbbing pulse . . . as in a fever.

———•••———

Note: I am entering some of these musings under dated headings because they not only bounce about in time, they were hand-written into a journal immediately after being hatched in my mind.

31 January 1964—late Friday afternoon

NOTES ON GIELGUD

Dear Bob . . .

There have been but two days of rehearsal and I've gone a bit breathless and juvenile, what with celebrities to the right and left of me. I'm used to celebrities, but only when they come by ones and twos. Fame in profusion rattles me a bit. Though I maintain a cool detachment in public, I sometimes pore over my private knowledge of the great and famous and am as avidly occupied as a small boy with a new bag of marbles. The current bag includes many a cat's eye and pearl-colored shooter. I once saw Henry Fonda get all excited at meeting Julia Meade. On Miss Meade's part, she later admitted she thought she'd faint. Fame of any degree does not make one immune to the old feelings of awe and delight. Not unless one *chooses* to be immune.

As for Gielgud, the man is *news*. In fact, he fascinates me beyond my wildest expectations. Example: while we confused and cerebrating actors stumble from scene to scene, struggling blindly for a specific sense of our surroundings, obeying whatever blocking is given us with a silent prayer that all will end well, he weeps profusely at our "beautiful" readings; he giggles childlike as Hume Cronyn conjures up invention after invention for what will obviously be a most unusual Polonius; he all but rubs his legs together like a drunken cricket when Richard Burton takes hold of a line such as "O, most pernicious woman!" and squeezes it juiceless as though he were strangling a wolf; and when Linda March takes her first, uncertain stab at "O, what a noble mind is here o'er-thrown," Sir John's forehead creases deeply between the eyebrows and tears gush from him like oil from the Oklahoma fields. It is her sensitivity which moves him. That she is self-conscious, tentative, afraid—these are human feelings which lie well within the compass of his understanding. They disturb him not a whit.

He smokes an arcane brand of flattened cigarette (imported) and is able to hold one of these smoldering white fingers in a corner of his mouth for minutes at a time without going either blind or into a coughing fit. His left eye, however, squints badly from the smoke as he suddenly stops the rehearsal, rises to the balls of his feet, and rushes forward digitigrade—one arm outstretched, the plangent voice crooning plaintively, "Try this! Try this!"—and then proceeds to rattle off King Claudius's entire first speech to the Court, beginning "Tho' yet of Hamlet, our dear brother's death the memory be green," which is surely one of the most convoluted and difficult in all Shakespeare. He uses the speech glibly and lightly, solely for the purpose of demonstration. It is a chastening demonstration indeed, since I am next to certain Sir John has never played the part. In the midst of chanting one of Gertrude's speeches, he will weep thin streams of tears and his face will turn red with feeling, and he hasn't played Gertrude, either. Once his point has been made, the weeping ceases abruptly and the speech is finished. He wipes his eyes with but the faintest trace of self-consciousness and the rehearsal proceeds. At times, he reminds me of Cyril Ritchard in one respect (*only* in one respect), in that Ritchard, when directing, ends all interruptions pleasant or unpleasant with the same adjuration: "Veddy well, then. Let's press on!" It is a reassuring sound, eventually—rather like the final notes of "God Save the King."

Undeniably, Gielgud knows perfectly well that some of us are moved when he demonstrates the magnificent words he knows as intimately as he would know a cherished friend; no doubt he also knows that he creates a moment of beauty. But to wallow in such ancillary beauty, to cover one's self with the emollient lotion of one's talent when the job to be done is as much administrative as it is inspirational is to extract only apricot juice from the rehearsal. Gielgud makes his point and gets off. Once he is in the wings, there is no need for further tears.

When he arrives at the rehearsal in the morning (he is always either on time or early, and so is Richard Burton) or when he leaves in the evening, he doffs or dons a Siberian-styled fur hat which looks suspiciously to me to be fashioned of sable. The look of it is ragingly chic. This devastating hat puts me in mind of an actor I know who is well acquainted with Gielgud. I ran into this distinguished acquaintance immediately before leaving for Toronto. He expressed considerable enthusiasm over my working with Sir John. He himself had worked under his direction a few seasons earlier and given one of his most successful performances. "You know," he said, "*his* Hamlet was not just the best Hamlet I ever saw—it was the best *performance* I ever saw. Something else, too: he's a marvelous director. He'll drive you right up the wall sometimes, but he's the right kind of director— an actor's director."

When I requested further details as to wall-climbing, my friend indulged himself in a fleeting grimace. "Well . . ." he said, "he loves to change things. He gets bored easily and often wants to discard something the audience loves. He doesn't give a damn about the audience. In the long run, as both of us bloody well know, this is the surest way to please them; but when you're trying out a show on the road and looking everywhere but in the bell captain's eyes for reassurance, it's only human to care about what works for the audience. Besides, *sometimes* they're right. Every now and again, I've gotten the same laugh in Eau Claire, Wisconsin, as I got in New York."

I didn't bother to ask him when he'd last played Eau Claire but confined my questions to Gielgud. We both ordered another drink.

"If you expect the standard British director," my friend continued, "all efficiency and a ruler across the knuckles, you're in for a surprise. What's hard is to get a run-through out of him, either the whole play or an individual scene. He wants to keep worrying over each little detail until he's touched all the bases. Then he gets bored with what he did yesterday and wants to change it again. How does that grab you? He's *not* just readings or postures or West End hauteur or any such business. He's down to earth and he loves the work and he can't settle for what will just get by. Time and again, he'd be talking my ear off about some little change or other and I'd say, 'That's wonderful, John, but for God's sake, let me *run* it.' He'd stall and pat me on the shoulder and say there'd always be time to run it later on. But there wasn't. Our first honest-to-goodness run-through was our opening night out of town. Still, as we both know, that can be a good way to work, even though it's scary. The polish always comes. The important thing is to make an honest pair of shoes."

I thought of what other friends had said who had worked with Gielgud: that he was a man of monkish discipline (an apple for lunch, broiled fish for dinner) and that he made of his theatre career a religious observance involving obedience and scholarship. One of these friends—a celebrated actor—told me of a "charming" letter he'd received stating that Gielgud had expressed impatience when all the publicity concerning Richard Burton and Elizabeth Taylor exploded in Rome. "Oh! Oh!" Gielgud was heard to cry. "I'm weary of Richard and these endless peccadilloes. It's all too fearfully immoral. Immoral, I say! Disgraces the English theatre. We're all grouped with him when he does these things. Oh, yes—we are!"

When I confessed surprise at this position, my friend nodded patiently. "Yes, of course," he said in his mildest Oxford don manner. "That's what's so charming." He meant it, too. He was not being sarcastic. He thought it was fun. He thought it was John. Quite obviously, too, Gielgud's disapproval was no more permanent than the swift rains of springtime. Having now met him, I am not surprised.

I have never met a gentler man. Or a more amusing one. Just before the release of Joseph Mankiewicz's film version of *Julius Caesar*, Marlon Brando said of Gielgud, "He's good in the movie —damned good. Now and then I can hear his metronome clicking away, but he sure knows his way around the meanings. I liked him very much. He made me laugh." When I told Brando that Gielgud had written an article expressing misgivings about traditional stagings of *Julius Caesar*, since even the best-intentioned actors, when draped in togas and seated upon marble benches, tended to remind audiences of so many softish businessmen in a turkish bath, Brando laughed. "See what I mean?" he said. "That cat is *down*."

In passing, it is interesting to note that the Brando performance in "Caesar," being a controversial one, has been staunchly defended by Gielgud and Paul Scofield. Since both men are qualified practitioners of the "traditional" approach, however modern-minded, their whole-hearted belief in Brando's talent for Shakespeare carries no little weight.

Perhaps all these observations helped me to observe Gielgud more efficiently during those first few days. I noticed, for example, how straight his back is and how often he stands with his surprisingly small feet absolutely together, as though he had been taught posture in a school for models. Much of his physical behavior resembles that of a well-behaved and self-possessed young gentleman of means. But the analogy shatters when he darts forward to demonstrate how he wants a scene to be played. Sir John speaks Shakespearean text and demonstrates its intention with a skill and drive and bright clarity which I imagine would have left Ben Jonson limp, let alone Shakespeare. Lee Strasberg once said, "When Gielgud speaks the verse, I can hear Shakespeare *thinking*." Mr. Strasberg is hardly addicted to the English view of acting, but once told a group of young students that he expected them to see Gielgud in *Ages of Man* and that, if they did not, there would be little point in their returning to classes.

Sir John is probably touched with some sort of genius, but genius does not normally stimulate me to speculation, since it cannot be held in the hand any more than quicksilver. More important than Gielgud's genius are the years of work and thought which drape about his shoulders almost visibly. He is a lifetime of experience and of practice. On the quieter, less electric days, he sits behind a rehearsal table and interrupts the staging of a scene with a murmured apology. He then removes his spectacles and rubs his reddened eyes. Perhaps he thinks for a moment. The silence is taut. Rarely does anyone move or speak. He then delivers himself of no more than a sentence or two, but these brief remarks are cornucopias filled with forty years of reading, studying, considering, and analyzing Shakespearean verse. The words are tightly packed, but Gielgud knows more than what can be gleaned from even the most serious reading, playgoing, and analysis. He remembers, bone-wisely, all the forty-plus years of playing Shakespearean roles; of directing his fellow actors in those roles; of observing Ralph Richardson rehearsing and playing this part, Laurence Olivier that one; of guiding or acting with Robert Newton, Wilfred Lawson, Diana Wynyard, Peggy Ashcroft, Celia Johnson, Lewis Casson, Sybil Thorndike, Edith Evans, Harcourt Williams, Gwen Ffrangcon-Davies, Alec Guinness, Paul Scofield, Alan Badel, Richard Burton, Carol Goodner, Noel Willman, Emlyn Williams, and on through every degree of accomplishment and competence.

At the center of him there sits a firmness, a certainty. Indeed, he is so fundamentally assured that he can admit the most serious doubts and confusions. At times, after delivering himself of what would seem a total idea, he will smile his Gioconda smile and say, "Of course, you yourself may find a better way." One might reasonably suspect the words to be disingenuous, but it is an attitude which can work psychic wonders on an actor—most especially a cagey one. Gielgud disarms the actor of his self-protective weapons. He does it by not pushing too hard. He combines an unspoiled intuition with a lifetime of learning. The *feel* of his rehearsals is most ingratiating . . . and persuasive.

The rehearsals are closed, by the way. No visitors allowed, whether local press or staff members of the O'Keefe Centre. Not even—at this point—Elizabeth Taylor, though she did arrive yesterday some fifteen minutes before the end of our rehearsal. Even this brief visit has caused some mild dissent.

As for Richard Burton, I think of him at this writing as reminiscent of earlier civilizations. A Rabelaisian man, yes, but also a Renaissance man. And that is interesting. For so was Hamlet.

> Best wishes,
> William

1 February—Saturday

Dear Bob . . .

I had dinner with Jessica Levy tonight. She is Gielgud's production assistant—an assignment which suffers from lack of definition since we also have two stage managers: Harry Young and Nat White. Jessica was Gielgud's only adviser on the casting of the play, aside from Alex Cohen himself, but now that rehearsals have begun, her only visible function seems to lie in the area of company morale. We shall later discover how highly or lowly such a function is valued by a theatrical management.

Later in the evening, we were joined by John Cullum (Laertes) and Linda Marsh (Ophelia). Mr. Cullum had chosen our first Saturday night as a fitting occasion to compete with Bacchus. He is an old-fashioned drinker—both hands and emotional. He drinks bourbon without branch water. You cannot get branch water in Toronto, and Cullum wouldn't want it if you could. A completely delightful young man, he works hard when working and plays hard when not working. He is also probably frightened to death, and he's got plenty of company, including me. All rehearsals are frightening, but Shakespearean rehearsals are doubly so for obvious reasons. And Shakespearean rehearsals for American actors are *triply* frightening since few of us have played him more than once. [Paul Ford asked me a few months later, "What the hell do you say if you go up?" * I told him that the late Robert Newton always said, "Is it not passing brave to be a king and ride in triumph through Persepolis?" which is not Shakespeare at all but a line from Marlowe's *Tamburlaine*. Ford grunted. "Can you say that playing Guildenstern?" he asked. I admitted that it would sound most peculiar. "So what do you say if you go up?" he repeated. "I *don't* go up," I said. "If I go up, I go off."]

We all ate together at a restaurant mysteriously named Letros (no apostrophe) which sits directly across King Street from the King Edward Hotel. Throughout our Toronto rehearsals and engagement, we were treated handsomely by this simple establishment, as well as by the staff of the King Edward. But more than the major pleasures of decent rooms and proper food, I shall remember the minor one of Letros' tireless pianist. He literally played "Melancholy Baby" and similar antediluvian tunes hour upon hour while seated above the bar, a single spotlight balding him. It was a charming, pre-jukebox note, and took me back to the days in New York when even Chinese

* Which means forget your lines.

restaurants had three- or four-piece bands for both luncheon and dinner. So much of Toronto is old-fashioned in the sense of New York or Chicago, circa 1935. Example: Yesterday, I wanted to purchase a cocktail shaker and a corkscrew (I drink martinis but, being eccentric, I shake them. Don't argue.), but I could not find either item in any department store, discount store, or drug store. Baffled, I made inquiries. A bellhop suggested a hardware store. There I discovered precisely what I wanted: an aluminum-copper cocktail shaker, marked $4.98. But the proprietor shook his head as I reached for my wallet. "That's too much for this thing. I've had it here for two years and it's the only one left. Give me . . . uh . . . two-fifty." I gratefully agreed, since I'd paid ten dollars for a far inferior one at Bloomingdale's six months before. The man then hunted around for a corkscrew (yes, he had to hunt) and finally uncovered the simple sort which any New York appliance store will sell for just under a dollar. It was marked 50¢. Again, the proprietor shook his head. "Give me a quarter," he said. I did so and then I kissed him. Well, no—I didn't *really* kiss him . . . but I wanted to.

Example 2: While shopping at Loblaw's Supermarket (a chain similar to our A&P), I inadvertently dropped a jar of shrimp. The jar broke into several untidy pieces. I immediately sought out a clerk. "I've made a mess over there," I said. The clerk replied amiably that it would be cleaned up in due time and not to worry over it. "But how do I pay for the shrimp?" I asked. The clerk shrugged. "But I *should* pay for it," I said. The clerk smiled. "Should you?" he said.

Example 3: I inquired of a cab driver about the subway system and he responded, "Don't take cabs from where you live. The subway's faster and cheaper." I told him that I hadn't the time to wait for subway trains. "You'll never wait for a train in Toronto," he said. I tested his testimonial several times and he was entirely correct. The Toronto subway runs every two minutes and most of the cars are empty. They are also clean, well-lit, and comfortable. Of course, I continued to take taxis because I am a self-indulgent slob, but that is not Toronto's fault, or the subway's either.

Back to our dinner. Following smash on the heart #2 (I was having stirred martinis), John Cullum began to show Saturday-night fangs on the subject of English acting. He is an old friend of Richard Burton from the *Camelot* engagement, but an *ambiance* of Burton idolatry which emanated from Miss Levy, Miss Marsh, and myself irritated him momentarily. "I love *Richard*," he announced forcibly, "but I resent Richard *Burton*. Not a lot, but a little. I resent Philip Burton, too, even though he's my teacher. I resent John Gielgud most of all, even though he's one of the kindest men I ever met and a great theatre artist. You don't understand, do you? I'm talking about *America* now and the *American* theatre. The American actor is an incompetent orphan being led about by an English uncle. I resent that."

If this be treason, make the most of it. Cullum meant nothing personal, and it was brave of him to speak up. In fact, I knew precisely what he meant. He stands four-square resistant to the unselective adulation of English acting which now rides rough-shod over the American theatre like a White Plague. So do I.

But he neglected to remember, for the convivial moment, that Burton and Gielgud have, in this instance, surrounded themselves almost entirely with American players. Eileen Herlie is an English actress, but she is also a resident alien who has played nowhere but in the United States for the past eight years. Dillon Evans is an English actor who wishes to remain on this side of the Atlantic for as long as he can be employed. George Rose is an English actor who has worked entirely in America for the past three years. With these "English" exceptions, the *Hamlet* company is entirely, utterly American (Richard Burton is Welsh, and do not ever call him English if you value your somatic well-being). I am persuaded that Alex Cohen and John Gielgud did not arrive at this pass by accident. Nor do I think Burton was uninvolved in the decision. To staff the current production with American actors was not merely a matter of public relations; it was a matter of financial recognition and successful production.

A Man for All Seasons imported four English actors into New York, one of whom left the company after two weeks of the

Broadway engagement. It was a decidedly English play performed almost entirely by Americans. It ran twenty-one months
in New York and one year on the road, returning something
over five hundred per cent to its investors *without* a motion-
picture sale. *The Rehearsal*, a very fine play, was entirely staffed
by English actors, received splendid reviews, and has closed after
a depressingly short run, losing nearly all of its capitalization.
Chips with Everything, a good play, was played entirely by
Englishmen, received excellent reviews, and did not regain its
investment, though it eked out a one-season run.

This *Hamlet* is intended to be a highly modern, fast-moving,
crowd-pleasing production and will likely be one of the most
successful Shakespearean productions of all time, even though
the American actors playing in it will be largely ignored or
criticized no matter what they do. But when it comes to the
public acceptance of such a production, American actors are a
flat necessity. British supporting actors, by and large, tend to be
stodgy and dull, and everyone seems to know it but American
critics. Granted, an American company must be carefully guided
by an English scholar such as Gielgud, for only the English
have had sufficient experience with Shakespeare's plays; but the
staffing of this company as it is can hardly be accidental. The
powers behind the production know precisely what they are
about. And Mr. Cullum's irritation, though quite understandable,
is unjustified in the present instance.

Best Wishes,
Wm.

2 February—Toronto

Dear Bob . . .

After today's somewhat discouraging rehearsal, I took advantage of Jessica Levy's hospitality and went to her hotel room
to make myself a drink. Jessica had to remain at the O'Keefe to
complete Gielgud's prompt book and type up the day's cor-
respondence. A director's prompt book should record the daily
alterations in blocking as well as whatever cuts and excisions
have been settled upon. Shakespeare has to be cut out of town

like any other Broadway-bound playwright. Each rehearsal day leads to snippets and droppings here and there.

Linda Marsh accompanied me to Jessica's room, and I immediately asked her to get as naked as possible. She refused, saying that she hardly knew me, and so we fell to talking. Love is not all, you see, and I accept rejection as well as the next man: thin-lipped and shaking with rage. In any case, Linda's room is next door to Jessica's. After she slapped me, she went inside to get into something uncomfortable.

Mr. Clem Fowler-Rosencrantz arrived a moment later (I'm not the only one Jessica is nice to) and we discussed stopping smoking. Since he has succeeded in doing so and I haven't, the conversation was a bit one-sided. When Linda returned, she seemed glum and was even brusque. Tension mounted furtively and we exchanged sharp words. I mention this unimportant tiff only to illustrate a point: actors often go a bit gritty during rehearsals. Especially if they like each other. Sometimes they snap and nip and challenge in much the same way relatives do. I like Linda Marsh and I think she likes me. Oddly enough, such flashes of temper can be a sign of mutual trust. What is strangest of all is that many actors, like Linda and myself, have barely met before rehearsals begin, and when these internecine clawings and scrapings erupt, the parties concerned have been acquainted for no more than a week to ten days. Rehearsing a play is an utterly emotional matter. The director and stage managers should remain eternally cool and above the crowd, but actors must be permitted to rant, to rave, to fulminate against the gods, if necessary, both in rehearsal and out.

Of course, there is such a thing as "carrying on," and it should be gently-firmly suppressed, but a few excesses are par for the course and must be winked at. Otherwise, the actor may never come to life. Though much of this depends on the temperament of the individual actor, I used the word "permitted" above and not by accident. A rehearsal atmosphere which does not *permit* of temperament is a bad one.

The theatre is not a temple of temperance, nor a Board Meeting of General Motors. Common sense and cool heads are important factors in any enterprise, but they are not enough in the theatre. Inspiration, on the other hand, is the word we often hear (and use) to describe creative process. I am not addicted to its implications. "Inspiration" too often connotes fragile-winged fairies and a good deal of weeping. *A*spiration, then! What about that? Well—no. For I find that aspiration, like inspiration, tends to energize people, which is good, but in the wrong direction, which is not. The aspirant begins to think he *is* Napoleon merely because he *aspires* to be Napoleon. He begins to value sentiment above reality. He *feels* something and therefore assumes that a tree of life is growing within him. Usually, he is mistaken.

Though an actor needs a warm heart, his mind must remain cold—even skeptical. Many an *inspired* or aspiring actor grows so full of himself that he finally resembles nothing so much as Vincent Price laying hands on the Little Lame Prince to cure his twisted leg . . . the Prince's leg, I mean, not Vincent's. So far as I know, Vincent's *legs* are all right. It's his *hands* I'm worried about.

At any rate, let me sum up the notion this way: Rasputin— *that* dirty old thing—is "inspired." He is also as nutty as a fruit cake and I don't trust him. Mozart may very well have been "inspired" and there is a bookful of evidence to indicate that he was nutty, *but* . . . he knew a ferocious amount about music and I trust him. Rasputin *aspired* to be in touch with God out of an *inspiration* for black magic. Mozart merely tried to write good music, and I don't think he thought much about inspiration *or* aspiration. What he *did* think about was how to get more heat in that damned garret, and how nice it would be to own a good scarlet coat. These are eminently trustworthy ambitions, and even the nuttiest among us must put our work in such a context or it will all get too "inspired" for popular consumption.

Once an actor steps on stage, he must be trustworthy. The audience can spot a charlatan or a nut as quickly as they would spot one on the street. They may accept him in the theatre, out of sheer boredom, but they will never accept him in their hearts. All this and so much more must be kept in mind by the actor while he digs around in himself for a suitable stage image.

But it *is* necessary to get angry, to bring one's blood to a boil, to think a lot, to tear at one's hair, to plunge deeply into one's throat for new sounds, new vibrations, and deeply into one's heart for new meanings. It is necessary to figure things out—to worry, to sweat, to strain. If this be inspiration, I'm for it. But I call it hard work and emotional nudity. Politeness in the theatre can be an enemy to excitement and creativity. Don't ask me to prove the point. I can't. But I know it to be true.

In any case, the fang-and-talon part of my exchange with Linda Marsh connoted nothing serious on my part, nor anything personal on hers. Simply speaking, she was upset and needed to lash out at something, and I knew why, for I was upset too. Sir John had put us through a conventional and rather impatient day —the first I could truly call "disappointing." Rumors are quietly circulating that one of Gielgud's oldest and dearest friends is dying in London and that Sir John cannot abide the thought of his old acquaintance passing unattended by himself. Whether the rumors are true is none of our business, but such a thing can deeply affect the producing of a play.

Gielgud seemed vague today—distracted and tearful—even rather bored by our crucial early efforts to avoid a pat staging of an intelligent first reading. Intelligence is a curious factor in the theatre. Point one: it is not enough. Point two: what seems "intelligent" during the first days must be carefully nurtured and tutored over the first week or it will soon be yesterday's intelligence. By the second week, it will no longer be news; by the third, it will be moribund, and by opening night it will no longer be intelligent. The most important days of rehearsal are the first week to ten days. Once the "tone" is set, everything else follows with a dead certainty.

Today's "tone" was sour—and confusing. Our ship was Captainless. As soon as one drink got comfortably down, Fowler and I fell inevitably into an exchange of Performers' Anxieties—Out-of-Town Variety, Severe-type Syndrome. Both of us feel, despite Gielgud's compliments and enthusiasm, that we are working ably but not really well, not deeply. Rosey and Guildy are *over there* and we are shooting ourselves at the parts like arrows. The arrows are perhaps well-feathered and professionally wrought and even the target is pretty, but acting is not archery. It is not a sport. It is an Art. It is Zen Buddhism. An actor must be both arrow *and* target. He must be *inside* his part, not standing in the hallway and thumping on the door. While Clem and I rehearse our lines, our scenes—which are so short, so small, and therefore require the utmost concentration—no blood courses through our veins. We speak out forcibly and distinctly, but we learn nothing new and we are headed nowhere. During all this, Sir John chews endless mints and Life Savers, weeps a bit, chain-smokes his exotic cigarettes, and nods and smiles with unvarying approval. "It's going to be excellent, that scene—just excellent. Oh, do believe me—it's quite true."

I am baffled. So is Fowler. Richard Burton is not baffled. He agrees with Gielgud. That baffles me doubly.

A bit over an hour had passed when Jessica returned from her chores. Linda Marsh again retired to her room and we began to suspect she had a body in there. Ignoring her suspicious behavior, Clem and I discussed our misgivings with Jessica. She was amused by our earnest terror and told us over and again how solid we were. When we insisted on denigrating our work further, she raised both hands to call a halt. "Are you trying to tell me," she cried, "that you do not trust John Gielgud?"

She had won the argument. But I was no less afraid. A moment later, the telephone rang. Jessica handed it to me and said it was Bob Wilson calling. Statuesque and intelligent, he is Richard Burton's dresser and catches all. Having worked with Burton for several years, he no longer functions merely as a valet, but doubles and triples as diplomat, strategist, bartender, part-time secretary, and full-time factotum. He asked if I could join Mr. Burton and Miss Taylor for a drink as soon as possible. I said I could and went alone to the Royal Suite (no joke intended; such was the official name of their rooms) after apologizing to Jessica, Clem, and Linda for being chosen jester of the night.

My exclusivity was short-lived. All three arrived ten minutes later. Burton was not yet in sight. During the interim, I was presented to Miss Taylor, whose clothing and make-up surprised me. She wore an enormous full-sleeved sweater fashioned from angora wool and dyed a flattering shade of orchid. Her eye make-up was heavy and Cleopatra-ish, but she was otherwise un-painted. From the waist down, she might have been naked so far as I noticed straight off, for I was fixed on the rest of her. Later, I saw that she was wearing tight-fitting purple slacks which looped beneath her arches, stretch-style. For some reason, her shoes escaped me. I believe they were jester boots crafted from soft leather and dyed yet another shade of purple. I do know that nothing mitigated the sublimely purple effect except for a double strand of pearls. They were white. The over-all impression would not have driven a fashion model mad with jealousy but for one as yet unmentioned factor: the lady was a knockout.

She stood up when I entered, which confused me, and insisted on mixing me a drink. "You needn't," I said. "I want to," she said and asked me for my preference. When I told her, with some embarrassment, that I drank Beefeater martinis, not stirred but shaken, and poured into a frozen glass with no olive or lemon, she smiled.

"You shall have one," she said and left the room. Moments later, she returned with my drink on a small tray. More to relieve my discomfort than anything else, I spoke to her of mutual friends, all of whom had begun acting as children: Joan Lorring (who attended school with her at M-G-M); Roddy McDowall, and Montgomery Clift. She got the message. "Were you a child actor?" I said that I had been. "But not in films?" I told her I had made but one film as a child and that in New York while I was playing in *Our Town* at night. "You worked only in the theatre?" And radio, I said. She nodded and pointed to my all but untouched drink. "Your frozen glass," she said, "is no longer frozen."

At that moment, Richard Burton appeared and asked me what I was drinking. "It is," I said, "a Beefeater martini, shaken—not stirred—with no olive or lemon and poured into a glass which is no longer frozen."

"Whisky is simpler."

I conceded that it was, but said that when I drank whisky I drank too much.

Burton pointed to my martini. "Those are potent?"

"Lethal."

He took a taste and scowled. "Couldn't bear it. I go raving mad on gin. Uncontrollable. Vodka's the thing—or whisky. Or tequila when I'm in Mexico. Do you like tequila?"

"Considerably. But when I drink it, I drink too much."

Burton poured himself a drink. "Martinis for sobriety. I wonder if you could start a movement."

"He was a child actor, Richard," Miss Taylor said.

Burton looked surprised. "Is there a connection between the two, or are you changing the subject?" Miss Taylor took a sip of her drink, which was (and always is) champagne. "Yes," Burton continued, "I had heard that ugly rumor. So it's true then that both you and my bride-to-be were neurotic little show-offs while the rest of us grew up normally?"

I replied that I was no longer little, and Burton was kind enough to smile. "Well—you've survived it," he said. "Not many do. There's Elizabeth and Roddy and Monty and a few others, but not many. You're a bloody good actor, by the way. Have I told you that?"

I said that he had.

"Bloody good. Damned good."

I was about to request that he repeat such sentiments as often as possible when the others arrived. The evening evolved into a dinner party, drenched in tales of the theatre, most of them too brief and parochial to be printed here, but the spontaneity of the affair still impresses me. I do not think they intended to entertain us so lavishly. It merely happened. In less than an hour, a splendid table was set, complete with wine and champagne. I talked too much, but neither Burton nor Clem Fowler took a back seat. Throughout the evening, it would have been a neat trick for the ladies to get a word in edgeways. Happily for the gentlemen, none of them tried.

Burton's tales are expertly garnished and beautifully dressed. He does them to a turn, as a good chef does a soufflé. If there are traces of rodomontade in his details, so much the better. I prefer line drawings to photographs. I have the feeling that Burton does also. At least, such a conviction shines through his stories, all of which are amusing, all of which bring his subjects instantly to life before one's eyes, thick-pulsed and electric. Then, too, perhaps some of the stories are factually true. Some of mine are. Some—perhaps—are not. Sometimes the teller himself doesn't know. Does it matter? I don't think so. The prominent tales of that memorable evening concerned Sir Ralph Richardson (whom I do not know), who is surely the English theatre's favorite eccentric as well as one of its two or three finest actors. Here are a pair of his legends.

Some thirty years ago, Richardson was rehearsing a play with a man whom I shall call Cyril Sunt. The latter was the last of the old-time directors on the British side of the Atlantic. By "old-time," I mean abusive, cruel, sarcastic, and contemptuous of actors. He had (and has) his American equivalents, of course, but let them be nameless here.

Richardson was an important actor at the time but not yet a film star nor one of the classic theatre's leading lights. In this particular production, it had been decided to open "cold," which means no tour of the provinces and no previews before the opening performance. Throughout the rehearsal period, Sunt was nasty and autocratic with most of his actors, but left Richardson strictly alone. In fact, practically no conversation, pleasant or otherwise, passed between them. "Good morning, Mr. Richardson"; "Good morning, Mr. Sunt"; "Good night, Mr. Richardson"; "Good night, Mr. Sunt" was about the long and short of it. The night before the play opened, the cast performed a dress rehearsal with only Sunt out front. He stopped the performance quite often, either to change entrances and exits, lighting and cues for the stage manager, or merely to abuse the skills and talent of one actor or another. Late in the evening—midnight or thereabouts—Richardson made an exit which Sunt considered important. He stopped the performance and asked the stage manager to bring Mr. Richardson back on stage. A moment later, Richardson stood soberly before the footlights.

Sunt rose from his seat and ambled down the center aisle. When he reached the first row, he spoke softly. "Mr. Richardson," he said, "do you think it possible that at some moment between now and tomorrow evening you could learn to leave the stage like a gentleman?"

Richardson gazed blandly back at his director and then all but murmured, "Yes. I believe I could." He thereupon turned away, left the stage, continued on past the wings, the dressing rooms, the stage doorman, the alleyway, took a taxi for the railroad station, a train to his country home, told his wife what had taken place, instructed her not to call him to the phone for any purpose, and never opened in the play. For several days, his telephone rang hourly, but only Mrs. Richardson heard the pleadings, cajolements, blandishments, and inducements offered by producers, playwright, and fellow actors. It would seem perhaps cruel to deprive one's innocent colleagues of employment, but if the play had been really good they would have gotten someone else. In any case, they didn't. The play closed before it opened, and Sunt's directorial charisma sustained a smarting blow. Richardson—single-handed—caused what amounted to a silent revolution in the treatment of English actors by directors. Of course, in the present era, such a *coup de force* would be impossible. Either British Equity or American Equity would insist the actor return until a suitable replacement be found, but Richardson's gesture was a majestic one, and it did not surprise his fellow players when he began to bring more and more of that majesty onto the stage.

This story reminded Richard Burton of another: "Rafe is one of life's truly memorable characters. He's a dear, really, but if he makes up his mind to something, his hauteur can alarm even his peers. When Tony Guthrie produced *Othello*, with Richardson in the title role and Olivier as Iago, a few pre-production conferences took place between Guthrie and Olivier. For years, scholars have debated Iago's motives. To many, Othello's failure

to name Iago his lieutenant, or even the casually mentioned possibility of Emilia's adultery with the Moor, do not seem sufficient
motives for Iago's relentless malevolence. Guthrie and Olivier
hashed it over for days and could come up with but one answer:
Iago was homosexual. In fact, he was in love with Othello.

"Guthrie determined to build his entire production around this
novel conception, and Larry went fiercely to work to bring off
one of his *tour-de-force* characterizations. But both agreed to say
not a word to Richardson about the matter during rehearsals.
They also agreed that at one moment toward the end of the play
Iago should embrace Othello and kiss him. But obviously it would
be best to hold off with this piece of business until the last minute.
At the dress rehearsal, however, time had run out, for even
though Olivier had minced about to some extent during rehearsals Richardson seemed either not to notice or not to care.
Finally, the die was cast. At the proper moment, Olivier embraced Rafe and kissed him, chocolate make-up and all. Richardson did not say his next line. He disentangled himself from his
friend's arms and stepped down to the footlights. 'Tony!' he
called. 'What was the meaning of that?' Guthrie came running
down the aisle and said, 'Well, Rafe, we didn't want to tell you
sooner, but . . . well, Rafe, I never *believe* Iago on stage somehow . . . Larry and I talked it over and Rafe . . . well, Rafe
. . . he's a *poof*—that's all there is to it. There's no other explanation. Iago is a poof.' Richardson said nothing but turned to
Olivier with a mad glint in his eye. 'He's a poof, Rafe,' Olivier
said. 'He has to be.' Richardson headed for the wings. 'Where
are you going?' both men cried. 'I'm going home,' Richardson
replied, 'until both you lads have come to your senses.' He didn't
come back for two days. But this time—at least—he did go on
for the opening. He even allowed the kiss."

Apparently Richardson's first experience with stage-leaving
got into his blood. According to many actors who have worked
with him, he can be blood-curdlingly grand. During rehearsals
for *Waltz of the Toreadors,* Harold Clurman, who was directing,
said to Richardson, "At this point, I'd like you to sit down."
Richardson replied, "I don't think that will be necessary."

Among English stars, both male and female, he is not alone in this attitude. Dame Edith Evans once found herself working with an eager young director who'd had very little West End experience. The young man came up with quite a few suggestions on the first day of rehearsal and Miss Evans, whose upper vocal register can easily shatter crystal, finally used it: "Young man!" she cried. "You must keep entirely silent for the first two weeks of these rehearsals until one of us *asks* for you!" The young fellow protested that he was the director, after all. How could he possibly sit out front in silence? What did she expect him to do? Dame Edith considered the question for a moment. Then she found her answer: "If you just sit quietly for a bit, never fear. We're bound to find *something* for you to do!"

Such imperious employees could hardly fail to be popular with their colleagues. We could have continued into the small hours, telling tales of them and others. But a decent time of departure arrived and someone was wise enough to point it out. We thanked Richard Burton and Elizabeth Taylor for a generous evening.

It seems to me that Taylor is a more striking beauty in person than on the screen. Her face is lozenge-shaped, which means that even when she goes a bit pudgy the face remains narrow at the chin and slightly depressed below the cheekbones. Her eyes are a truly slumbrous color and shaped like the almonds of Near Eastern legend. Her mouth is perfectly defined—what kiss-fanciers call "shapely." But more important than all this (to me), she is possessed of a modesty and self-effacement which surprised me a great deal. Granted she may have been on her best and most cautious behavior, I nevertheless believed her softness to be genuine. Possibly she is not consistent in this respect, for movie stars learn quickly that they must fight hard when a fight is called for lest they wake up days later no longer movie stars. The lady must be tougher than she seemed, but still, assumptions of humility cannot fool me often, and I suspect her ego is rather less expanded than that of the average Movie Queen.

As we reached the door, she mentioned her desire to attend at least an occasional rehearsal. I was beginning to say "Why not?" when I saw Burton shaking his head. This surprised me, since she had already appeared at rehearsal toward the close of the previous day. Seeing my confusion, she told me that one of the stars had objected, claiming that any visitors were distracting until the actors had learned their lines. The objection was mildly expressed and friendly in manner, but it was also sincere, and Burton wished to take such an objection seriously. Taylor repeated her wish to attend, at least now and again. "I'd rather die than irritate anyone or disturb their way of working, it's just . . . well, I want to *learn*."

Burton interrupted his good nights to the others, turned round, and shook his head again.

Taylor lowered her voice. "Did my being there disturb you?" she asked.

I said that it hadn't.

"Are you sure? Tell me the truth."

I told her I had enjoyed seeing her there—which was true. She smiled and thanked me and said good night. "Maybe he'll change his mind," she added.

"Maybe he will," I said, but I could almost feel Burton's head shaking behind me as I left the Royal Suite. It was as though he hoped so small a thing would not become complicated. There is such a thing as too damned much good will.

The whole notion of "rehearsals" is misunderstood by the public and even by some of the workers in the theatre. It is a period during which the actor is willing to look silly or even a bit insane. It is an experimental time. A singer, in order to make beautiful sounds eventually, must make some ugly sounds while studying. Actors, when rehearsing, should be willing to do the same. It is a difficult process but a brave and necessary one. Uninitiated people do not understand this, and actors *know* they do not understand and tend to become inhibited and embarrassed. Miss Taylor is hardly uninitiated, but as she herself had said, "I'd like to see how *theatre* actors work."

By the way, *this* theatre actor was elected Equity Deputy today and over his living body, more's the pity. I have performed this thankless trade-union function in more than ten productions, each time vowing solemnly never to do so again. The present shanghai was accomplished through the hugger-mugger efforts of Hume Cronyn and Philip Coolidge, both of whom are false friends and dirty dogs. Since they mutually detest any sort of social service, they decided they could protect themselves best by nominating me in very loud voices. I was washing my hands at the time and these two Brutuses managed to carry the day in my absence. When I protested their unfriendly and assassinatory action, Coolidge delivered himself of the following remark: "If you have the bleeding gall to accept star billing for playing Guildenstern, you can damned well be the deputy."

I thought this argument unfair but everyone within earshot thought it funny, so I am trapped like a snipe in a canvas bag. I'm beginning to wish *I* weren't allowed to attend rehearsals.

Grumpy good wishes . . .

William

3 February—Toronto

Dear Bob . . .

We have now staged—or blocked—to the end of Act Two, having completed only five days of work. It is a rapid pace . . . *too* rapid. Much of this initial staging is glib and unreal. Some of it must inevitably lead the actors *away* from the meaning of a scene rather than toward its center. However—there's a bit of Hobson's choice here—too much delay or palaver over primary blocking can bog down the spirit of a rehearsal. Gielgud is obviously one of those old hands who feels: Let's press on, ping-pong, so that we can get a crack at the whole thing! If it's not up to snuff, we'll fix it later! It's a reasonable position to take *if* we ever get around to the "fixing." Before these rehearsals began, Alex Cohen told me that Gielgud does everything necessary during the first ten days and, thereafter, does not know what to do with himself. At least, not until the play opens before an audience.

Well, oddly enough, I agree that the first ten days are crucial, sort of like the first five years of a human life. The tiger has been bred, nor will he change his stripes—not for paint nor flagellation. But when Alex says "everything," we must underline the word carefully. What *is* everything? More important, what does *Gielgud* mean by everything? If what we have done up to now is five days' worth of everything, it follows that it is half of everything. If it is *Gielgud's* idea of half-everything, we are canoeing rapidly into turbulent waters.

For the sake of those Shakespeare lovers and scholars who are wondering what I mean by "Act Two," I do not mean Shakespeare's Act Two, which ends rather early in the play. Had we spent five days on the first two acts according to Shakespeare, I would consider our tempo to be rather Polynesian. Shakespeare wrote most of his plays in five acts, but they have not been played in such a form for generations. Our production will be broken into three acts, the longest by far being Act One. Instead of lowering the curtain—as is customary—after Hamlet's cry, "The play's the thing wherein I'll catch the conscience of the King!" we continue on through the nunnery scene and into the brief, conspiratorial exchange between Polonius and Claudius—the latter saying finally, "Madness in great ones must not unwatch'd go." This sinister line takes on new weight as a curtain cue, I think, and may raise gooseflesh on the napes of some necks.

Our second act opens in a sprightly fashion with Hamlet's Advice to the Players (a speech which Burton, at this point, treats with surprising indifference), and we then move headlong into the Play Scene. The act ends after Hamlet's final soliloquy—"How all occasions do inform against me"—which concludes "from this time forth, my thoughts be bloody or be nothing worth." Hamlet is on his way to England. We shall not see him again until Ophelia has gone mad and drowned herself. Both these divisions are felicitous, I believe, as well as original. They are Gielgud's notions and they are good ones.*

In point of fact, our blocking has been accomplished in a mere four days, since the first day of rehearsal was more than halved by travel, the press conference, and the reading of the play. Sir

* After our Toronto opening, the second interval was removed. This made a shorter evening for the audience and a less lucrative one for the stagehands. The actors didn't care. They don't get overtime.

John moves us swiftly indeed—as though the hounds of heaven careered in hot pursuit, barking and snorting, "Do it now, before we catch you!" Perhaps we will all be excommunicated if we slow down. Waste not, want not. Quick decisions, right or wrong. "We'll fix it *late*-ah, dahlings! *Late*-ah! Trust me!"

And so we come to *trust*, an atomic word in the theatre. Since the theatre is a community effort, and all plays are put on by committees, trust would seem integral to the production of a play. Actor must trust director; playwright must trust director and actor; director must trust scenic designer; producer must trust everyone.

But *trust*, surely! At all costs, mutual understanding, interdependence, and *trust!* Nothing of the kind, my ingenuous friend. Most theatre workmen (particularly actors) would rather fight than trust. Is this because show business is dog-eat-dog and we must all look out for Number One, yes sir, hoo-hee, sing the Corruption Number for me? Not really. It's not good hearts that are wanting, it's good judgment. Too many actors have loved too many directors only to discover (after the New York opening) that Broadway is not in love with the offspring. More bad performances have been given by more good actors who trusted their directors than you can shake a book of *What's Polite* at. The actor must be as sly as a sneak thief. He can no more trust an unknown director than he can walk through Central Park at midnight and expect not to be mugged.

Richard Burton, for example, may not be sly but he is a long way from being naïve. Which reminds me of a fan-letter written to Marlon Brando by a sixteen-year-old girl. It was a typewritten note, acceptably phrased and impeccably spelled but for one baffling, Nathanael West-like lapse. "Oh, Marlon!" the final line rhapsodized. "I love you because you are so suffisticated. Best wishes and kind regards."

Very well, then. Richard Burton is suffisticated. He never says no to John Gielgud. That would be rude. But he frequently does not do as Gielgud asks. In fact, he *usually* does not do as Gielgud asks. He says yes; he does otherwise. This is one of the most ancient of actors' techniques. Some actors practice it consciously. With others, it is a matter of intuition. Ideally, the actor should hash out all creative matters with his director and even his author. But "taking direction" is a much misunderstood cliché of the theatre. When I was a boy actor, a white-maned and impressive character actor said to me sagely, "The most important thing an actor can learn is to take direction. Always remember that, son, and you'll be a success."

I *did* always remember it. I remembered it so well that I gave more than one grotesquely poor performance while following the advice of some grotesquely poor directors. I also now remember, with bitter hindsight, that the old poop who told me that was a lousy actor. The only acting he *really* knew how to do consisted of placing one finger alongside his nose and giving a wise old wink while affording young colleagues bad advice. Forgive my spleen, but I do not believe in theatrical Kris Kringles.

Put it this way: One need neither argue with a director nor "take" direction with unquestioning, childish obedience. A proper instruction, carefully worded, would be: *Digest* direction. Be in or out of agreement, as your intuition dictates, but *listen* to the direction. If you don't like it, don't do it, but taste it, savor it—roll it about in your mouth. Then swallow it, digest it—it may work out. It may stretch you to an achievement you did not imagine. Do not confuse stubbornness with integrity. Be blown by the wind. Imagine yourself a kite.

This is Burton. He will move to any position, do any sort of "reading," whisper when asked, shout when asked—but nothing is merely obedient, nothing is fixed. And a good thing, too. Because acting is not made up of a reading here, a gesture there. It is not a pattern of mosaics. It is far more a matter of long, sweeping lines of action. Should the actor work out the details of his part in personal terms, should he succeed in engaging his own secret anxieties and enjoyments—his private beliefs, his dream-life characteristics, should he then insinuate these secrets into the ebbing and flowing of the play, he will be inevitably swept into the main lines of the action—he will be forced unconsciously from point to point in his performance. The more certainly and firmly these guide ropes have been rigged, the more the actor can afford to forget them and begin to shade his playing.

Most observers say to actors, "How do you remember all those lines?" What a lovely irony, since the actor's most elusive achievement is to forget them! Or, to put it more clearly, to know them so well and to understand their implications so well that he can *afford* to forget them. Marlon Brando once said, "I am good when I forget. When I can sit on stage and think of catching a fish. I have just sunk the hook, there's a tug on the line, and at that preoccupied moment, I hear my cue. My God, what is my line? And then I say my line, because the motor memory will save you if you really believe. So I say my line, the line I thought I'd forgotten, and it's good, man. It's really good."

Sounds mysterious, but it isn't. It is merely a neat trick. Catching Pegasus by the heel is a neat trick. It proceeds not from hard labor but from a knowledge of the self. Such knowledge is hard-bought, but it is not like digging ditches. It is a giving-over of the ego.

All the technical memorabilia of acting; all the "moments" which audience and critics prize dearly or cheaply: pieces of business, readings, vocal flights, outpourings of tears or laughter —all the fine follies an audience remembers are of little or no significance to the performing actor. I don't mean they're no good. Nor do I mean that they are less than what they seem. If audience and critic speak of them with praise, such moments are probably good ones, but they are of *no* moment for the actor. They are the *result* of what the actor does. They cannot be planned; they cannot be fixed. The actor's work is something else.

Line readings, gestures, bursts of sound, waterfalls of tears, cachinnations of laughter, the deft handling of objects (Jack Lemmon, for example, handles objects with a personal glee which makes me yearn to watch him do five minutes of uncut pantomime)—none of these things are of more than competent significance should the actor fail to identify the depths of his personality with the implications of his role. So we come to more than inflections and gesture, tears and laughter. We come to secret switches and the spurs which gallop the soul. Subtext? Living the part? Yes, but also *words* and the implications of words; the subcutaneous tales within tales suggested by the play. I do not care what ignites the actor: the sniffing of lemons, the shape of a line, the touch of your hand, or the cut of his jib. Ignited he must be, and only he knows the secret.

Still—this business of "living the part" has been much misunderstood. It should not mean a state of frenzy or emotional trance. No good actor ever forgets that he is a workman performing in a play on stage. To be real is to include what is real around you. The audience is there; the stagehands stand casually in the wings; your fellow actors are irritating; your leading lady is wonderful; you are not good tonight; you are slick as a whistle tonight. Each performance, each set of reactions, will be different from those of the night before. Such responses are not to be ignored but included.

During our everyday lives, we see things about us which are unrelated to our momentary line of action. While we speak to the pretty girl on the street corner and play out our "intention" (seduction, I hope), we are aware of a passing taxi as well as the driver's plaid cap. We wish we hadn't noticed. The girl becomes aware of our distraction. Dug the taxi; lost the girl. Such is life. Such, also, is the theatre. Actors must never subtract. Not during a performance. Subtraction is for rehearsals.

The actor loses himself in his part, *but not entirely*, for he also *finds* himself, and a damned good thing. He finds himself because he is watching for himself. He is on the lookout. A large part of his job is to lie in wait and trap his unconscious. He is a guerrilla against his id: a secret member of the Viet Cong who spends twelve hours in the mud, sucking air through a straw and waiting for his chance. He is filthy, degraded, and losing hope. A tiny clot of mud leaks into his mouth; his last straw is wilting. Soon he must surrender his position, but he hears footsteps! He jumps at his chance, springs like a cat from the mud to find— not an enemy, but himself. He loses the battle. He wins the war. He loses as he finds. At the precise moment when the actor is entirely lost, he shall be entirely found. There he stands! A fleshed-out mannequin, dripping mud, but ready to act out the fantasies of those whose words are trapped below the throat. He is the Lost and Found of contemporary souls.

The actor's art and business are completely of today. This year's good acting is next year's extravagant ham. Well, not quite. But as little as ten years can make considerable difference. Acting styles change abruptly, perhaps because they are so attuned to the mores of the day.

Shakespeare, referring to actors, said, "They are the abstracts and brief chronicles of the time." No one ever said anything sharper about the profession. Shakespeare more than once delivered himself of subtler and more specific advice to players than he put into Hamlet's famous speech. The well-known Advice to the Players is in fact more general than valuable: don't overplay, don't underplay; don't use your hands too much, but don't stand still like a stick; be bold but not too bold, and for God's sake hold the mirror up to nature.

A high-school drama coach could tell me that. So could John Dover Wilson. The speech is famous because academicians, critics, and various other non-actors can understand it, thereby electing themselves experts on the oh-so-simple art of acting. But to professional players (the ones who can think) the speech is amateur night in Omaha. A competent stock-company leading man will practice Hamlet's advice at every performance and *still* manage to put his audience to sleep. Moreover, many an actor unawed by Shakespeare has wondered just what in hell that band of strolling players would *really* have said to such an arrogant amateur, had he not been a Prince and but recently bereaved. The scene is saved from absurdity not because of Hamlet (who was not an actor) but because Shakespeare (who was) knew what his public and patrons wanted to hear on the subject. He was right, too. They still want to hear it. Earlier, I mentioned Richard Burton's indifference to the speech. I have since discovered that he loathes it. I don't yet know why, but the reasons just mentioned might interest him.

Shakespeare, however, was a many-faceted chap, and that's putting it mildly. He knew perfectly well that he spoke to more than one audience. Like the baseball pitcher who would rather outsmart hitters than mow them down with speed, he was what ball nuts call "a cutie." He serves meat and potatoes to the hoi polloi but caviar to the professionals. Hamlet admonishes Polonius to see the players well bestowed, adding, as I just mentioned, "For they are the abstracts and brief chronicles of the time. After your death, you were better have a bad epitaph than their ill report while you live."

These two lines touch effulgently on what Tyrone Guthrie has called the actor's fate: to be "writ in water." A good book lives, a good play lives—just as it is with music, painting, and sculpture—but a good performance lives only in the memory of a witness.

Acting is the most mortal of the arts. Like perishable foods, it must be taken fresh or not at all. To hear Staats Cotsworth describe John Barrymore's Hamlet is a pleasurable experience. But to *see* John Barrymore's Hamlet, played exactly as it was played in 1924, could cause its many admirers acute discomfort. Richard Burton recently implored some young actor friends to see Laurence Olivier in *Henry V*—a fairly recent film. They returned from their duties bewildered. "He's so *old-fashioned,*" they complained. "The battle scenes are good—the rest is eye-wash."

But, at the time the film was made, Olivier was modern; just as Jelly-Roll Morton was once modern. Today, Morton's records are relics, possessing little more than antique charm. And Olivier's Harry rocks with age. Or so the young folks say. Still, the continuing stature of Olivier proceeds largely from his ability to change, to give modern performances year upon year out of an unusual sensibility and a scholastic command of the theatre.

On film, oddly enough, certain performances wear better than others quite aside from their original reception. Laurel and Hardy are one example; Jean Harlow is another. She was not a good actress, not even by Hollywood standards, but she is delightful to watch today because the spirit of her era all but shines from her eyes. She synopsizes the late twenties and early thirties, just as she carries a tattered flag for all good little bad girls. She is *fun*, which is what movie stars should be.

It is interesting to note with what merciless consistency her contemporary critics mauled her. Mae Clarke was always getting better notices: "Mae Clarke steals the picture." "Mae Clarke gives the inept Miss Harlow an acting lesson." And how well do you remember Mae Clarke, may I ask? Perhaps the displeasure of a film critic provides an accurate incidence of what will survive.

A theatre performance can survive only in the mind. Shakespeare's comment is significant on more than one level: abstracts from briefs and briefs from abstractions. Could it mean that the actor is a newspaper? A periodical? But he is alive!

Line drawings, quick sketches. An intuitive understanding of what reaches people today—loving, hating, and struggle. The actor must be deep in his heart and quick with his hands, catch Pegasus by the heel while riding a tiger, have the soul of a fairy and the hide of a walrus, change himself from night to night and alter his psyche from year to year. He is a chameleon gone aesthetic; a shade with a purpose. A second-story man who breaks into your house not to take but to give. Actors who do not keep pace with today will go under. Like lemmings, they will drown even in the neap tide. For the actor, today is the future.

Shakespeare had more to say. He was nobody's fool. A further jewel of advice nestles near the center of Hamlet's third soliloquy. It is like a pearl set into a diamond bracelet. Hamlet broods over the Player King's emotional display while reciting Aeneas's tale to Dido. Finally, Hamlet cries out with bitter envy, "What would he do had he the motive and the cue for passion that I have?"

And what would *you* do, young actor? The spine of a role is the motive (the intellect, the reason); the juice is the cue for passion—the inner switch which ignites the heart. Though we color ourselves with limps and canes, with green umbrellas and purple suits, we cannot escape the motive and the cue.

It is a professional thought, and only a professional actor could have set it down. Shakespeare, we are told, was a mediocre player, but he was an actor all the same, and knew more about the profession than the cleverest critic writing today.

Kenneth Tynan?

Who did he ever fight?

Best wishes
Wm.

4 February—Toronto

Dear Bob . . .

About our arras. That is, about our lack of arras. As you know, *Hamlet* cannot be produced without an arras. Polonius hides *behind* it. Hamlet stabs him *through* it. Gertrude's bedroom (or closet) doesn't look ladylike *without* it. Where's our arras?

We don't have one. Our set is informal. Hamlet and his Mama must play their wild, incestuous scene on a raised platform about five feet square while Polonius—well, dammit, what *about* Polonius? What about anyone in the play who must conceal himself? Appear suddenly? Be visible to the audience but not to other characters?

Gielgud's answer is to dress our stage with two wardrobe racks which can be wheeled on and off by hard-working supernumeraries, as in a Japanese Noh play. Polonius will do his eavesdropping from behind a wardrobe rack. But who picks up the eaves Polonius drops and what keeps the audience from watching the process? Sir John has thought of everything. The racks are hung with greatcoats, velvet, and fur. Again, we are inconsistent in concept—there would be no such carryings-on during a rehearsal—but at least there will be places to hide. One last question: how is Hamlet's sword to get through the greatcoats, velvet, and fur, and into Polonius?

The subject came up at today's rehearsal and consumed considerable time. John Gielgud—as director—has several ideas. He naturally wants the moment to seem convincing and colorful. Richard Burton—as both star and stabber—wants to find precisely the right crevice between clothing so that his sword be not wrenched from his grasp by fuzzy velvet, making him seem a weak-fisted pantywaist.

But Hume Cronyn—as He Who Gets Stabbed—has ideas of his own. Understandably concerned that safety precede spectacle, he has thought up a way to kill Polonius short of killing Cronyn.

One could see the gathering fear in Cronyn's eyes as Burton and Gielgud calmly discussed what would "look best." There was a glazed look at first, followed by a tightening of the shoulders, and, finally, a continuous opening and closing of the hands.

Suddenly, there was no one but Cronyn talking. The moment was being staged, with no further discussion. Mr. Cronyn was handling Richard Burton physically, pushing him this way and that, politely but firmly. He was asking Gielgud to observe the action and demonstrating what he would do when stabbed; how he would fall through the greatcoats a few moments later. There was nothing novel in Cronyn's staging, but a certain intensity of purpose caused the next few moments of rehearsal to seem electric.

It is Cronyn's notion that when Burton thrusts his impetuous sword through wardrobe rack jam-packed with velvet cloaks and fustian blouses, the concealed Polonius Cronyn should carefully place the extended blade between his right arm and side just below the armpit. All the while he will be howling death throes as Polonius but feeling just fine himself, thank you. These plans may seem excessively cautious, but Richard Burton does not strike me as a fastidious swordsman, and Cronyn's concern seems warranted therefore. Once the blade is tightly tucked in a safe place, Hume can take hold of the hilt with his free hand and Burton—after saying "Is it the King?"—can slowly pull both sword and dying Polonius through the costumes, watch his unintended victim sink to the floor, and release the sword handle strategically so that the weapon all but hums.

There we have Mr. Cronyn, then, very much unharmed, while Polonius lies supine, dead as the Aztecs, and somehow recollective of a mounded military grave, complete with officer's saber standing at attention. This queer little salute would then gently obtrude throughout the closet scene between Hamlet and his mother. The latter part of the idea didn't work out. Gielgud decided that the erect sword was disconcerting and the moment was quickly restaged. Burton merely withdrew the weapon from Cronyn's body while saying, "Thou wretched, rash, intruding fool—farewell."

As you can see, not all theatre effects proceed from a beautiful vision. Necessity is the mother of invention in the arts as well as the home. Aesthetics aside, it is safety first which now concerns me. Cronyn did not wait for anyone to tell him how to die. He figured it out for himself. That is as it should be. Dying is a private affair, and a man should go about it his own way—with no help from careless outsiders. That's the way Hume Cronyn did it. Hooray for him. Not only that, there's not a mark on him.

And we don't need an arras.

Best . . .
Wm.

5 February—Toronto

Dear Bob . . .

This afternoon, Alfred Drake expressed concern over two aspects of our rehearsals. He feels that he is learning his lines too quickly and that too few moments in the play are being questioned, examined, and made logical. He also wonders why Richard, Eileen, Clem, and I—among others—already know our lines and seem to be giving finished performances. "It is too soon for such things. It is not enough to play things ably. A performance must be *inevitable*."

He is right as rain, but what the hell. I can't speak for the others, but my own motives add up to nothing less than sheer terror. I have played Shakespeare in public only once before. I feel compelled to get a head start, to work quickly. If Gielgud asked me to take it easy, I'd do so, but when I'm left to my own devices my slogan becomes: All Deliberate Speed, with more speed than deliberation. To put it plainly, I don't want to goof, and I said so, but Alfred shook his head. "The atmosphere of this rehearsal seems to be, 'Let's all give the best performances we can in the shortest possible time and don't ask any questions. It's *infra dig.*' Dammit, that's the way you put on plays in school. There are so many questions I want to ask about Claudius, I get dizzy. Iago is a snap by comparison. But when I ask John a question, I feel as though I've stuck a knife in him. All he wants to talk about is mechanics."

Drake was not whining or even complaining. He was just plain resigned. I admire this man. I appreciate his professionalism, intelligence, and sense of humor. I also respect the unconventional approach he is taking to the role of Claudius. It takes courage *not* to play the part as Hamlet's "bloat King," *not* to play him as a lecherous alcoholic. But if the actor is so daring as to avoid the traditional attack, he must take considerable pains to discover what to play Claudius *as*. I doubt that it's a good enough role to support *original* interpretation. Unhappily for an actor try-ing to be subtle and novel, Claudius *is* a lecherous alcoholic and a man of deplorable character. His self-flagellating prayer mid-way in the play implies no true change of heart; it is merely a hymn to his guilt. He berates himself, yes, but he denies himself nothing. He cannot give up Gertrude. He cannot surrender the crown. He cannot confess. He cannot repent. Even *after* the prayer, when Hamlet supplies him an excuse for further chican-ery by killing Polonius, Claudius does not hesitate. He exiles the Prince to England and prepares sealed orders calling for his execution. He is one of the blackest of Shakespeare's villains, irremediably written.

Alfred is trying to play him as a sober and competent states-man, deeply in love with his wife. One of the oldest of actor's axioms is: A villain is never a villain to himself. Obviously, Al-fred would like to play Claudius with such a maxim in mind. He wants to create the role from *Claudius's* standpoint rather than *Hamlet's*.

Commendable, but dangerous. Some roles are written so darkly that they can be successfully played not through *avoiding* vil-lainy but only through *loving* villainy. The love of crime can justify crime, not only from the standpoint of the criminal but from that of the audience as well.

Why, then, did Shakespeare write the prayer? Why even the

lip service to guilt and morality? I don't know. But I *do* know that Shakespeare's writing cannot always be counted out as one might count clay beads. He is not always susceptible to a careful probe. Since he is the least pedantic of writers, his logic moves in large blocks, not tiny mosaics. From the standpoint of the actor, the links in Shakespeare's chain of events are sometimes rusty. Alfred's determined tugging may break Claudius's particular chain. One thing is certain: if he is to give the revolutionary performance he has in mind, he will need the most careful attention and guidance.

But Gielgud says so little to him. Occasional remarks such as, "Frightfully good, your opening speech. *Such* a difficult speech. Bit slow, don't you think? Pick it up a bit next time. Frightfully good, though. Many thanks," and then he dances away to confront Problem #2—whatever it may be. Alfred is left to wonder just what was so frightfully good and just how much to "pick it up."

The speech, in fact, should be twice as quick and thrice as wide in scope. But Drake would have to be clairvoyant to know this without being told. Whenever an actor tries to give a low-keyed performance in the theatre (films are the reverse) the director must watch him with the eyes of an owl to see that he doesn't over-relax. This is especially crucial when the performer intends to sidestep a traditional interpretation of a classic role. Old plays are harder than new ones. Both critics and audience bring trunks full of preconceptions. To be "relaxed" in a Shakespearean role is next to impossible from the start.

Hume Cronyn, on the other hand, is off and running. His perils and pitfalls, if any, will take a different form. Will he over-play it? Will he be too vigorous, too agile? It's a great part, but the Polonius who advises his son so beautifully and humanly does not seem to be the same man who would connive so shamelessly, or pry with such slavering prurience, or "loose his daughter" to Hamlet in the manner of a pimp. Ben Jonson called him senile. Good point. For a man in his dotage becomes a patch quilt of man—behaving sensibly at one moment, idiotically the next. But such an interpretation would not sit comfortably on Cronyn. He

is too young, too trim, too vigorous, and a modern-dress production makes disguise impossible. If Cronyn were to make himself up with age lines, much white hair, etc., the effect would be
too elaborate for Gielgud's *mise en scène*. He would seem like
the medieval knight in the Ajax commercials: stronger than dirt,
perhaps, but basically incongruous.

Instead, he is playing Polonius as a wily, conniving politician—
a professional. He is also playing him for laughs. Too many? At
this point, it's hard to say. Most members of our company think
he's a scream. So do I, I suppose, but I also find him interesting,
which is far more important. It is twenty years now since I
heard George Abbott say to Red Buttons, "Don't worry so much
about being funny. Be interesting instead. Funny is your lines.
Interesting is you."

As for the laughter Cronyn educes from his fellow players, I
hear it with a skeptical ear, but my skepticism proceeds from an
awareness deeper than envy. I am always suspicious of "inside"
laughter—the sort which explodes from one's colleagues at some
excruciatingly delicious moment. High camp among the pros.
Such moments rarely make an audience laugh. The moments
which *do* have usually been overlooked by the actors. In fact,
Hume Cronyn's only worry has to do with becoming, as he himself has said, "just too cute and funny for words." He questions
Gielgud often as to "cutesey-pie stuff" and an abundance of
"tricky business," the sort of thing which Jack Lemmon has
called "a bad case of the cutes."

Light comedians are particularly susceptible to this disease, an
infectious virus which causes the victim to believe that he is not
only amusing but adorable.

This is an area of performing which has nothing to do with
talent but has, instead, to do with taste. Some actors (Joan
Hackett, for example) believe that talent and taste are insepara-
ble; that talent, in fact, cannot exist without taste. Another professional friend of mine goes so far as to insist that Jerry Lewis
is utterly giftless, pointing to his excesses as proof. Wrong. Lewis
is an absolutely crackling example of what I mean. Since he is
less than the most tasteful creature of the twentieth century and

makes Mickey Rooney seem positively Savile Row by comparison, it is disquieting to those who wish justice triumphant that he is also stupendously talented. Frustrating, perhaps, but precisely the point.

Hume Cronyn is debating questions of taste, of choice, of selectivity. His talent is not at stake; his judgment is. Since he is a cultivated gentleman, his dilemma is less dramatic than Lewis's or Rooney's, but the issue is the same.

Some years ago, Alfred Lunt—a smashingly fine actor—was appearing in one of many plays with his wife, the formidable Lynn Fontanne. As always, the couple continued to work on this and that detail of their performances long after the success of the production had been assured. Mr. Lunt was especially concerned with a moment when he asked for a cup of tea. Under the circumstances of the scene, "May I have a cup of tea?" was an absurd request, and Lunt believed the line should get a laugh. Night after night he failed. He experimented with different readings, bizarre inflections. He tried shouting the words. He tried whispering. He made his hands shake. He stood stiffly. He stood limply. He spoke quickly, then slowly. Nothing worked. He was desperate. He was frustrated. At last, he was enraged. His wife endured several weeks of his agony. One magic night, she took him by the hand to soothe his shattered nerves. "Alfred," she suggested, "tomorrow night, instead of asking for a laugh, why don't you just ask for a cup of tea?" Mr. Lunt did so. And yes, he got a laugh. Simplicity is a wonderful thing.

Hume Cronyn has nothing to fear. His grip on the part is firm and joyous. Excesses? Gielgud must edit him carefully, just as Hume must edit himself.

Other key performances will be those of Linda Marsh as Ophelia, Robert Milli as Horatio, Eileen Herlie as the Queen, and John Cullum as Laertes. None of these performances has taken shape as yet, although Miss Herlie's Gertrude will obviously be knowledgeable and hard-working. For the moment, it seems to me that Miss Marsh is trying too hard to justify Ophelia in naturalistic terms; that Mr. Milli is the sort of nice, polite man a director must *push* into center stage; that Miss

Herlie is playing as fully as though today's rehearsal were opening night; and that Mr. Cullum is endeavoring to be "*conversational*" with Shakespeare. As for me, I have already mentioned my uneasiness: I am still uncomfortable and uninventive. Guildenstern is not a character, nor am I at one with him. I am "indicating." Sir John allows all of us to continue along these questionable byways and praises our efforts generously. This makes us love him a great deal but it does not necessarily improve our preparations.

William

5 February—Toronto

Dear Bob . . .

Gielgud, it seems, does not wish to play God. Or even Samuel Johnson. He *has* no interpretation of Shakespeare's play. Or, if he does, he is keeping it to himself. I speak of meanings here, not effects. We know, of course, that John wants the production to be swift and forceful. We also know he wants a "run-through" feeling and that we are to wear all manner of experimental clothing to the daily rehearsals. He has spoken a few words here and there as to "informality—no declaiming, please," but nary a word as to what the play is all about. Perhaps he thinks we know. Perhaps we think so too, but what is to keep Clem Fowler from playing *his* version while I play mine and Eileen Herlie plays another? It is folly to think that actors automatically agree on the interpretation of a play. They almost *never* do. Which is why directors must risk the charge of pedantry and bloody well tell the actors what the damned play means. It is better for a director to misinterpret a play entirely than not to interpret it at all.

One of the ironies of the theatre is that a well-cast play sometimes works out well despite wishy-washy direction. Nevertheless, directors should choose. That is their job. Actors should be willing and able to execute the choices. That is *their* job. These are the rules of the game. When I think that a roomful of English professors would bend my ear for hours discussing the meaning and interpretation of *Hamlet* while John Gielgud will not even declare openly what *period* we are choosing, I could turn myself inside out and play leapfrog with my liver. Several things puzzle me: Gielgud's direction of *Five-Finger Exercise* was most impressive; his direction of *Big Fish, Little Fish* was positively brilliant. Did he go about his business silently in these instances? Is his direction communicated by osmosis? Is he in league with the devil? Don't laugh. Actors in rehearsal are as dependent as infants in cribs. They can hardly hold their own heads.

Only one remark of Sir John's so much as brushes at what I would call a *concept*. "Hamlet," he said sadly to me, "must be the star of the play. All must serve him. It hardly seems fair, since it's such a good part, but it must be so. Hamlet has to steal the show." Well, I don't know how Hamlet could avoid stealing the show, especially as played by Richard Burton, the sort of actor who compels attention even at his worst, but at least I'll defer to the notion as being a notion. The rest has been silence. Over and again I tell myself that Gielgud is biding his time, that he is not an English professor—his tongue is not painted with chalk. He is an actor, not a theoretician; a director, not a lecturer. Disapproving of Freud, of J. Dover Wilson, of Hubbell and Jones and Grebanier and perhaps even Granville-Barker (in theory), he does not wish to "dope" the play. He has played it so often, seen it so often, directed it so often that he has perhaps doped it too often. Either that or he has found it to be undopeable. Obviously, Gielgud wants the play to just happen. It is not an uncommon technique. Arthur Hopkins built a distinguished career around a similar idea. Cast good actors and let them alone. It's the deliberate absence of a technique which theatrical liberals call a technique in itself. Lee Strasberg is committed to such freedom and relaxation, but at least with him there's a lot of discussion and at least he speaks of faith. But Gielgud? It doesn't seem *like* him, somehow—it is not what I've heard about him. It is not what I *see* when I watch him act. Gielgud is not Arthur Hopkins, he is not Strasberg—but when is he going to be Gielgud?

I have mentioned some of the scholars and theoreticians. Before rehearsals began, I read most of the prominent ones, with behoovement at my left hand and a tumbler of scotch at my right.

I also plowed through the New Variorum edition and the Yale and Kittredge editions, and listened dutifully to the Shakespeare Recording Society's full-length text with Scofield as Hamlet. Is all this cramming necessary? Damned if I know for sure, but it's part of my nature. What I *do* know, however, is that the theatre is no Palace of Justice. It is not Solomon who stands in the wings but only William James's Bitch Goddess. She dispenses favors, not justice. As G. B. Shaw said, "Oh, it's *justice* you want, is it? Nobody's ever had it since the world began, but *you* want justice!"

The theatre gives no dividends. We either get a great deal more than we deserve or far less than our due. These dispensations have to do with talent, self-promotion, and plain damned luck. We must swallow the Ipecac of reality and *then* go to work. Once an actor gives up any idea of fair play, his joy in the theatre begins.

Anyway, the scholars popped into my mind today because of a dispute between Burton and Gielgud. For the first time since rehearsals began, Burton openly rejected a suggestion from his director. The Closet Scene is being pinned down, root and branch. At the intense moment when Hamlet thrusts his avenging sword through the wardrobe rack and into Polonius, Sir John wants Burton to cry out triumphantly, "Is it the King?" as if to say, "Have I done it? Have I killed the filthy pig?" but Burton demurs at this . . . his passionate head trembling, his fingers twitching. "He's a gentle man, John. Gentle, gentle. He doesn't want to kill anyone."

It occurs to me while watching Burton's shifting insistence that gentleness has come hard to him, that violence sits hunkered behind his eyes like a watchful Cheyenne, and that his explosive power as an actor proceeds from a warlike energy, a secret love of blood—sublimated only by his fear of being killed. "He's gentle, John. Gentle, gentle," but the two men are poles apart emotionally. It would make perfect sense for *Gielgud* to cry out, "Have I killed the hated one? How wonderful!" but Burton's cry would have to be, "Oh, God, have I done what I always feared I'd do? How awful!"

It is bewitching to watch both men struggle for *Shakespeare's* meaning while they squirm as individuals beneath the weight of their own psychologies. This is a problem for every interpretive artist who ever drew breath. He must be true to the writer and true to himself. He literally serves two masters. To expect the interpreter to be a puppet who conceives and executes the *ideal* Hamlet (or Puck or Lady Macbeth or Merton of the Movies) is to deny the human condition. An actor can discipline his effects in order to avoid distortion of the play—giving up, sometimes, his most popular tricks—but to expect him to reject the totality of his personality in order to imitate *The Character* is madness.

The actor is stuck with the character, but *the character is also stuck with the actor.* Directors sometimes pretend that the character is everything and that the actor must adjust no matter how uncomfortable it makes him, but the actor's job is to preserve himself somehow—not by distorting the play, although many modern actors do, but by admitting his own limitations, by knowing what he can make real for the audience and what he can't. If the actor has been miscast, he cannot compensate for the error by destroying his God-given nature on stage. It is the *producer's* job to know beforehand how flexible the actor is.

Here's a daisy-chain of ironies: Time and again on Broadway, actors whom the local reviewers approve are cast into roles which they proceed to distort. Their distortions are so successful that the plays they appear in often fail. But the critics continue to praise the very players who made the operation of the play impossible. Why? Because noninterpretive actors tend to look relaxed and comfortable on stage. Therefore, why pick on *them?* There must be something wrong with the play. We close Saturday night.

Still, I maintain that the offending actor is not chiefly to blame. Why should he stop doing what gets him good notices? The critic is to blame, as well as the producer and director who hire an actor to play Restoration comedy because he was well received in *The Toilet.* Pity the poor playwright! How often he has seen his play buried by the actor who got the best reviews!

Critics like an actor who makes them *watch* him. But what if the whole point of the play (or scene) is that they should *not* watch him? What if the actor is charming and attractive but his timing is bad? And what if he's playing a farce, where timing is everything?

The argument between Gielgud and Burton touches on a choice between effect and personal belief. It is not a matter of black and white, right and wrong. In fact, it is the sort of honest dispute which should take place constantly between actor and director. We feel the electricity between the two men. Such electricity puts belief on stage; it sets the locomotive on the tracks and makes it move.

Gielgud wants "Is it the King?" to lift the audience from their seats. He feels that the moment demands an upswing—a thrill and exultation. Burton shrugs and says that thrills and upswings are always desirable but Hamlet is still a gentle man and blahblahblah couldn't we bring a brass band into Gertude's closet—what a thrill and exultation and upswing *that* might give us! The argument goes on for some ten minutes. It is finally compromised by Gielgud (his expression is pale and discouraged, like a man who has been cheated at cards), and the good gray eminence says, "Perhaps we can get both. Let's keep working at it, shall we?"

It's a cliché, a cop-out, a confession of helplessness, the surrender of a stubborn man to a more stubborn adversary. Still, what was he to do? For I knew what Gielgud meant whether Burton did or not. Gielgud wants anxiety, fear, guilt, and triumph. And he wants them all at once. He doesn't know *why* he wants these things but he wants them in much the same way a conductor wants the climax of Beethoven's Leonore #3 to saw back and forth like a pair of lumberjacks in Sequoia. You either want it or you don't. If you want it, no one can talk you out of it. If you *feel* it as part of the texture and rhythm of a play, no amount of psychological or photographic cant or even ten-cent-store logic will dissuade you. It is an effect you desire: an image, a dream. But it is also a tall order. And Richard Burton, for reasons of his own, does not wish to fill it.

As it is, numerous Shakespearean scholars have maintained that for Hamlet to say, "Is it the King?" defies logic entirely. In fact, they say, such a question is patently absurd since Hamlet has just left the King at prayer and surely knows that Claudius could not make his way from *prie-dieu* to Gertrude's arras so quickly. Apparently neither Burton nor Gielgud (despite their other disagreements) take the scholars seriously, and how right they are! For if Hamlet, logically or otherwise, did not entertain the notion of his victim being the King then why, a moment later, would he say to dead Polonius, "I took thee for thy better"? Several truths and possibilities lurk about in the shadows, and I intuit strongly that Burton and Gielgud are aware of them all.

(1) Why do the scholars assume that Hamlet did not dawdle on his way from Claudius to Gertrude? He is a dawdler of considerable fame. The entire play concerns itself with his dawdling and the reasons therefor. In this particular instance, he was *first* told that his mother wanted to see him by Guildenstern but he stalled, dawdled, and made fun of his false friend by means of a recorder. He was told again by Polonius and he delayed again, saying, "I will come by and by." He sees Claudius at prayer and debates the killing of him. His mother's message is many minutes old by now. Is there any reason to doubt that Hamlet stops somewhere on the staircase to debate the question further? Or— for that matter—to go to "The Toilet"? Remember, he is having a difficult day.

(2) Flippancies aside, Hamlet is so agitated, so beyond logic by this time in the play that he likely stands past a recognition of ordinary circumstances or even a chronology of events. Surely he is infuriated enough to thrust his sword ferociously through the arras while less than sure of his victim, but he is hardly in proper possession of his senses. He comes to his mother to "be cruel, not unnatural" but quickly exceeds his intentions. His beration is fierce. To expect him, upon hearing a muffled male voice, to stop and think, "Oh, that can't be the King. He's downstairs praying," is to turn Hamlet from a frenzied and desperate

avenger into cool-headed, cold-blooded Raffles, playing hide-and-seek with Scotland Yard. By the time Hamlet begins to tell Mom off, he hardly knows where *he* is, let alone Claudius.

(3) Perhaps most important of all, *Hamlet* is a revenge play written during the Elizabethan era when the sort of dovetailed, natural logic we demand of plays today simply was not considered. Over and over, Shakespeare's plays will prove to those who *act* them that neither Will nor his players cared much for the details of logic. Richard Burton has said to me, "The play is a series of theatrical effects. If you try to figure them out pedantically, you're lost." Gielgud has said, "It is a poem." The two statements are conjunctive.

Much of the research done by Shakespearean scholars is invaluable. No production of the plays should be undertaken without a careful study of the several good editions. But—unhappily—scholars suffer from the same malassimilation as do critics: they know next to nothing about the acted theatre. When they write of folios, quartos, variant readings, the dimensions of the Globe stage, and like matters, they speak from strength. When they write of interpretation, they speak from the shadows. Most scholars (like most professors) think exclusively in literary terms and along protracted linear threads of logic.

Scholars and critics can afford to be wrong. They can even afford to be fools. One of my favorite critics, Lionel Abel, has written of Gogol's "The Gamblers." The central character considers his mother's advice at the end of the play: *If you are stupid, resign yourself to being stupid. If you are intelligent, try, try to be stupid.* It might be good advice for us all, but whether stupid or intelligent the scholar and the critic have leeway. Actors do not have leeway. They have hardly any room at all, particularly in the American theatre. Actors, too, are fools, no doubt, when it comes to girls and whisky and the stock market. But they are a different breed of fool altogether when it comes to the theatre. A critic (Lionel Abel) or a scholar (J. Dover Wilson) can err in print and it does not really matter; but when an actor errs on stage, the woods burn. Worse than that, the play closes. Actors simply must be pragmatic and adult about the theatre or the curtain will never rise. Some may feel they could say the same of a factory worker, a reporter, a shoe-shine boy, but such analogies are inexact. The theatre is more ruthless than a factory, more expensive than a newspaper, and more closely watched than a shoe-shine boy. The theatre's product is fearfully expensive; the theatre's guarantee of employment is nil; the theatre's competition is savage; the theatre's employer's are gamblers with the odds a good eight to one against them. Do you think the actors don't know this? In fact, you will not meet a more tough-gutted and realistic group of people *professionally speaking* during your lifetime than actors. Why? Because when a play fails, Armaggedon is upon us. It even costs money to cart the scenery away.

Show me a working actor and I will show you a man with a cement stomach. Again, I exempt film stars. When Lance Reventlow married Jill St. John he said, "I like Jill because she doesn't want to be an actress. She wants to be a movie star." Mr. Reventlow is no fool. Neither is Jill.

Lionel Abel once delivered himself of the following bromide in print: "Actors are, in general, childish." On that occasion, Mr. Abel was being stupid without really trying.

Theatre actors are not children. They can't afford to be. They are losers. That is quite another matter.

> Cheery regards . . .
> William

9 February—Toronto

Dear Bob . . .

Several days between letters but there has not been much to report. Gielgud talks little, rehearses even less. Many of the people grow uneasy, myself included. It's all too smooth, too relaxed, too easily approved. We break too early. We take too many fives. Every five we take will get us ten. Gielgud does not frequently enough pin down what the scene is about—not specifically, not with a firm thumb. Crucial sections of the play go unrehearsed for days. "That's all right for now. We'll come

back to it. Press on!" Sketched in with a promise of return—
like Douglas MacArthur to Bataan. But MacArthur *did* go back
. . . will we? And what will we find when we do?

But accuracy compels me to hang a bit of pink crepe before
all this black bunting. And some paper lanterns, too. We have
our moments. Many of them gay, some of them thrilling. Whenever Gielgud *does* get down to business, the effect is galvanic.

To Burton: "Have a care as to your playfulness. It's splendid
that you've such humor and wit and quickness in the part, but
the long lines of Hamlet must be sad. If you frolic too much too
often, you may not be able to stop the laughter later on. No,
don't scowl—you're going to make them laugh quite a bit, have
no fear. But if they laugh too much and you can't stop them, you
will have won their stomachs while losing their hearts. Look to
it."

To Burton again: "Have a care as to shouting. You shout brilliantly; both you and Larry Olivier do—two splendid cornets. I
am a violin, I'm afraid, not too good at shouting. But these hunt-
ing calls you do so well can be tiresome when sounded too often. Don't overuse it. It's a wonderful weapon but it's your *last*
weapon. Use it only when all else fails." (A really wise, understanding bit of direction this, for Burton's shouts and outcries
are truly electrifying, and most directors would simply go giddy
with excitement at the very sound. But Gielgud is looking ahead:
peering carefully past the fragments of a stop-and-start rehearsal
onto a future highway where the lights are always green.)

To Hume Cronyn: "My dear fellow, when you say to Claudius, 'What do you think of me?' you simply *must* say 'What do
you think of *me?*' You must emphasize the word *me*." Cronyn
finds this inflection baffling, since his intelligence indicates the
reading to be, "What do you *think* of me?" When he asked
Gielgud for an explanation, Sir John shook his head. "I can't
give you one," he said. "Just read it that way."

Phil Coolidge has a theory. "Gielgud once heard some other
Polonius say it that way and it got a laugh. He wants that laugh
for us." I suggested that, laugh or no laugh, the reading didn't

make sense. Coolidge pursed his lips. "If it gets a big enough laugh," he said, "it'll make a lot of sense."

American actors, by and large, are fanatically opposed to this business of "giving readings." I am not sure it matters one way or the other. The late William Eythe once pleaded with George Abbott not to give him readings. Abbott grunted. "If you don't read it right, I have to give you the reading, don't I?"

But a reading never alters the heart of a scene—it merely changes the sound. We strike A-flat instead of G. A lot of good directors have given me readings. A lot of bad ones haven't.

Gielgud has asked me for a reading I don't want to give him. During our first scene with Hamlet, a flourish of trumpets interrupts the conversation and Guildenstern cries out, "There are the players!" Sir John insists I say, "There *are* the players," which seems contrived. My strong feeling is that the line's inflection is unimportant. What really counts is for the audience to feel Guildenstern's flustered embarrassment, his relief at the players' arrival. If his *feelings* were to speak they would say, "Thank God! The *players* are here!" Hamlet has caught us in a fib. He is beginning to behave in a sharp and hostile manner. In fact, as Burton plays the scene, he all but calls us snakes-in-the-grass. If I am to be pinned down to a particular word emphasis, I would far rather underline *players* than *are*.

I have three times said yes to Gielgud's request and three times I have refused to read the line his way when we ran through the scene. I remind myself of Julius Caesar refusing the crown . . . dimly . . . very dimly. In any case, Gielgud has caught me each time. He even interrupts the scene to say, "There *are* the players." In other words, he is obsessed. This particular reading is not a mere whim. He really *wants* it and I suppose I'm stuck. What's more—he may be right.

Further intelligence: Most directors, when they want to illustrate a point by quoting from a play, will ask the stage manager to find a particular line. There is no such thing as a director knowing "the lines" of a play. Even authors directing their own works have but a sketchy notion of the dialogue. But Gielgud needs no prompting in *Hamlet*. Whenever the spirit moves him, he leaps from his chair crying, "Nononononononono, deah boy! Much fastah!" and proceeds to act his ass off. The voice is sometimes hushed and haunted; the speech is rapid, desperate, pursued: "Thoughts black, hands apt, drugs fit and time agreeing; confederate season else no creature seeing; thou mixture rank of midnight weeds collected . . ." and hastily on to a shattering climax. His complexion reddens, his knuckles go white; he stands on pigeon's toes; he is tense, excited, stimulated—his brow shows deep creases as though he were in pain; tears appear in his eyes. Then, like a thunderclap, the speech is over and his actors stand about him, silent and breathless. He brushes at his eyes, turns away from us, and resumes his seat. Sometimes he says nothing more. Sometimes he blows his nose and murmurs, "Try it that way, deah boy."

After the first few days of rehearsal the entire company realized that Gielgud knew every line in the play. We decided to enjoy the spectacle. But one afternoon he couldn't remember a particular line in the Polonius-Reynaldo scene—possibly because the scene is so often cut. He turned to our stage manager (Harry Young) to say, "Mmmmm, how odd. What is it?"

An angel of silence passed above us. Harry did not immediately give him the line. Finally, Hume Cronyn laughed aloud, which broke the tension, and the entire company joined in. Gielgud blushed until he was all but purple and then announced loudly, "Well there you are, you see! My reputation is exaggerated and fraudulent. I'm just a silly old goop who can't remember his lines."

Philip Coolidge (the Yankee Clipper) leaned close to me. "Thank God he missed it," he whispered. "Even an idol should have one clay foot."

Gielgud demonstrates the Shakespearean roles and reads the Swan of Avon's verse with a clarity and a musicianship no other living actor supplies. He does not preoccupy himself with what I would call "acting" but instead allows the shape and weight of the words along with the *sound* of his own carefully tuned voice to do the acting. The results are cello-like, plangent, mellifluous —and quite disturbing. For if this *is* acting . . . then what are the rest of us up to?

Gielgud's clarity is brighter than Burton's. His music is sweeter. One can actually *see* the line when he chants it—like a printed slogan, a rubric. One can also *feel* the line: the throb, the thrust; the pulse of its accents. And yet there is something nineteenth century or at least Edwardian about this good gray Knight, while Richard Burton (Lochinvar in his thirties) bounces vigorously onto the contemporary scene with the ease and stamina of a professional boxer. Burton is rhetorically brilliant and certainly as well educated as Sir John, but he is also immutably of today and embroiled in the self-examinations of today's acting.

One colloquy between Gielgud and Burton went as follows: Sir John wanted Burton to pronounce the word "express" with the accent on the second syllable. Burton insisted that the accent should be on the first syllable since Shakespeare's obvious intention was to use a poetic truncation of the word "expressive" for the purposes of meter. "What a piece of work is man . . . in form and moving, how *ex*press and admirable." Gielgud could not understand Burton's argument. He insisted that ex*press* sounded better. After several minutes of listening to the argument (Guildenstern is in the scene) I was cheeky enough to speak up. "Perhaps," I said, "we should change it to local." Gielgud was painfully embarrassed by my remark but it endeared me to Burton. From that time on, he said *ex*press.

There is a conversational quality to Burton's playing (what laymen mean when they say, "Oh, he's so *natural!*") which Gielgud never achieves. Between the two men there is an artistic disagreement, an aesthetic split. It is a fundamental difference of both belief and technique. Burton is a method actor who knows how to sing: a naturalist with a voice. Gielgud is a baroque actor entirely uninterested in the "natural" grunts and groans with which people punctuate their conversation.

In private, Burton has said. "I grew up on Gielgud—his recordings, his writings, and the stories my father told me about his acting. By the time I was twelve, I saw him act and he was in his prime then. Great. Simply great. My father loved him. I loved him. But that singsong approach to the verse—that mellifluous-voice business. It's old-fashioned now, I think. He does it better than anyone alive but it's the easiest thing in the world to do if you shut your mind to anything else. Try it sometime. I don't think audiences want that sort of business any more. Not from me or you, at any rate. They'll take it from Gielgud because he's an elder statesman. But it's out for the rest of us. Don't you think so?"

Why do two such opposed men want to work together? The answer measures the excellence and flexibility of both. Burton wants Gielgud's discipline. Gielgud wants Burton's spontaneity. Both are men of strong conviction and large accomplishment. Both are men of exceptional capacity but neither is so arrogant as to believe that he alone has all the answers. They balance because of their differences. It is most ingratiating to watch them in operation together. The thrilling bad boy and the watchful don.

Alfred Drake is still having difficulty with his words—just the plain damn memorizing—and I can understand why. Claudius is an unusually complex and convoluted text. Tricky to make clear and hard to keep interesting. An experienced actor friend of mine said recently, "Claudius is the fifth longest role in all Shakespeare, but you'd never know it when you see the play."

By the way, what's the *longest* role in Shakespeare? Lear? Hamlet?

Iago, buddy. Look it up.

This afternoon I received my first bit of real direction from Gielgud. Since our rehearsals are now ten days old, it would seem high time. On the other hand, I disagreed with what he wanted, so there you are. The poor man is damned if he does and damned if he doesn't. But, as Nick the Greek has pointed out, the next best thing to winning at cards is losing at cards.

Gielgud referred to the brief Rosencrantz-and-Guildenstern scene with the King and Queen in which we tell of our meeting with Hamlet. "Be crisper, Bill," Sir John said, "more authoritative and expansive. Be even smug with achievement. You're in the King's good graces now. You're a personage at court. You can afford to puff up a bit."

I took the note in silence, nodded, and walked away. After a quick pull at the water fountain, I stood scratching my head for a moment, playing a few frames from an old Henry Fonda movie: baffled country boy trying to decipher big-city ways. "Authoritative," "smug," "puffed up"? Impossible! Our report is *bad*. We've failed to ingratiate ourselves; Hamlet has unmasked our pretended innocence; we've received neither information nor encouragement from him; and Claudius, in this very scene, might justly say, "Oh, you two are no help whatever. Go back to your lands. I'll find someone *clever* to keep an eye on the Prince." Moreover, Guildenstern, in his way, is an honest reporter. It is he who confesses to Hamlet, "We were sent for." It is he who tells Claudius and Gertrude that Hamlet "with a crafty madness keeps aloof," just as it is he who admits straightforwardly that Hamlet received them "with much forcing of his disposition." And this after Rosencrantz has deviously tried to put a good face on things.

I discussed the matter with Clem Fowler and he agreed that our report is a sorry one, but for the arrival of the players—a lucky break indeed for which R&G can hardly claim credit. After taking two deep breaths, I edged forth to discuss the matter with Gielgud. Since I have already discovered that he does not concern himself with a play's circumstances but only with its effects, I approached the issue on cat's feet. Admitting to him that both Fowler and I were confused by his note, I suggested that such behavior seemed to contradict the facts of the scene. He thought for a moment and then said the following: "Ah, yes, I see. Well—it's more a matter of *change;* that's what's really important. Granville-Barker once said to me, 'You've already shown me that—now show me something else.' It was a wonderful direction for me because I tend to be monotonous. After that, I always made sure that each scene I played had a different color, a new shape. Even the lines should change every few moments or so. If I do one line this way, then the next should be that way and then the next should change and the next. It's good to keep the audience off balance, you know—always interested—perhaps even a bit confused."

He walked abruptly away from me and stood in a corner. He lit a cigarette and then quickly returned. "Deah boy," he continued, "I suggested you be smug. Perhaps that isn't right—but whatever you do find *something* new. It must be different from your introductory scene as well as your first scene with Hamlet. You have so few words in the play; therefore you must change your attitude very dramatically each time you appear. You need a new note for every entrance. My suggestion for this scene is: less groveling, a bit of pride. But if you can find something else that makes more sense, very well. Don't worry *too* much about making sense, though. Words should make sense. But not feelings."

Gielgud wrote the preface to Stanislavski's most famous textbook, *An Actor Prepares*. You would never know it from the above remarks. And yet, who is to say what is right and what is wrong? Gielgud thinks of acting the way a composer thinks of music: a bit of fast music here, some slow music there; something poignant now, a stroke of brave defiance to follow. Many a painter looks at a colleague's half-completed work and says, "It needs a touch of red." What Gielgud was asking of me is directly analogous. American actors—the modern ones—have no traffic at all with such thinking. Logic is the root of every scene, of every play. The circumstances are of prime importance. Pace, shape, color, arbitrary differences in attitude—all such things are considered results, externals. They are the business of the playwright and the director, but have nothing to do with the actor. I wonder if we are right.

There are exceptions, of course. Some actors say, "I do as I'm told," and shrug philosophically. Jason Robards, when confronted by an analytical director, will say, "Come on, man, do you want the sad face, the glad face, the fast face, or the slow face?"

Nationality included, not all actors are the same. Those for whom logic and clarity are important will not be bullied out of their preoccupations by being told that they are pests. If they give up their inquiries, the director will have won a Pyrrhic victory. The actor who questions the thought behind an instruction is usually an intelligent actor as well as a valuable one. Obedient actors are beloved by stage managers, whose profession demands that they bird-dog a play in production as well as conduct understudy rehearsals twice a week. They are also beloved by understudies, because misery loves company. And no one serves so admirably in the fields of summer stock and television. Obedient actors are the salt of the earth as well as good soldiers.

But the theatre is not a military academy, nor is virtue always rewarded. The obedient actor is often a bad one (or a dull one), and most Broadway directors do not really want what they ask for, nor should they. Only a puppet can blindly obey instructions night after night on cue. Even Dr. Frankenstein's monster turns on his maker once a flicker of human feeling ignites his heart. Sooner or later, a living creature expresses some sort of preference. I believe this is true even of plant life. And what is a preference?

It is an opinion.

Without his opinion, the actor does not exist. He is a mindless Pinocchio. And all puppets, no matter how much they may entertain us *mitten drinnen*, want to be *real* little boys.

Who was it who said, "I *think*, therefore I *am*"?

Ah, yes—Jay Silverheels.

I knew it would come to me.

———••••———

This afternoon we escaped from our rehearsal room and got onto the stage of the O'Keefe for the first time.

Today being Sunday—and our advance sale being fat enough for Alex Cohen to shrug off whatever expense an on-stage rehearsal requires—the sets for *Little Me* have been pushed flush against the rear wall of the theatre while our huge platforms and staircase have been dismantled in the rehearsal hall and reassembled on stage.

We are now ready to take a good whack at Shakespeare's tragedy before a Sahara-like expanse of empty seats. As I have mentioned before, the O'Keefe seats well over 3000 viewers. It seems as deep, if not as wide, as Yankee Stadium. It is a Canadian Ocean.

How awesome to inhabit so vast a stage, bedeviled by feelings of inadequacy: the incredible shrinking man! How truly forbidding so gross an auditorium can be! *Come on, you teentsie-tinies, fill me up. Acres and acres of me and I'm all yours.*

As always, when I am deeply disturbed, I laughed. But my mind conjured fantasies all its own: We should be doing *Die Walküre*, not *Hamlet*—and what a splendid Brünnhilde Richard Burton would make, complete with blond wig, like Bert Lahr. And, if he didn't work out in the part, he could be replaced instantly by Eileen Farrell.

Gielgud did not permit us to run the play. As soon as he saw the early scenes from a distance, he began reblocking like some mad revisionist. Most of the day was eaten up by the first scene: the Battlements. When some of the actors (including Burton) complained, Sir John began to move things along. "Yes," he said, "you're all perfectly correct. I can't fix *all* of our crimes in one day. But they'll come back to haunt us, never fear."

He's right about that.

By the end of the rehearsal, we had gotten up to the Closet Scene. At seven p.m., we quit for the night. Before we toddled off to various rendezvous, Gielgud spoke briefly: "As you have all seen and heard, it is a large and ominous theatre. We all want to act simply and we all wish to avoid old-fashioned posturing and declamation, but we must act with great sweep and fire and drive in this theatre or we shall be lost. Get a good night's rest. Tomorrow, we return to our little room. But this time with our eyes and ears open."

Oddly, he had failed to mention the resplendent fact that our ultimate goal has nothing to do with O'Keefe's or any theatre like it. Cynical it may sound, but rehearsals should concern themselves exclusively with a production's important opening. For a Broadway production, that important opening is New York City. Being loved in Toronto is like being loved in Sheboygan— no one ever paid off a show in Toronto. A Toronto audience comes to see a tryout which is headed for New York. Both the audience and the reviewers must appraise what they see on a tryout basis or they are out of touch with theatre reality. If Toronto —or Chicago or Los Angeles or Anyplace, U.S.A.—doesn't want it that way, then their theatre managers must refuse to book a production until after its New York engagement. Adjusting performances to this theatre or that *after* a Broadway run does little damage to the destiny of a show. To do so beforehand is to invite ruin. Not only that, most people—in most cities—*prefer* to see shows before the New York engagement. Although it is true that even *My Fair Lady* was less efficient in Philadelphia than it was for its New York opening, a sense of excitement pervades an out-of-town opening that cannot be duplicated thereafter.

If I were an "out-of-towner," I would find the pre-Broadway openings an exciting hobby. I like calling the tune on a new show. I like pitting my judgment against the smart money. Moreover, I believe that most out-of-town folks who love the theatre feel more or less the same. They like being used as guinea pigs because they like being told that they've got something valuable to say. Out-of-town audiences, for the most part, are very good audiences. More than that, they are instructive. Unfortunately, most out-of-town reviewers are not too good at instructions and tell the creators of a show nothing useful at all. Here's a cardinal rule for tryout productions: Listen to the audience, never the critics.

Back to Sir John. His "special instructions" for me threw me a bit off my stride. For over ten days of rehearsal, Gielgud has seemed simply delighted with my playing of a particular scene. I refer to R&G informing Hamlet of the King's "choler" and adding that the Queen would like to speak with her son ere he goes to bed. It is the same scene of which I auditioned a brief portion last October. At that time, too, Gielgud could hardly restrain himself from burbling into overt laughter.

The note that I have been striking in this scene, with recognizable if not boring consistency, has been one of exaggerated servility and astonishment, the sort of behavior reserved for someone who has committed an indecency in church. Since the scene follows hot on the heels of the Play Scene (which is perhaps the most active, dramatic, and busy-busy in all Shakespeare) a different note altogether must be struck. Guildenstern begins the scene saying, "Good my lord, vouchsafe me a word with you." He is—as I see it—in a state of shock. He is nervous. He is upset. He is doubtless convinced, by this time, that Prince Hamlet is as nutty as a fruit cake, and that he (Hamlet) must be forestalled from further peccadilloes lest he embarrass all Denmark with his unpredictable, disrespectful behavior. Guildenstern refers to the King as "marvellous distempered." It is not too much to assume that the King has said *directly* to R&G that they'd bloody well better talk to their young friend and tell him to get his saucy self to the Queen's closet. Surely, Guildenstern is anxious and apprehensive; he is exaggeratedly polite and cautious; he is circling watchfully around this dangerous Prince who used to be such a carefree companion. Over and again, Gielgud has watched this basic approach and approved it. Imagine my surprise when he suggested that the scene be played in an entirely new way! "Much *stronger* in that scene, Bill," he cried out from deep in the orchestra. "You must bully Hamlet now! You must tell him off! He's behaved disgracefully—let him have it!" No doubt I looked nonplused, for Sir John rose from his seat and strode down the aisle. "You've got the King on your side now. You're not afraid of Hamlet any more. His behavior is shocking. He was unnecessarily rude to you in the first scene. Stronger!"

I nodded and did as he asked, but how I longed to say, "*Stronger?* Truly, John? Do you really mean stronger than that? Well, forgive me, but I'm already showing you my peak output. This is it, *mon vieux*—there's no more wattage!"

I mentioned my puzzlement to Richard Burton and he was

roundly amused. "Well, look here," he said, "since the old boy loves *change* so much, why don't you tiptoe over to him and say this: 'Er—John, dear—instead of my being stronger in that scene, why don't I just be *different?* '"

I said I hadn't the nerve to try it.

Burton chuckled. "Bloody well better not," he said, and then another thought occurred to him. "You know what he'd say if you did? He'd go a bit erect, and lift his chin. That active little muscle next to his nose would twitch a bit and he'd turn on his Royal Family smile and say, 'Different, is it? In a farthingale, perhaps? And a derby hat?' "

Burton does a dazzling impersonation of Gielgud—as does George Rose. Many years ago, as Burton tells it, he was standing in a hallway amusing some fellow student-actors by "doing" Gielgud. At one point, the faces of his auditors froze and the giggles went silent. Burton turned round to see Gielgud standing behind him, looking as fearfully imperious as Catherine of Russia. "Generally speaking," said Sir John, "very good impersonators do *not* make very good actors."

In any case, I did approach him again before the rehearsal broke up. It was a frightfully cold day and he was donning his sable hat. For a brief, arrested moment, I paused to note that he indeed resembled a Romanoff dressed for winter. Not Catherine, to be sure, but possibly Nicholas II—a rather inbred and lonely creature, regal as an Afghan hound. "Sir John," I said, "forgive me for troubling you, but I . . . I don't quite know how to get *stronger* in that scene. I'm sure you're *right* about it, but it seems to me I should be more amazed or astonished—er, taken aback—alarmed, I mean, well . . . Do you see what I mean? I mean—rather than *bullying* him."

He lit a cigarette and the small nose muscle went diligently to work. One nostril dilated while his head moved subtly on his neck. "I *do* see," he said, "but remember this: Richard has a *veddy* strong personality. And Hamlet is *such* a good part." He then smiled, turned quickly on his toes, and dashed away. His exit reminded me of Nureyev leaving the stage in a series of leaps. Anyway, I got the point: Richard's a tough actor; Hamlet's a good

part. You're a good actor; Guildenstern's a bad part. Don't be
softish. Bully him.

Very well. I would bully the hell out of him.

Later that evening, I discussed the matter with Clem Fowler.
He inclined to my view of the scene but pointed out that Gielgud could be seeing things from a different standpoint now that
the staging perspective had been altered. And *how* it had been
altered! Anyway, Clem had a new thought about our basic
"characters." He spoke of what manner we should use, if any. I
told him I thought a special style of behavior might well be
useful. He suggested certain modern parallels for the courtiers,
dukes, and earls of monarchic days: the big-time agents inhabiting
the hallways and cubicles of William Morris, GAC, Ashley-Fa-
mous, et cetera. Such men are always on the lookout for someone to *woo*. *Let's woo Marlon Brando, Kirk Douglas, Gregory
Peck; or—for that matter—Richard Burton*. Clem's point was
that we *do* buddy up to Richard Burton. No matter how hard
we try not to, we tend to flatter him, to gather around him a bit
too often, to listen to too many stories and tell too many. He is a
Prince of the profession just as Hamlet is Prince of the realm. He
is by no means, as the Gravedigger says, "your even Christian."

Though it may seem we are straining at gnats, the truth is
that one tends to work harder on the small parts than on the
long ones. More meticulously, at any rate. Long roles move in
long waves. Some of what is to be done can be left to the rhythm
of the play once it is performed before an audience. Short roles,
however, move in quick, sharply defined jabs. Much of what is
to be done must be *forced* upon the audience.

Some fifteen years ago, when *A Streetcar Named Desire* was
the sensation-hit of its decade, a Chicago company was formed
and a long out-of-work character actor was selected to play the
small role of the doctor. This character appears in the final minutes of the play. He speaks few lines. He is there to take Blanche
away to an institution, and he is gentle enough to cause her to
say, "I have always depended upon the kindness of strangers."
So much for the assignment. There is no more to it than that.

When the actor playing this role arrived in Chicago, some

long-unseen relatives called him to invite him to dinner. The gentleman accepted and was greeted royally by his relations. At one point during the festive dinner, one breathlessly inquisitive niece said to her uncle, "We've heard so much about this 'Streetcar' play. Please would you tell us what the story is?" The old gentleman put down his soup spoon and smiled at the young lady (character actors are notoriously courtly) and said, "Of course I'll tell you what the story is, my dear. It's about a doctor who comes to New Orleans because he's received a telephone call from a young lady whose sister is having a nervous breakdown."

I'd hire that old fellow for *my* play any day of the week. Why? Because he's right. Because, to the actor, *his* part should be the biggest in the play. Let the director be objective, never the actor. An actor should be objective (theatrically speaking) only when the meaning of a scene is at stake, only when his sense of character is somehow spoiling other performances—other moments. At that point, the actor must be willing to surrender his subjective position in order to comprehend the problem of the scene. But any director who attempts to bring an actor "into line" by emphasizing the smallness or lack of importance of a role is a foolish leader as well as a bad one.

Gielgud, of course, gives no such impression. He has never elaborated upon the relative importance of one role to another in *Hamlet*, except for his pained admission that Hamlet, the character, simply must "steal the play." Still, it is not hard to be aware of John's feelings. He wants each actor to be happy and to fulfill himself. He also believes (I think) that a happy, satisfied actor will probably give a good performance. And—except for particularly perverse personalities—that is true.

More tomorrow.
William

10 February—Toronto

Dear Bob . . .

We are back in our Rehearsal Hall, cozy as ever. Somehow I am attacked by the subtle suspicion that yesterday's "vastness" will be forgotten too quickly.

At the close of today's rehearsal, I was one of those invited to join Richard Burton in his upstairs "Dressing Room" for a spot of wassail. This room has been made available to him until *Little Me* departs the O'Keefe and Sid Caesar vacates the #1 Dressing Room. Actually, Burton needs no dressing room as yet, but he does have interviews and conferences and needs a room for greeting visiting dignitaries. True to his nature, however, Burton prefers actors to dignitaries. Each evening, five or six members of the Hamlet company gather there as Mr. Burton's guests. This is not only fun, it's good for morale. Stories abound and spirits are high. Twilight relaxation.

Richard told us a valuable story of Laurence Olivier. Some years ago, he attended the opening-night performance of *Titus Andronicus* in which Sir Laurence starred. Midway in the play, there comes a famous scene during which Titus is compelled to chop off his own left hand with a hatchet. The performance was going entirely well but the audience began to murmur with anticipation as this scene approached. Olivier was already famous for bold physical effects and a certain Grand Guignol appetite for letting visible blood. How would he handle the hand-chopping scene? The next words are Burton's: "If only I knew the speech by heart—but I don't. Titus says a fond and rueful farewell to his hand; that's what it amounts to. As usual with Shakespeare, no sentiment is left unturned—when he gets through with his hymn to the hand, there is nothing left to be said. But what was more impressive was the way Larry was *handling* the speech . . . (Laughter) . . . Lord, but you've all got quick ears! Very well, *handling* the *hand* speech. Now, as you know, the speech takes place *before* the removal of the hand, and there was Larry crooning and moaning and kissing his dear hand for all the world like a lost, pathetic child. I tell you it was thrilling! I had never seen him so truthful, so real. You see, there's something I've always withdrawn from in his acting—just a tiny bit, I mean. Oh, don't misunderstand—he's brilliant, absolutely brilliant, and—of course—beautiful, too; but I've always felt this *technical* thing, a sense of cogs and wheels going round and round. Well, *this* time it was gone. *This* time, there was a freshness, a newness, an illusion of the first time, a spontaneity unlike anything I've ever seen from Larry. It brought me bolt upright in my seat, my eyes and ears wide open. I'm speaking only of this particular scene, mind you, not the rest of the play.

"Up to this moment, he had been the same old Larry—expert and crisp—but now he began to moan and whimper and kiss the hand he was about to lose. He brought each finger to his lips, he pressed the palm to his cheek, he turned it this way and that and held the wrist with his right hand as though to memorize the thumb, the mound of Venus, the wrinkles in the knuckles, each tiny blue vein, each fingernail. He murmured to it lovingly, like some passionate Casanova. Some of the lines were swallowed— which isn't *at all* like Larry—but the effect of the scene was overwhelming. It was so *intimate*, like something played out behind closed doors. At one point, he all but turned his back on the audience for several lines, several kisses, as though he too was aware that this was all too private. I was absolutely bewitched by the way he moved his mouth about the hand while his other hand caressed it, stopping here to pinch and there to touch—it was as though the whole business had been choreographed! A beautiful dance of the hands! It was such an artistic pattern; such as enchanting *design*. . . .

"Well, indeed it *was* a design—as we soon found out. For when he finally neared the end of the speech, he stopped his crooning and caressing; he straightened his shoulders and placed his beloved hand flat against a table top; then he accepted the hatchet from a soldier, swung it a great roundhouse whack through the air, brought it down into that butcher's block as though he were chopping firewood, let out one of his hair-raising shrieks, and bounded across the stage leaving—*his own hand*, dismembered, sitting all alone on that mad little table. I tell you, the audience was thunderstruck. We gasped as one person—a few ladies fainted! And I swear to you that, for one awful moment, I believed it! Truly, I thought he had gone round the bend and chopped off his own left hand: the last and most spectacular of all his effects!

"Well, do you begin to smell out the sordid facts of all this business? Method? Sincere feeling? Psychological drama? Nothing of the kind. He *had* to do the speech in just that way. He needed all the pauses to give himself time to undo the artificial hand which was attached to his arm and his costume. The bent shoulders, the passionate-looking hunch came from having to withdraw his own true hand carefully up his sleeve. The kissing and caressing and back-turning and touching with the other hand were all necessary to conceal the nuts and bolts and ratchets, the springs and screws he was putting carefully into place. He didn't *choose* to play the scene that way—it was *thrust* upon him. It was *inevitable!* Method indeed—it was a magic act! And beautiful, too. He's the Harry Houdini of the Old Vic—the greatest trickster of them all."

I could not help retaining the words "inevitable" and "thrust upon him," and then I thought of Lee Strasberg. For the point of Stanislavski's Method (or System) was to contrive circumstances which would make the desired behavior *inevitable* and in the most personal possible way. Wouldn't Strasberg say that a series of objects (such as Olivier's ratchets, springs, and bolts) would first engage the total attention of the actor and then relax him utterly; that the task to be done with these objects would help the actor to experience private feelings in public; and that the *intention* or *action* (not to *really* lose one's hand and to avoid pain of any kind) is so clear and strong that it need not be imagined, faked, or even *acted?* Wouldn't Strasberg say that, Manny?

Sure he would, Moe.

Let many flowers grow.

William

Note: A cold, hard look at Act III of *Titus Andronicus* shows me that Titus himself chops not his own hand. One Aaron the Moor does him this service. Moreover, Titus delivers no long speech before the hand is severed. He merely gives the ax to Aaron and says, in effect, "Faster, you fool!" Well, many liberties are taken with Shakespeare these days, and perhaps Olivier created an extensive pantomime which Burton remembers imperfectly. Either that, or you're drunk.

One thing I'd like to clear up once and for all, however: Aaron the Moor is not, as some scholars have insisted, the half-brother of Erin O'Brien Moore—the lovely film star of the thirties. Instead, he is best friends with Irish Davey Moore, former lightweight champion of Tierra del Fuego. The two gentlemen are currently living in Spain. As for Titus's hand and how it *really* got chopped off, Aaron refuses to talk about it.

W.

12 February—Toronto

Dear Bob . . .

At today's rehearsal the subject of Laurence Olivier again intruded itself upon our attentions. During a five-minute break Gielgud and Burton had a chat about their brilliant fellow player. He is evidently something of a hobby among his peers. Burton repeated his contentions as to Olivier's magicianship and technical supremacy. Gielgud acknowledged the point but eagerly added, "He's also a great observer of life, you see. I've not met anyone in the theatre who *sees* more. A great, great deal of what he does on stage derives from what he's seen in life. It's a highly developed faculty in him, and it's truly brilliant. Yet at times I think that his observations interfere with the poetry. And it's the poetry that pays, don't you think? Larry *imposes* such dazzling things on the text. But what of the text itself? Simply the text."

Burton nodded politely but I had the feeling he was in only partial agreement. When men of skill and capacity talk shop, their disagreements are often silent—only areas of agreement are given voice. Something to do with courtesy, I suppose. But a sharp eye and a listening ear will record more evidence than is spoken by the tongue. What if Olivier, too, had been present? Well—in a way—he was.

To hear Burton, Gielgud, and (indirectly) Olivier speak of the theatre is to realize straight off that none is a man who preaches one art while practicing another. Olivier has not often written about the theatre, but what little he has set down amounts to no contradiction of what can readily be seen in his playing. Much the same could be said of Gielgud and Burton. One can see the poet in Gielgud, the peasant in Burton, and the magician in Olivier. There is more to each man by far than a glib label, but the labels are signposts nevertheless. The old saw, "You can't tell a book by its cover" is not always true. Sometimes you can tell a little.

In any case, Richard Burton is an actor who functions almost entirely on Celtic temperament and vocal technique. He is not, strictly speaking, "inventive"; he does not *dream up* much. He decides upon the long lines of his role and he flings himself at every implication of such decisions, but finally—he stands center stage and cuts loose. He is a bardic actor—crooning, humorous, and exotic—but there is also a bit of soil on his boots with all his education. He is an intelligent man but a plain man, still. There is not a little blood and guts about him. He would not seem entirely out of place in a slaughterhouse.

Gielgud, of course, must be removed from that slaughterhouse at once and trundled off to a musicale. He is the verse-speaking musician among us, but he is also a man of stubborn opinion. He believes, heart and soul, in the text. Ever and always, when it comes to Shakespeare especially, the *text*, the *text*, the *text*. He is not interested in blood. He is not even interested in thunder. He is interested in beauty and clarity; in pure, cold water. Olivier is quite demonstrably interested in bringing his audience bolt upright with excitement. And, indeed, he succeeds quite often. Since Burton calls Olivier's acting "tricky"—as well as great— and Gielgud calls Olivier's acting "anti-poetic"—as well as great —is it too much to assume that Olivier might call Burton's acting "brilliant but inflexible" and Gielgud's acting "magnificent but mental"?

After his chat with Gielgud, Burton spoke to me again of differing acting styles. For himself, Richard believes deeply in what he calls "stillness." Two days before, he had murmured during a run-through, "I'm not still enough yet. Stillness is most important."

Though the remark was uttered quietly, it was thick with conviction. I am now convinced that Richard Burton, at bottom, is a *plain* actor. By plain, I mean simple, of course, yet I avoid that overused word out of my belief that so complex a man could hardly be a simple actor and that the word "simple" is too often interpreted as meaning "simple-minded." The meaning of plain is beyond confusion, I hope.

Burton gains his stage effects largely out of the strength of his personality. He is by no means a character actor—as Olivier is, as Paul Scofield is; he knows nothing about make-up and does not seem interested in the use of it; he is not addicted in any way to limping, laughing, Inverness capes, or humps upon his back. All he knows of costume, make-up, and the use of his voice goes to buttress the on-stage image of Richard Burton himself.

I did not see his London performance of *Othello*, but something about the photographs leads me to believe that even so simple a necessity as chocolate make-up gave Burton an air more of masquerade than of Moor. He is a rhetorical actor, of course (plain does not mean naturalistic) but he is not a Fancy Dan. Save some rather predictable vocalisms, such as extreme voicing of consonants and a frequent use of the nose, his acting tricks would not last him more than one act when playing the great and challenging roles. What *does* support him, I believe, is the personality, the intelligence, and—above all—the stamina.

But the bag of tricks is there and might as well be looked into: his favorite trick, if it can be so called, is the one he refers to as "stillness." It is a puzzling word for him to use, since I do not believe that he means "standing still." He is so often in motion; he so often employs gesture, and rather wild gesture to boot. No, he speaks of an inner stillness, which produces a stillness about the eyes and an uncommon steadiness of the head. These rare qualities often create an effect of what theatregoers call "simplicity."

By common consent, simplicity is an acting quality much sought after and seldom achieved. Nearly anyone, particularly a professional, will recognize "simplicity" instantly. But what the actor does (or is) to create this effect is by no means simple, nor does it project across the footlights merely because the actor thinks and/or behaves "simply." Actors who are merely simple (because they are not complicated) are but a negative and useless example of the quality. Laurence Olivier, on the other hand, is a splendid example of the opposite. Sir Laurence is by no account simple. Indeed, he is as intricate as an IBM Calculator. His mind is intricate, his body more so, his work with make-up the most developed in the modern theatre, and his courage is, well, earth-shaking. But he is not simple. Burton, on the other hand, *is* simple. That is not all he is, but he is certainly simple in several important respects, and the following tale he told me may further illustrate the point.

"I don't know whether you know it or not, but the biggest success I ever had in the theatre was *Coriolanus* when I was twenty-six years old. After the opening night, Larry Olivier said no one could ever play the part again. It was a beautiful and graceful lie, since Larry himself was and always will be this era's definitive Coriolanus. Anyway, Bobby Helpmann did me a favor during rehearsals. When I died—as we all must—he had me do an absolutely shattering fall down a great flight of stone steps. Helpmann is a magnificent dancer and choreographer, and he taught me how to do the fall by bumping my fanny against every step—one at a time. It was like teaching an elephant how to play tennis, but it worked. I was young, I didn't get hurt, the fall thrilled the audience, and I could do it every night with very little risk. Now, then—when Olivier played Coriolanus before me, he did the most spectacular death scene in the history of the modern British theatre. He rigged some sort of harness—like a vaudeville knife-flinger—which sprang out short spears at the touch of a button so that it appeared he'd been turned into a pincushion by ten or more assassins, and then he fell backwards —yes, I said *backwards*—off a six-foot platform where two ter-rified young apprentices had to grab him by the ankles at the last possible moment. The final image was of Larry upside down, spears stuck out all over his chest, breathing his last while being kept from a skull fracture by the strong arms and fingers of his two young soldiers. A devastating effect, of course, but the two young men spent night after night examining their sweating palms and absolutely dreading the end of the play. So much for Larry's first breathtaking Coriolanus.

"Ten years after I played the part, Larry again decided to play Coriolanus. He called me at my home and asked me if I would teach him to do 'that splendid fall down the steps.' I told him to come on out for fanny-bumping lessons. By that time I was thirty-five, and Larry himself was fifty-three or thereabouts. He was bloody damned if he was going to let frightened boy supers grab him by the ankles again—he had stretched both Achilles' tendons painfully during the engagement—but he wanted some other spectacular effect and had hit upon the notion of re-creating mine. We spent the entire afternoon thudding down the main staircase of my house and both of us came perilously close to a fracture of the coccyx. Because I was younger than he, I could not give up first—I have my pride, dammit!—but I was in excruciating pain. Finally, Larry broke down. 'I'm too old for this!' he shouted and stopped the bumping. 'I should pack it in, that's all. I'm just too blasted old!' I leaped at his suggestion like a starving dog at a hamburger patty. 'For Christ's sake, I'm too old myself,' I said. 'Let's have a drink and a hefty one, too.'

"After I'd served our grog, I said, 'Look here, old chap, why must you bruise your fifty-year-old bum doing an effect for this production? If you insist on playing the part again, well, just play the bloody part and to hell with the rest!'

"The old boy looked at me with that amazed look he gets sometimes. 'Are you round the bend?' he asked. 'I have to do *something*, after all,' and I replied—quick as a hare, you'll see—'Yes, by God, you *do*—you have to *die*—but that's all. Shakespeare writes, Coriolanus dies . . . and that's all he writes. And that's all you have to do.' The old boy looked at me with pure and total hatred and then he lifted his glass to me and said, 'Give me another drink, you bleeding halfwit.' We laughed the rest of the afternoon away.

"But that's Larry, you see. There's always got to be a dazzler, a knocker. Something that pulls a gasp from the audience and turns them into a thunderstruck mob. He loves his power over them. He loves to make them jump. More than anything else, I think, he wants to homogenize them into one entity, one mass impulse. He's brilliant at the task, but I sometimes wonder if it's all that necessary or if it isn't more hypnotism than art. I have never approved of mass hysteria, and Larry tends to induce such reactions in an audience. He's like a rabble-rouser or one of your Chautauqua speakers. In the rabble-rousing parts, such as Henry V or Hotspur, he has no peer, but I wonder if his Douglas Fairbanks derring-do quite suits some of the other roles. One cannot really disapprove of Larry ever. He's too good, for one thing, and whatever excesses he's guilty of emerge only from his love of the theatre and his love of excitement. His love of excitement knows no bounds and his love of the theatre is simply overwhelming. But his Hamlet, for example, must have been quite something.

"Aside from the film, he has played Hamlet only once—on the London stage, that is; he played it once at Elsinore—and Michael Redgrave, of all people, was his Laertes. It was in 1937. Vanessa Redgrave was born during the engagement. Since I've worked with Michael quite a lot and we are good friends, I felt disposed on one occasion to interrogate him on the subject. I was so bold as to inquire what Larry's Hamlet was like. Michael stared at me gravely for a moment and then lifted both his hands to the top of his head. With nary a change of expression, he parted his luxuriant hair and revealed an absolutely livid scar at least four inches in length. 'He was a *spirited* Hamlet,' Michael said. 'He was a *most* spirited Hamlet.' I asked still another actor —I cannot name him—about Larry's Hamlet and he smiled benignly. 'It was,' he said, 'the finest performance of Hotspur that I have ever seen.'

"Perhaps that's what dear old John G. is driving at—that Larry simply cannot leave well enough alone. If the part needs that inventive, imaginative touch, Larry will provide it. If the part is so well written it needs no such gingerbread, Larry will provide it anyway. He will carry coals to Juneau—where they are sorely required—and he will carry them to Newcastle as well. All that he does, he does from love, but we do many things from love that perhaps we should not do. Larry is no exception. Are any of us?"

Have I said yet that Burton is as bright as he is romantic? For that matter, have I said that he is as eloquent as he is phonetic? Moreover, have I said that he is as profound as he is deft?

I don't think I have said any of those things. To tell the truth, I don't think they need to be said.

> More tomorrow, Bob.
> William

Note: I later discovered that Burton's story of Coriolanus is all out of chronology. Olivier, in fact, did his spectacular fall *after* the production in which Burton thudded down the stairs. Albert Finney, who was standing by for Olivier, had to play an uncommon number of performances because the trick tended to stretch Olivier's Achilles' tendons so badly that he lost control of his feet.

When I confronted Burton with this inconsistency, he laughed. "Well, of *course*, you silly lump," he said, "the whole point of the story is that he whined and complained about bumping down the stairs and then went ahead and did something three times as difficult *ten years later*."

I tried to collect my thoughts. "Well, did he or didn't he come to your house just before he went into rehearsal?"

"Did I say that? Oh, he may have—but what I remember best is that he asked me to teach him the fall the very night I opened in the play. He came backstage and said, 'Dear boy—how *did* you do that fall?' We went right onto the stage and I showed him. Clear, now?"

No.

> 13 February—Toronto

Dear Bob . . .

So little is happening creatively these days that my attention wanders. My scenes are seldom rehearsed and I have stopped watching the rehearsals of other scenes in order to fix my concentration upon my own acting problems rather than those of others. This is something of a forward step for me. Many knowledgeable actors fall into the trap of subconsciously *directing* other actors during rehearsals rather than *rehearsing* their own roles. As these letters amply demonstrate, I have no more conquered this habit than I have managed to stop smoking before breakfast, but I am keeping both sins to a minimum, thank you, and a damned good thing, too.

As for new scenes (which I would certainly watch at least twice), there have been none. George Voskovec (Player King) and George Rose (First Gravedigger) have only recently arrived, which leaves them less than two weeks to prepare their roles. Moreover, Gielgud has not yet scheduled a rehearsal for either of them. One can only assume that Sir John considers both parts "cameos" and not needful of much rehearsal. I do not agree, but who am I? Just a middle-aged juvenile, shuffling along.

I busy my mind with tales of the past. I busy my ears collecting more of same from Burton, Gielgud, Alfred Drake, and Philip Coolidge—to name but a few. I even spend my midnights retelling my own favorites. One follows.

During the highly successful run of *A Man for All Seasons*, Noel Willman, who directed, called occasional brush-up rehearsals at which we listened to whatever "notes" he had jotted down concerning the removal of our improvements. Now and again he also read letters to us which he had received from members of the audience. Most such letters were paeans of praise, but Noel eventually opened a rather disturbing one. The correspondent concerned herself with a crucial moment in the play: When Sir Thomas More removes his Chain of Office as Lord Chancellor, he effectively separates himself from the beneficent affections of an irascible Henry VIII. Lady Alice More, understandably fearful for her husband, asks him pointedly, "What will you do now?" to which More replies, "I'll write, I'll read, I'll play with my grandchildren." The letter in question praised our production highly and considered Paul Scofield's performance an exceptional achievement but went on to say, "I am a student of the sixteenth century and one anachronism in the play offended me deeply. When Thomas More resigns his office, he says to his wife, 'I'll write, I'll read, I'll play with my banjo.' Let me assure you, Mr. Willman, the banjo had not been invented by 1545. Couldn't you persuade the playwright to change this one line in an otherwise estimable play?"

Mr. Scofield is considered one of the great elocutionists of the contemporary stage. If even *he* can make "grandchildren" sound like "banjo" what on earth must the rest of us be up to? The customer, after all, is always right.

Some years ago, Mr. Johnny Weissmuller, having become famous as the monosyllabic Tarzan, essayed the role of Mowgli the Wolf Boy in a play the title of which escapes me entirely. Quite possibly, it was called *Mowgli the Wolf Boy*. Anyway, I hope so, but I did not actually see the play. The novelty of the production proceeded from Mr. Weissmuller's scantily clad presence at a well-furnished mansion in the city of San Francisco. Precisely why Mowgli the Wolf Boy should have been stopping over at a well-to-do San Franciscan's I cannot imagine without considerable aid, but he *was* all the same and his mode of dress remained a loincloth, a pair of sandals, a band round his head, and a knife angled into his whipthong belt. At a climactic second-act moment, Mowgli and the villain of the piece struggle to the death for possession of a pistol with which the villain has attempted to shoot Mowgli. On opening night (in Los Angeles, I believe) the powerful Mr. Weissmuller wrested the weapon from his snarling but flimsy adversary and fired it at him. But the prop weapon misfired and the tell-tale clickclickclick of the trigger told a sad story: villain of play will not be shot tonight, dear friends and neighbors. Mr. Weissmuller, showing commendable presence of mind, immediately went for his knife. Unfortunately, the knife bent visibly double against the villain's chest because it was made of rubber. This amused the audience a good deal but caused the villain to break out in a cold, trembling sweat. Actors who are supposed to be killed become frightfully nervous when things don't go as expected—more nervous, for some reason, than fellow actors who are supposed to kill them.

Weissmuller himself? Unfazed, apparently. He began to growl and grunt and stomp. He dragged the villain to the window. He then wrapped window drapes around the hapless chap's neck and the latter, being only too happy to cooperate, commenced to expire. But the audience would have none of it. "He's not dead," several cried, and "Hit him again!" When Mr. Weissmuller ripped the drapes away from the villain's throat, the audience burst into applause. "No more strangling," a man cried derisively. "Think of something else." Weissmuller did. He stared hard at his fellow player, who—terrified—began to sink slowly to his knees. Weissmuller then lifted his right fist threateningly. The villain mumbled and whimpered. Suddenly, Weissmuller pressed his fist against the villain's forehead and croaked ominously, "I keel you weeth my poison ring!" The villain gasped his relief and fell over in a heap, quite theatrically dead. I believe that even the audience was satisfied. If they weren't, they should have been. Mr. Weissmuller deserved a standing ovation that night. If he didn't get one then, he gets mine right now.

I am illustrating, in rather circuitous fashion, the perils of live performing. Such nightmare thoughts begin to bedevil the mind of every actor toward the middle period of rehearsals. When not enough rehearsing is being done, these goblin-infested fantasies run absolutely riot. As for *Hamlet*, even the English actors among us are beginning to mumble lines from *Macbeth*. This is a sure sign of deteriorating morale. So far as English players are concerned, to mention the title of "that play" or to quote even a single line from it while inside the walls of a theatre is to invite disaster. It is a far worse tempting of fate than whistling in the dressing room, say, or seducing the wife of the theatre manager. I have not yet encountered an English actor, mystic or otherwise, who debunked this superstition. Mr. Olivier has written of it; George Rose has informed me that no production of *M.....h* since World War II has opened without at least one catastrophic inadvertence, and Richard Burton has confirmed Rose's word. Aside from physical injury to players, productions of *Macbeth* tend to incite the most devastatingly awful reviews. From the actor's standpoint, it is hard to say which fate is worse.

According to Burton, the late Diana Wynyard—who was a lovely-looking woman as well as a dedicated and gifted actress —insisted on playing Lady Macbeth's sleepwalking scene with her eyes closed. Having done some Stanislavkian research on the subject, she discovered that sleepwalkers do not pursue their nightly rounds with their eyes open, as most actresses playing Lady Macbeth would have us believe. Lady Diana was devoted to the truth and refused to make matters easy for herself. She closed her eyes and kept them closed. Unhappily, this particular scene was staged along a rather narrow parapet which jutted impressively into the audience. Miss Wynyard practiced her sightless walk over and again, going through the dress rehearsal without a hint of mishap. On opening night, however, she fell from the ramp and broke everything in sight—including a disheartening number of her own bones.

On another occasion, the actor playing Macbeth died in the midst of an opening night. I do not mean he gave a bad performance; I mean he plain dropped dead. Mr. Geoffrey Toone, who played Banquo on Broadway with Michael Redgrave and Flora Robson, was nearly dispatched one evening during the scene with the Three Murderers. An over-zealous Third Murderer shoved a dagger into Mr. Toone's ear. Later, Mr. Toone was discovered sitting at his dressing-room table, his ear heavily bandaged, and staring at himself in the mirror. He was also murmuring, "He's too keen, that chap. He's just too keen."

A list of all *Macbeth* disasters could easily be the subject of a lengthy article in *The Saturday Evening Post*. For now, suffice it to say that Mr. Burton has put me on to the talisman for curing a *Macbeth* spell. Whenever the play is referred to backstage in any way, all actors present are to turn round three times while whistling "Yankee Doodle."

Back to business now.

———•—•—•———

Thursday afternoon
February 13—Toronto
Shortly after today's luncheon break, all actors were dismissed from the rehearsal with one exception: Mr. Richard Burton. It is Sir John Gielgud's wish that a half day be spent in private rehearsal. No other cast members, no stage managers, no mem-

bers of the production team, nor any visitors were allowed admittance. Even Miss Jessica Levy was asked to leave, which disappointed her not a little, since she is presumed to be Sir John's one assistant and confidante. Only one outsider remained. Call him observer, reporter, philosopher, or what you will. I call him the Enforcer: Mr. Bobby LaSalle.

He is personal bodyguard to Mr. Burton and Elizabeth Taylor. A small but dangerous-looking man, Mr. LaSalle is often asked, "Are you—or were you—a prize fighter?" to which he invariably replies, "Well, I sure wasn't *born* with this face."

The point is well taken. His face clearly spells combat. He is fifty-four years old and entirely gray on top, and he has the gnarled fists of a woodsman . . . or a prize fighter. He wears bow-ties exclusively, which I at first assumed was a matter of stylistic preference. He later showed me that a clip-on bow tie made it impossible for an adversary to grab him by the tie and cut off the action of his windpipe. A clip-on bow tie comes off in an opponent's hand while Mr. LaSalle throws the left hook. "That's the one," he has informed me, "with the steam in it."

I also noticed his shoes. The heels are as high as a flamenco dancer's and the toes are sharply pointed. Very stylish indeed, but again I confused couture with contingencies. Mr. LaSalle is not a vain man. He is a fighting man and he wears a fighting man's footwear. The heels are good for grinding an aggressor's metatarsal arch into bone meal, and the toes will all but kick a medulla oblongata into a cranium. Such street tactics are employed only *in extremis*, of course.

He is a skilled masseur, as most old fighters are, and he once manipulated the soreness out of a stiff shoulder of mine in less than fifteen minutes. "Heat mentholatum," he grunted, refusing any more than an agent's share of the credit for my miracle cure, "that's the trick. Get yourself a jar o' heat mentholatum an' I'll garntee ya'll feel okay in the mornin'."

Mr. LaSalle is a Southwestern American. He sure fixed my shoulder, though. As for his current assignment, he openly admits that neither the theatre nor motion pictures interest him (to watch, that is; he has been working in films since 1932, when he served as a technical adviser on the Max Baer–Myrna Loy classic *The Prizefighter and the Lady*), but the story of *Hamlet* seems to be relaxing his resistance. Several times during our rehearsals he has commented positively on the play's text. On one occasion he gave Mr. Shakespeare the following notice: "Say, I can't hardly b'lieve my eyes 'n' ears. I mean, this Hamlet is terrific. It's funny an' it's sad an' it's gotta lotta action, too." I realize that all this sounds too good to be true—rather like some part once played by Nat Pendleton in a William Powell movie—but it *is* true, nevertheless, and while Richard Burton and John Gielgud explored the intricacies of Hamlet's soliloquies and the long, sweeping corridors of Hamlet's aggressions and delays, as well as the niceties of interpretation and rhetoric, only one pair of outsider's ears could eavesdrop—and they were cauliflowered.

———•••———

Because our afternoon off came as a surprise, Alfred Drake made a civilized suggestion—namely, a drink on him. Also present were Eileen Herlie, Hume Cronyn, and Philip Coolidge.

Current production plans have it that we will also be given the week end off after the rehearsals on Friday afternoon; practice sessions to resume on Monday afternoon at 2:30. Many cast members have decided to go home to their families. Isn't that wonderful?

No, it isn't. Vacations are for salesmen. For the actor (or any artist) life itself is a vacation, and one's creative work is a celebration of that conviction. A vacation in the middle of rehearsals? It's insane.

When we return next Monday afternoon, we will be shaking hands with the 17th of February—a date exactly eight days previous to our first public performance. Calendars and clocks play large and darkling roles in the fantasy world of the actor. Rehearsal time ticks madly in his ears while his blood pressure rises. It is a thin-lipped parody of "The Tell-Tale Heart." Opening night approaches. He dreams of Black Masses and Walpurgis

Nacht. A party is in progress, but the top-hatted guests are skele-
tons and warlocks. Fear arrives in a funny hat, saying, "Hurry
up, please. It's time."

Over our cocktails, which tasted just fine, by the way, Hume
Cronyn again expressed concern as to being too adorable and
comic for words. We reassured him. I expressed concern as to
being merely negative as Guildenstern, having brought no special
edge to the role. They reassured me. Eventually, we all expressed
certain misgivings about this and that (excepting Miss Herlie) and
we all reassured each other (including Miss Herlie) until we
were quite as drunk on reassurance as we were on alcohol. In
fact, I do consider Hume's anxieties groundless. The conception of
his role is neither excessive nor precious. Nor do I think that
Gielgud is pushing him too far, although he *is* pushing him. If
I were pressed for a negative comment, I'd admit that he seems a
bit nimble, that's all. It's all very well to play Polonius as a
vigorous politico rather than as a doddering old poop, but he is
still far from being a young man and Hume must guard against
reminding the audience of a Canadian businessman at the prime of
life.

Alfred Drake is still disturbed by the logic of some of the
staging. Our patterns seem to him facile and contrived. "When
stage movement is dreamed up glibly and quickly and when the
physical blocking is used completely in terms of such-and-such
a pattern making an effective choreography with so-and-so a
pattern, the management might as well hire a chorus line. Unless stage movement proceeds from logic, it degenerates into
pageantry, and empty pageantry at that. What's worse is it's so
damned hard to play! But who wants to be the one to say,
'What's going on here?' Not I. I've fallen down that chute too
many times before."

Even fellow actors regard a dissenter as hot-headed and eccentric. In an interesting autobiography called *Early Stages*, John
Gielgud wrote (nonverbatim): "Don't resist your director. If
you do, you are at odds with him and nothing can be accomplished. Either swallow your disagreements or resign."

Among the Jivaro Indians there is an unsettling saying: "Only fools and children ask questions." The notion shakes me up a bit, but questions are the lifeblood of the theatre and I doubt that the Jivaros have put on many good plays lately. As far as management is concerned, however, inquisitive actors are troublemakers —"methodists"—pompous intellectuals who should be directing rather than acting. In the theatre, interrogators don't win unless they are stars.

Only at the Actors Studio (granted its drawbacks and parochialism) can the actor ask question on question with impunity. Only there can he seriously explore the mysteries of his craft without being looked on as a neurotic pariah. The basic framework of the Studio is narrow and rigid, but within that framework anything goes. Should the framework ever expand, the Studio would be a truly great academy. This important issue aside, the Studio remains a house of questions and stands, therefore, as an oasis in the lip-cracking desert of pay your dues and take your orders and grab the money and run for the cat-house. And most of all—for God's sake buy Xerox. One can ask any question at the Actors Studio, so long as it does not relate to the solid challenges of England's Royal Academy, Laurence Olivier, Albert Finney, and the undeniable power of the human voice. I can think of no other theatre area where such permissiveness exists. With nine directors out of ten, whether they function on Broadway, in television, or on film, I am fearsomely aware that a question or any sort of conceptual conversation will weaken my position beyond repair. I cannot say that I have stopped asking questions, but I have certainly stopped believing that honesty is the best policy. Because it isn't. Not when directors are kings.

Good directors understand all this, of course, though they don't often say so out loud. Good film directors understand exactly the reverse, and they are quite correct. During the filming of *The Greatest Story Ever Told*, George Stevens (a really excellent film director) was queried by an actor as to "motivation." "Young man," he said, "while you were resting yesterday, I went up in those hills over there and I shot a lot of sequences with a herd of cattle. Not one of those cattle asked me a question about motivation and, believe you me, they did just fine."

Questions could not be less appropriate to the movies if an international law were passed to that effect. But questions *are* appropriate to the theatre. What irritates me is to see theatre people embrace a directorial concept (which is filmically appropriate) instead of an actor-and-playwright concept (which is theatrically appropriate). The late James Agate wrote, "Theatre consists of two great arts: acting and playwrighting; and there is no third art necessary to coordinate them."

I said most of these things in the Olde Kinge Cole and His Merrye Fiddlerres Three Roome of the King Edward Hotel in Toronto. Much of it excited approval; some of it didn't. Occasionally I found myself staring into the faces of bemused adults indulging the polemics of an adolescent socialist. Alfred frowned tolerantly whenever I mentioned the Actors Studio, but he embraced my fundamental premise. "Questions is the right word. And to question is the perfect infinitive for the theatre. If 'Why?' is life's most pointed question, it is also the theatre's most pointed question, for the theatre is life. *This* rehearsal all but breathes an atmosphere of: No questions, please. And I can't understand it. It's like a classified news conference. When Gertrude Stein was dying, she said, 'What is the answer?' Nobody said anything so she said, 'Well, then—what is the question?'

"There are no answers without questions. I've gone pacifist about it, but only because a director who is convinced of his superiority can't be talked to anyway, so what's the point? Gielgud is a sweet man and a preoccupied man. Therefore—no questions. Not because he's a tyrant but because he plain doesn't want to converse. Very well, then. Like the saying goes: Shrug your shoulders and say, 'He's the director.' Like another saying goes, That's show business. But I can't help feeling uneasy. The whole damned thing is just too smooth, too slick, too quick, and too *mah*-velous."

Eileen Herlie rose to leave. She had completed a drink and a half. We all tried to seduce her into another toddy, but she would have none of it. "No, no, dahlings—my hair, my rest, my supper, my lines. That's my regimen. I'm a soldier. Can't you see my medals?"

Eileen has beautiful eyes. She retires to her hotel room, medals and all, by eight every evening. She dines alone and works on her role. She has played the Queen twice before, on stage and in the Olivier film, but still she works nightly. And still—she smiles and never complains.

Does she worry? Apparently not. In fact, she reacted to our anxious explorations with a certain amusement. I even detected a trace of female disdain. "Dahlings," she caroled, as she bade us good-by, "it will all work out well on the night!"

Is she truly so philosophic? Is she indeed untroubled? I doubt it. Probably she is frightened to death like the rest of us. But optimism and brightness constitute her style. It is a most winning style. And—as some anthropologists maintain—a winning style is a trick of survival.

Philip Coolidge proffered a dollop of solace to all before we downed our final drops. "Remember this," he canted. "Any bunch of actors who have been around as long as this unholy four can always look in their dressing-room mirrors and say, 'I've been in worse jams than this.'"

Alfred Drake gave him a skeptical glance. "Philip," he said, "I think you rehearsed that."

He probably did. He's no good, that Coolidge. He should be the deputy.

William

Friday
14 February—Toronto

Dear Bob . . .

At today's rehearsal—our final session before adjourning for a very long week end—George Voskovec was at last given an opportunity to practice his important and exacting speech as the Player King: Aeneas's tale to Dido of Priam's slaughter before the eyes of Hecuba. Few theatregoers understand the crucial nature of this monologue, since, on the surface, it seems no more than a set-piece: a golden opportunity for an old school actor to show off his resonant technique. On the contrary, the actual purpose of the Player King's speech is all but seminal. It stimulates in Hamlet the notion to "have these players play something like the murder of my father before mine uncle." In other words, the Player King teases to the surface Hamlet's quite probably latent impulse to rewrite *The Murder of Gonzago* as a mousetrap for Claudius.

I once saw a production of *Hamlet* in which the actor performing the Player King literally stole the show. This is not to say that other players did poorly; there was an excellent Ophelia, a fine Horatio, and an interesting Hamlet, and the production— over-all—was more than enjoyable, making the Player King's achievement especially surprising. Although I have forgotten his name, he gave a performance I can recall in every particular as though I had seen it last night. I refer to the Jean-Louis Barrault production (spoken in French) which was shown here about 1954 and which, though imperfect and confusing in many ways, and tending to substitute sexual aberration for dramatic event, could on no account be called boring. Interestingly enough, the Player King—after making an entirely natural entrance—did the speech itself in a manner I can only describe as Comédie Française. Once requested by Hamlet to proceed, he turned straight front to the audience, stood with his feet no more than six inches apart, intoned the words in an impressive, cannon-like voice, built the pentameters one upon the other like musical bricks, moved his hands hardly at all, seemed altogether to be in some sort of trance, and finally wept copious tears from crazed and widened eyes without altering his facial expression more than a jot.*

This is a typically French possibility, since the Gallic tradition of *tirade* in the theatre is a long and honorable one.** But what this actor accomplished was more important than a palimpsest of Shakespeare and Racine. He managed to synopsize the purposes of the play and set its wheels in motion as surely as though

* I once described this performance to Wally Cox. "It sounds awful," he said.
** If you are at all research-minded, listen to any phonograph records you can find of Sarah Bernhardt as *L'Aiglon* or even Charles Boyer in *Don Juan in Hell* for specific examples, one old-fashioned and one modern, of the *tirade* approach.

he had shifted the gears of a manual transmission. To begin with, it is of value for the Player King to suggest to the audience (emotionally) that he is an *actor acting* and, even more important, that he is an actor of the fourteenth century. One of the particular fascinations of the part, in fact, is that the actor playing it need have no qualms as to being old-fashioned or "hammy" or excessive or even singsongish. The more he is these things, the more sharply the point is made, *but*—on no account must the actor evade the subtlest and most touching truth of all: ham or no ham, the Player King genuinely "forces his soul to his own conceit." He is genuinely moved, genuinely distracted, genuinely tearful. To put it another way, he is both old-fashioned *and* modern. He indirectly illustrates that although *styles* in acting change constantly, the fundamental ability of the actor to capture the shadows of his own unconscious and force his deepest feelings to his will does *not* change. Not among good actors, at any rate.

Hamlet regards the Player King's control of his soul as "monstrous." Indeed it is. And precisely because it *is* so monstrous, proceeding as it does from a mere fiction, a dream of passion, Hamlet is galvanized into action. After the self-berating of the "O, what a rogue and peasant slave am I" soliloquy, he never really retreats from his purposes again. Those authorities who regard either "To be or not to be" or "Now might I do it pat" as evidence of weak-willed procrastination are, I believe, mistaken. Hamlet, in fact, is not really a languid or defeated man at any time in the play. He is merely a man with some very serious problems. Until he catches the conscience of the King in the Play Scene, he cannot be certain of the Ghost's reliability. Until the Player King stimulates his imagination, he cannot be certain how to go about either trapping the truth or effecting his revenge. I believe Hamlet to be a highly temperamental, exacerbated, and distracted man—he is, in a sense, a man on the verge of a nervous breakdown—but I do not believe him to be at all weak, at all feminine, or even excessively thoughtful. He does not *like* the assignment the Ghost has handed him—who would? On the other hand, if the Ghost's story is true, Hamlet's duty is clear. But how in hell is he to go about killing a King without the direst consequences to both the nation of Denmark and himself? Those moments in the play which scholars have used to buttress a "soft" interpretation of the part can be quite as soundly interpreted otherwise. For example, is it unreasonable to assume that the real meaning of "To be or not to be" is not mere speculative philosophy any more than it is purely melancholy? I am persuaded that Dr. Samuel Johnson was on the right track when he interpreted the speech as a quite logical consequence of the previous soliloquy. Many scholars have been puzzled because Hamlet's soliloquy of decision ("The play's the thing wherein I'll catch the conscience of the King") is followed by a soliloquy of ambivalence ("To be or not to be"); and, indeed, a few nineteenth-century actors reversed the soliloquies in the running order of the play. Dr. Johnson, however, insisted that Hamlet— having committed himself to a hazardous course of action and almost surely having *written the new lines* for the players in the interim—is also having entirely natural second thoughts based on the supposition that to pursue Claudius is to get himself killed. From that quite logical supposition he proceeds to another: Well, why *not* get myself killed? Life is not worth living, anyway. But —how do I know I'll really be dead when I die?

Shakespeare's sequence of thought, although it is sometimes elusive for the modern actor as well as the modern audience, is often remarkably spontaneous. He quite soundly *proceeds* from one thought to another. The soliloquies are rarely pat notions which have been figured out beforehand. They are examples of the human mind in action. Shakespeare does not write as people talk, not even Elizabethan people, but he definitely does write as people think—and beautifully, too. He is more than just a great formalist; he permits a character to think one thought and then to surprise even himself with the next. He is in deep connection with the intricacies and contradictions of human thought. The scholar Malone has disagreed with Dr. Johnson, claiming that "To be or not to be" is clearly the speech of a man contemplating suicide. True, but that doesn't make Johnson wrong. Hamlet begins by thinking of the death which will doubtless be his should he take arms against his sea of troubles. Such apprehensive fantasies lead him into a colloquy with himself on the merits of death as well as the nature of death.

He is then interrupted by the sight of Ophelia at prayer, becomes recharged by his growing awareness of the eavesdropping Polonius and Claudius, and crackles through the Nunnery Scene recklessly and cruelly—back on the tracks of energetic action.

It is the Player King who has induced in Hamlet the brilliant idea of putting on the play. It is the Player King who has pricked Hamlet's conscience by showing him tears for Hecuba. This shortly written role is long on implications. It is quite a substantial jewel in the watchworks of Shakespeare's most intricate play.

Perhaps it is no wonder then that Sir John Gielgud today behaved in a most un-Gielgud-like fashion. Mr. Voskovec, not having been here at the beginning of our rehearsals and not having participated therefore in the first readings of the play, has not once gone through a single line of his part. Sir John put him immediately on his feet and quickly sketched in the Players' entrance as well as Hamlet's effusive greeting, but when Voskovec began, "Anon he finds him, striking too short at Greeks . . ." Gielgud suddenly stopped the rehearsal, crying, "Nononono, deah George—do it this way!" He then did the entire speech from beginning to end at a dazzling clip. I have mentioned before that Gielgud's demonstrations are breath-taking, but I also feel that an actor should have at least *one* chance at his part before he is shown how to say the ifs, ands, and buts. How contradictory, too! The strong leadership he was giving George Voskovec (*too* strong, indeed) he has not once given to the rest of us. I believe I know why.

Gielgud realizes utterly what a turning point in the play the Player King represents. He also has firm ideas as to the meaning and effect of the speech. The demonstration in itself was, of course, electrifying. Within seven or eight lines, there were tears in his eyes. When Polonius interrupted him, Sir John looked about distractedly as though he had heard a dog barking or a distant loon at midnight. When Hamlet bade him continue, he re-attacked his emotions with renewed vigor. Once more, tears appeared in his eyes. A moment later, he flung himself to the floor. I do not believe it was planned. It merely happened. When he spoke of Hecuba's "instant burst of clamour" at the sight of her husband's slaughter by the bestial Pyrrhus, he looked to the sky, as if seeking the Gods for mercy, and when he spoke the final words, "And passion in the Gods," his voice choked; the words were all but lost in his throat; and he collapsed in a heap on the floor. Then he rose quickly, demonstrated a slight, shy bow—still in the character of an actor accepting his due—and then turned to Voskovec, saying, "Try it that way, deah boy."

The pace and spirit of his reading had been sparkling, truly beautiful. Although his tempo was rapid and feverish from the beginning, the tone remained somewhat muted until the end; and—even at the end—his volume stopped short of absolute climax. It was all stylized, even a bit "hammy," but so sensitive, so enlightened, and above all so totally *committed* as to transcend cavil.

When the tears came for the third time, Richard Burton laughed aloud, turned his back upon the demonstration, and descended from the platform. He glanced at me and winked. To me, he seemed to be saying, "How about the old boy, eh? He's a miraculous old stick, isn't he?" but Clem Fowler was afraid that Gielgud might have thought himself laughed at—even mocked. I was startled by such an interpretation, but it intrigued me too. For Clem had honestly got the impression that Burton was not taken with the demonstration. Since we both observed the same event and interpreted the evidence of our eyes and ears in diametrical ways (sort of like *Rashomon*, isn't it?) I decided to compliment Gielgud at the end of the day. After all, his performance might have been unfair to Voskovec, but it was a hell of a performance nevertheless, and if he was to feel that his actors thought him an old-fashioned, sentimental fool, future demonstrations of even greater value might not be forthcoming. I tugged at his sleeve around five p.m. and cleared my throat. "You astonished this cry of players today, sir," I said. Sometimes it is necessary to play the fool in order to help one's auditor feel less like one. In any case, Gielgud blushed scarlet and his knees twisted shyly toward each other in an agony of pleasure. When he feels flattered and appreciated, he rises to the balls of his feet and blushes. Sometimes his eyes fill up with tears. They did on this occasion. Then, very rapidly, he said, "Oh, I can only do it in bits and pieces, you see—just gabbling, that's all, nothing but gabble—but thank you so much." He then danced away with the speed of a deer. I found myself wondering if he would meet up with Margot Fonteyn at the water fountain.

Best,
William

Sunday—February 16th
New York City

Dear Bob . . .

Our rumors have become reality. At the close of Friday's rehearsal, Sir John announced that we would not meet again until Monday afternoon. His farewell included a rather heraldic wave (one could have called it a Roman salute) and the following words: "Rest, perturbed spirits."

With or without rest, our rehearsals were over for two and a half days. For those of us who chose to go home to hearth and family, plane reservations were made by affable, imperturbable Seymour Herscher, who obviously believes all actors are lunatics but doesn't say so out loud. Seymour also helped me to make arrangements with the King Edward Hotel concerning the transfer of my baggage from the Waldorf-Astoria as well as the renting of a refrigerator and phonograph for my return. The renting of creature comforts in Canada is not so easy a business as in the U.S.A. Hertz may very well put you in the driver's seat but they will not send you an egg beater or a short-wave radio, as they will in New York.

With much regret, I said good-by to the Waldorf—where I have had space enough for two—and stored my bags at the King Edward Hotel, which is one block from the theatre and where I will have space enough for one.

I arrived at my New York apartment on Saturday morning,

approximately four a.m. For reasons I have never been able to understand, I am possessed of an attractive, intelligent wife and two highly amusing children. Nevertheless, my week end was an edgy, uncomfortable one. Nothing seemed right or natural. No amount of comfort could please me. Since our production had elected to rehearse in Toronto (which was unusual to begin with), then why in hell didn't we *rehearse* there, instead of vacating the premises at a critical hour? I cranked and grunted about the house for two days mumbling incantations to myself and humming snatches of old tunes.

Though it is always a pleasure to be with one's family, such pleasure is considerably diminished by an emotional state which I will call the Mid-Rehearsal Blues. This form of dejection is by no means less purple than the sort we hear about in St. Louis or at the St. James Infirmary. As Wally Cox used to sing, "Basin Street is the street where all the light and the heavy folks meet." This particular actor (me) felt very heavy indeed throughout Saturday and Sunday. As for the natural devotion felt by a father for his young, I am saddened to confess that parental feeling goes damned chilly when Opening Night begins to wave the bloody shirt. Very well, then. If I was to be of no use to my family, and even hurt their feelings by my preoccupation and indifference, why not stay in Toronto? Why not sneak over to the rehearsal hall every day and give myself a bit of a run-through? Rather like washing one's hands in rubber gloves, not having the others around, but perhaps something could be gained in the process.

No, nothing could be gained. Aside from the fact that an actor working alone is like a bat without a ball, I knew perfectly well that I would not once glimpse the inside of the rehearsal hall. Most of the company members who remained in Toronto were among the more lonesome and inventive members of the company. Through nothing other than weakness of will, plus an absolutely hysterical gregariousness, I knew that I would be seduced into all manner of museums (most of which I loathe) as well as cocktail lounges (most of which I love) and an amount of socializing, late-at-night drinking, and compulsive conversation which would make Samuel Pepys seem a recluse. Had I believed for a fleeting moment that I would spend my anxious weekend reading Gibbon or Gideon, or lending a thought or two to my unsatisfactory performance, I would have wrapped myself warmly in bed and remained in Toronto for sixty hours of meditation. But if I was to devote my time to empty frolic, then I surely owed a deeper debt to my loyal dependents.

As usual, I am driving at something. The ambivalent thoughts listed above may not be the secret world of every actor—though I doubt it—but I will chew the beret of any actor alive who hasn't at least a faint notion of what I am talking about. During the rehearsal circumstance, the actor is a two-faced lunatic. He is not only Janus, he is Janus gone dotty; and, as the rehearsal period draws to a close, his symptoms become acute. Under the circumstances of rehearsal, a fellow cannot really win. Whatever course he pursues in his private life, he is damned if he does and damned if he doesn't. Why? Because he *has* no private life. Many years ago, Lynn Fontanne said to me, "I think you are weak-willed. You talk so much of your wife and your mother. I say to blazes with both of them. Do you *want* to be Edmund Kean? You *could* be—you have the talent. I think so and Alfred thinks so. But you must forget about wives and mothers. For the actor, there is no such thing as a wife or a mother. There is only his part. And, after that part, there is the next one."

I do not think Miss Fontanne meant to be taken literally. I think she expressed herself as strongly as she did because she wanted to shake me out of a "niceness" which she thought lacked iron. Actors are not supposed to be nice. They are supposed to be dangerous. Even James Stewart (Mr. Nice Guy) possesses a hint of danger, of recklessness. Mildness is not a virtue in the theatre. It is not even a virtue in the movies.

So far as I know, this is the one quality theatre and film have in common. Both mediums are ruthless, granted other differences. Any successful player must reject a substantial hunk of living in order to achieve his ends. It is for this reason that so many film stars are unhappy people. Where movies are concerned, the game does not seem worth the candle. Unless one cares only for money, the rewards of film acting are not sufficient to compensate for the loss of life. There is no glory, there is only fame. There is no real sense of achievement, there is only money. Film stars do not choose their profession because of money alone. They choose it because of narcissism.

All actors are narcissists. Otherwise, they would not be actors. But the wise actor surpasses narcissism and faces the brutal challenges of the theatre. Once he has conquered that challenge, he knows that he is not only a narcissist but also a man. Kim Stanley has said of acting, "It is really a very brave and honorable thing to do."

She's right, but back to *Hamlet* and its interruptions. Time off for the actor represents time spent in a dilemma: to work—or not to work? To relax—or not to relax? Perhaps I should define my terms. What is work? What is relaxation?

For myself, I have always believed that good work proceeds from monklike concentration as well as anti-Rabelaisian deportment. As a human being, however, I am about as monkish as a call girl, and Rabelais is one of my idols. Nevertheless, once the work I have chosen has been successfully done, I am the Lord's happiest man. And, ironically enough, it is *only* when this work is done that I can really appreciate the pleasures of living. In these quite possibly sick sentiments, you will discover the seeds of the actor—and, perhaps, of every artist who ever drew breath. It is monkishness which makes art. But, strictly speaking, who could possibly enjoy so small a cell, so bare a diet?

> Until Monday, then . . .
> William

> 17 February—Monday p.m.
> On plane

Dear Bob . . .

At two-thirty this afternoon we return to our rehearsals. Seymour Herscher tells me that Gielgud will begin with the opening of Act III (Shakespeare's Act IV, Scene V). This final section commences as Queen Gertrude says to Horatio, "I will not speak with her." It is Ophelia with whom she will not speak, and the famous Mad Scene follows. Richard Burton has told me that he assumes a certain amount of behind-the-scenes hanky-panky from Ophelia's Mad Scene: Globe Theatre hanky-panky, that is. Mr. Burton's imaginative re-creation of history goes as follows: Since Richard Burbage (the first Hamlet and the Globe's leading tragedian) was a rather chubby forty by the time *Hamlet* was put on and since the role of Hamlet would tax the stamina of Cassius Clay, Burton is convinced that Burbage, who was well-to-do by then as well as a co-partner with Shakespeare in the theatre, said to his playwright, "Look here, old boy, I'll play your bloody four-hour part, but I'm damned if I'll do it without a twenty-minute break somewhere for a tankard of rum and a bit of rubbing on my feet. Here's a notion for ye: give the little girl a Mad Scene. Audiences like that sort of rot. Let her just go stark staring afore everyone's eyes and spin it out to twenty minutes or so. No arguments now. Once I spit out all that guff about thoughts being bloody or nothing worth, I'm off to my room for a bit of a lie-down and that is simply that!"

Not a bad guess. Laurence Oliver has conjectured that Burbage got a bit spiffled one night and said to Shakespeare, "I can play *anything* you can write. *Anything* at all." This moment of gasconade cost him dear, according to Sir Laurence, because Shakespeare then went home and wrote *Othello*.

In any case, Gielgud has elected to rehearse the final act of the play and I (with Rosencrantz) am as dead as the Petrified Forest. This leaves me free to check out my living arrangements at the King Edward. Have I a phonograph? Have I a refrigerator? An actor not at work on his role might as well become imperious about his lodgings. Happily, any hopes I had for the playing of a regally offended scene were quickly dashed. Upon arrival at the hotel, I discovered all to be precisely as requested. Having nothing to complain about, I fell to thinking. This noisome habit first afflicted me when I was just past four years of age and could not put together certain pieces of my Erector set. Since that time, I have taken up the most damaging hobbies imaginable in order to muffle the buzzing in my brain. Jed Harris once said that actors are not supposed to think and that any intellectual activity whatever is bad for them. He is probably right, but it's too late now.

Last night I was as depressed as ever I have been in my life. Why? Because an interruption of rehearsals—of any creative act, communal or individual—is kissing kin to coitus interruptus, and can leave an over-analytic chap with a bad case of the slack lip. But I have practically gone past the borders of *savoir-faire*. The more I dwell upon the uncertainties of this production, the more I resemble a basset hound who has been banned from the house on a rainy night. I am simply hangdog, that's all, and it is all I can do to keep myself from whining out loud. It's a bad business, believe me, and I shall therefore look on the bright side of things.

I have already told you that Gielgud's division of the play seems to me expeditious and clear. We do not lower the curtain after Hamlet's momentous decision, "The play's the thing wherein I'll catch the conscience of the King!" but continue with the Rosencrantz-Guildenstern report to Claudius and Gertrude, through "To be or not to be" and the Nunnery Scene, and do not finally come down until Claudius's subtle and insinuating sentence, "Madness in great ones must not unwatch'd go." I still think it's a nice idea, but the uncustomary nature of our first intermission has led me into a careful examination of both the play itself as well as its four centuries of commentary in order to discover why the tradition of an interval following "The play's the thing" has so seldom been violated. The answer was not hard to find and, indeed, it is unarguable. Hamlet first says to the Players, "We'll hear a play tomorrow." Moments later, he requests of the Player King that some "dozen or sixteen lines" be inserted into *The Murder of Gonzago* and repeats "We'll ha't tomorrow night." He then dismisses Rosencrantz and Guildenstern and soliloquizes about entrapping the King with the rewritten play. It is here that the curtain is normally lowered, for, in the short scene immediately subsequent, Rosencrantz, speaking of the players, declares that they have already been ordered *"this night* to play before him." And immediately following this scene, Hamlet enters speaking "To be or not to be." Surely he has written the extra lines for the play by this time. In other words, between "The play's the thing" and R&G's report to the King and Queen, there is a demonstrable time lapse of twenty-four hours, give or take a few. Not only does Gielgud's continuum tend to obscure this time lapse and bring the two soliloquies too close together for either comfort or clarity, the misinterpretation is further compounded when Mr. Burton exits *pointing his finger* at the oncoming Claudius. This implies no time lapse whatever, which is immediately contradicted by Rosencrantz's line. Since no one seems to *hear* Rosencrantz's line, let alone understand it, one puzzles over ancient arguments: integrity or effects? Mr. Burton's exit is most "effective," since he not only points but whispers the line loud enough for the audience to hear him, but presumably not loud enough for those of us who are entering to *over*hear. Effective indeed, but it makes no sense.

Then again, maybe it doesn't matter after all, since riding roughshod over logic has never been unusual in the theatre.

Shakespeare himself cared little for the logic of time and/or geography. Two months pass between Hamlet's seeing the Ghost and putting on the play, but we have only one brief line of Ophelia's to prove it ("Nay, 'tis twice two months, my lord.") and most audiences cannot decipher the matter since her direct reference is to the death of Hamlet's father four months before. In fact, the one-day time lapse between the arrival of the players and the staging of the play (which coincides with the far more important time lapse between "The play's the thing" and "To be or not to be") is often lost upon the audience, unless the director finds some way to point it out. Shakespeare was a bit like a magician. Sleight of hand is a matter of telling white lies at heightened speed. No card sharp can do his trick slowly and still fool the observer. It is much the same with Shakespeare. Examined too closely, he leaves many a stone unturned and many a seam in need of repair. Since he is neither a novelist nor a painter, one cannot notice his oversights or jerry-building unless one reads him with the utmost care. A theatrical performance moves swiftly, and I defy any audience member—even those who have seen the play more than once—to catch Shakespeare at his occasional shell game. Doesn't it seem justified, then, to pack another fifteen minutes or so of the play into Act I, ignore the time lapse entirely, and gain the benefit of Claudius's excellent line for a curtain?

At first blush, the answer seemed to me to be yes. Upon examination, it now seems to be no. But I wonder if Gielgud has been influenced by the temperament and personality of Richard Burton himself. Since Burton seems to "throw away" "To be or not to be," de-emphasizing it in favor of the preceding soliloquy, and since he all but slaps the Advice to the Players in the face, why worry over too great a proximity between the soliloquies and why not open Act II with the Advice to the Players, since it will be largely lost in the fuss and bother of the audience returning to their seats? One further·point (equally cynical): Not only does Gielgud's restructuring blur the intended time lapse, it actively supports a quite different concept in the mass-audience mind. Since intermissions often connote time lapses, we will surely seem to be saying that a day has passed between Claudius's line and the Play Scene. This is a perfectly good time lapse, indeed. Perhaps it is a better time lapse. But it is not Shakespeare's, it is Sir John Gielgud's and no one else's. You pay your money and you take your choice.

———•━•━•———

Gielgud's handling of Richard Burton puts me in mind of the words he spoke to me at my audition last fall. That is, of the thoughts behind those words: *Since Richard must play Hamlet as thirty-five, I cannot surround him with callow contemporaries. Rosencrantz and Guildenstern, for example, must be mature in manner. Also, because Richard is such a strong personality, I must have unusually able players in even the smallest roles. Only a strong supporting company will help him to give his best performance. It is my job to do everything possible to make him look good.* He could quite as easily have said: *The name of the play is* Hamlet.

But now that sufficient rehearsal time has elapsed for an observer to draw at least tentative conclusions, I find myself dividing Gielgud's effort into musical themes: one major and one minor. It seems to me that his major "theme" with Burton is to soften him, gentle him, and make him mild, like today's carefully filtered cigarette smoke. His minor theme is to dissuade the Flying Welshman from breaking up the long sweeping lines of Shakespeare's verse and rhetoric. Burton's commitment to "modern" playing often leads him to chop the verse into smaller and smaller segments. It is not that he plays Shakespeare "conversationally"; no one can. But he *seems* to be doing so. The effect is not an accident. Gielgud's verse speaking, on the other hand, is intensely musical: not only a traditional melodic line but a very long line, indeed. Burton knows perfectly well how to act that way, but it is decidedly not his style nor does he believe it appropriate to a modern-dress production before an American audience.

As our rehearsal time passes, one senses a tension between the two men. There can be no doubt of their mutual affection and respect, but some of Gielgud's manner and conversation implies the helpless resignation of a man whose leadership is being denied. Mr. Burton is entirely courteous, but two of his remarks are worth quoting. To one of Gielgud's suggested readings involving heavy emphasis on the word "I," Burton replied. "John, dear, you are in love with pronouns, but I am not." It caused a good deal of jocund laughter, Gielgud's included, but it must have stung a bit. Another time, when Sir John proposed a rather elaborate staging around a table during one of the soliloquies, Burton rested his chin in one hand and murmured, "It is a possibility, of course, but so is sitting still."

It is not that Burton is wrong about either of these things. Such discussions are entirely appropriate to the actor-director relationship. But it begins to look as though Richard is not especially interested in being directed by Gielgud or anyone else, except in the most general terms. He surely does want Sir John to curb any excesses, and he does want to appear "gentle" in the role of Hamlet. It is in these respects that Gielgud's "themes"—

both major and minor—seem to have been meticulously considered.

A director must know more than merely what he wants. He must also know how to evoke what he wants from his actors. Whether Richard Burton "should" or "should not" conduct himself more obediently is not the point. Whether he should play Hamlet this way or that way or sideways is not the point, either. All that matters is how he *can* play Hamlet, and it is Gielgud's job to chart the various possibilities as carefully as a navigator plots the course of a ship. On one occasion, he said to Burton, "Nononono, it's too cold. It's too cruel. Take him by the arm when you say that. You could even put your arm around his shoulder. What you are saying is: Come, let's go together. And we must feel that you *are* together. Hamlet is so in need of friends. When Horatio, Marcellus, and Bernardo behave in a friendly manner, we simply must feel Hamlet's gratitude."

Richard Burton's fundamental quality as an actor is so strong, so quick with competence and stamina, that it is hard to see how any director could blunt the impression. But such is quite obviously Gielgud's intention. Even though Burton stands easily in the classic mold of a Heldentenor, Gielgud gambles against such an effect. In fact, he places his largest directorial bet against the very grain of Burton's personality, hoping—I assume—that the actor will be flexible enough to emphasize certain secondary aspects of himself in order to approximate more closely a part which must, in the final analysis, escape him. This is not to say that Burton will be "a bad Hamlet." That would be impossible, just as it would be impossible for John Gielgud to be a bad Hotspur. None of these brilliant Shakespearean actors can be bad in any of the roles, simply because such men know how to play Shakespeare, period. I am speaking not of skill but of interpretation.

On the less than Olympian plateaus of achievement, where interpretation is nudged aside by excitement, Burton's performance shapes up to be an absolute dazzler. But there are other plateaus to be scaled, and even a cat like me should be able to look at an unblemished King. If these unstained performances are not at least imagined, from whence shall our criteria proceed? John Gielgud is an ideal Leontes, for example, and it would be next to impossible for any contemporary actor to match him in the part. Richard Burton is an ideal Prince Hal and a perfectly suited Iago, and would surely be a blindingly effective Hotspur. One cannot conceive of Gielgud matching him in these roles the longest day he lived. But both men are superlative practitioners of Shakespeare's plays, and until equally superlative players come to light who are more suited to the various roles there can be little argument as to their performance.

We shall open our play in less than a week. Light many a candle.

William

Saturday—22 February

Dear Bob . . .

Five days have passed since last I wrote to you. Since we give our first public performance this coming Tuesday evening and open officially the following night, a reasonable man would surely assume that these crucial, final, disappearing days would be rich with decision and backstage drama. Curiously enough, such is not the case. These days are rich with fear but not with incident. A young man named Richard Sterne, who plays a small role and understudies Laertes, has been operating a tape recorder from the first day of our rehearsals. At the end of each session, he returns to his room and plays back the dialogue of the day. Immediately before the start of today's rehearsal, Sterne informed me that Gielgud has not expressed one *new* thought in nearly a week. "He keeps saying the same things over and over. It's as though he cannot do anything but fill out the remaining time."

Richard Burton, too, although he seems anxious and nervous, has not discussed his part with anyone or even rehearsed it with any special vigor. I have the feeling he begins to see next Tuesday night as a slowly enlarging abyss at the bottom of which sidewinders and cottonmouths abound. Therefore he is doing no more than gathering the strength to make his death-defying leap when the time is upon him. Silence can bring solace to those about to make parachute jumps or fight critical duels, and Mr. Burton has fallen silent. In his position, I am persuaded I would do the same.

Today's rehearsal is a full-out run-through without stops—to be followed by copious notes from Sir John. It will constitute our last practice session until we get onto our set on Monday night. Many of us are already in "costume" since we are supposed to be wearing rehearsal clothes, but I have the strong feeling that many a change will be made in this business before we open in New York. Personally, I would rather wear a full suit of iron armor than decide for myself what proper "rehearsal clothes" should be.

Speaking of suits of armor, Richard Burton recently told me a harrowing tale which is further evidence of the possible disasters confronted by actors in the living theatre every time they emerge from the wings. An expert player named Geoffrey Toone, whom I hope you will remember from my Tales of Macbeth,* began his career at the Old Vic some years ago in a most auspicious manner. During his first season, he appeared in secondary but important roles and was entirely successful in each of them. Because he was intelligent, graceful, and unusually handsome, the Vic management catapulted Mr. Toone into major assignments the following year. He played Hamlet, Henry the Fifth, and one other demanding role: either Petruchio or Benedick. All in all, quite a season, but unfairly stacked against the young man, since he was not quite ready for such an exacting tour of duty.

Since those days, he has developed into one of the best and most consistent second men of the British theatre, but because he was a scarce twenty-two years of age when pushed too fast and since he was not possessed of a ferocious temperament, his performances were graded as able but lacking in power. All this is par for the course in an advancing career, but fate reserved a particularly horrendous booby trap for Mr. Toone in the production of *Henry V*. Whoever directed decided, somewhat academically, that it would be an interesting and decorative notion

* His ear was assassinated by the Third Murderer's dagger.

to dress Shakespeare's fighting men in authentic 15th Century armor fashioned from iron. Mr. Toone was consulted in the matter, but, being a friendly and rather ingenuous young man, he agreed. It was also determined that young Harry's "Imitate the action of the tiger" speech, in which he exhorts his troops to further battle, should be done straight front to the balcony rail —as though the audience itself were a troop of soldiers and Henry stood challengingly on a promontory before them. This naturally dictated that Mr. Toone's Henry would be alone on stage when he began the speech.

On opening night, several actors endured almost insurmountable difficulties while trying to move about vigorously in their suits of armor. The rehearsals had been sketchy (as they often are at the Vic), and Toone himself had practiced in his armor only once. When he bounded onto the stage, all confidence, and began crying, "Once more unto the breach, dear friends, once more!" he realized that the armor was simply not going to cooperate with his agility. By the time he had completed his first pentameter, he fell down flat on the stage. Worse than that, he could not get up. The armor was simply too heavy. Having fallen on his back, he was turned Kafka-like into a helpless turtle or beetle or shell-backed what-you-will. Saddled with a burden of inhuman metal, he could do no more than wave his arms desperately and shout his battle cries from a supine position. The barely suppressed giggles of the audience made it clear to him fairly soon that any continuance of such an erect speech from such a prostrate position was positively grotesque. He paused for a moment but could do nothing but wave his arms again. He tried to move his feet but they lacked sufficient power. He gave a lurch with his body but the armor undid his efforts. He finally did something very brave indeed. He turned his head to the wings and shouted, "Help!"

Several supernumeraries appeared on the double and lifted their Prince to his feet. They appeared to be nothing so much as the derricks of Agincourt in human form. Once on balance again, Mr. Toone made certain to move neither his feet nor his hands too abruptly. Though he was bound and determined to avoid a second fall-down, he nevertheless conducted himself in such a robot-like fashion that he recalled nothing so much as the Tin Man in *The Wizard of Oz*. The laughter of the audience became gradually unrestrained. According to Richard Burton, Toone tells this tale on himself. Not only does this prove him ultimately courageous, we clearly see that he is blameless. Moreover, a man who swallows his pride sufficiently to shout for help when all else fails is a man with an obvious talent for survival.

For many a year, Mr. Richard Maney—Broadway's super-publicist and master of sparkling jargon—has entered an actor's dressing room after an opening to say merely, "Well, nobody got hurt." I used to think Maney was just an unimpressible wise guy, but lately I begin to get the point.

As for our particular band of mummers, we face a relatively idle week end after the conclusion of today's run-through. Sunday will be devoted exclusively to striking the *Little Me* sets and moving them to Cleveland while our own platforms and staircases are dismantled in the rehearsal room and reassembled on the O'Keefe stage. We will have neither a technical rehearsal nor a dress rehearsal until Monday night. On Tuesday we will not rehearse at all, since it is Burton's privilege to spend a full day resting before facing his first audience.

Since today's run-through is coincidental with the final Saturday-matinee performance of *Little Me*, a marvelously corrupt admixture of show-business fluids has been stirred together and could easily be drunk off by an adventurous theatrical potsman. What I mean is, we are playing *Hamlet* without stops while Sid Caesar and his colleagues are playing *Little Me* without stops. It is not that they are strangers to us. Several of our boys, in fact, have made significant contact with several of their girls. But professionally speaking, we encounter them only on matinee days and we have never before found ourselves performing while they were performing. Rehearsing and performing are two entirely different things.

Picture this: Several of us would-be Shakespeareans now find ourselves wearing swords slung into sword belts—the belts being secured around our modern-dress jackets. We also now remain in the hallways until it is time for us to enter. A rehearsing actor will usually watch his fellow actors rehearse, but a performing actor wants to concentrate on his own assignment and does not like to be distracted by what is going on before and after.

We quietly intone iambic pentameter and play cursory tricks with our weapons while near to naked dancing girls scurry among us making quick changes and skipping toward the wings for their next entrance. Sid Caesar makes myriad costume changes and make-up alterations (he plays seven roles) and moves relentlessly back and forth between his dressing room and the stage, constantly surrounded by costume and make-up helpers. The chorus singers and dancers, both male and female, are over-made-up—which is traditional in musical comedy—and this affords them a grotesque appearance face to face. They stare at me and my fellow Shakespeareans as though we were a breed apart—both admirable and peculiar. This is something akin to a Hungarian staring at a Sikh. He knows the Sikh is human, but what's the rest of the story?

All performers are congruent, when scratched an inch beneath the skin, but actors and dancers sometimes look at each other as though they were strangers. The same is true of "show folk" and "classical players." Though it is probably true that vaudevillians and musical performers—clowns, comics, night-club entertainers, and farceurs—are not so intellectually disposed as their verse-speaking brothers, we are not so far apart as we seem. Alfred Drake, Hume Cronyn, and Eileen Herlie have all played in musicals and farces. So have I. Richard Burton, for another example, gave an exceptional musical performance in *Camelot*. Like the rest of us, he knows perfectly well that playing Shakespeare is in one important respect like playing anything else: the more muscle the better. One does not use all of one's muscles ever, but they have to be there. The theatre actor must be in good shape. He needs stamina, strength, and the correct preparation to act or sing or dance.

Are some plays and some parts easier than others? You bet your sweet little make-up kit they are. To play *Under the Yum-*

Yum Tree is a cinch, if you are a *farceur*, although some very fine actors would not be able to bring it off, but to play *Hamlet* is difficult no matter how good you are. All these things are relative, but nothing in the theatre is easy. Perhaps the painted faces of *Little Me*'s dancers and singers seem to be baffled and bewildered because they recognize that Shakespearean players have bitten off a difficult chew of tobacco. Perhaps, too, they are musing upon what sort of creatures would choose to make so difficult a profession even more difficult.

There are the wardrobe women, too, and the dressers—a few of them youngish but most of them middle-aged or older. One positively ancient lady of unusually warm demeanor sat near me sewing a costume while I both murmured sections of my part and strode about the hallways searching for the feel of a nobleman's walk. I noted that she was glancing up at me from time to time, but this did not prepare me for what she finally said. "May I ask," she inquired sweetly, "if you played Shakespeare with Sir John Martin Harvey?"

I replied that I had not.

"Pity," she said. "My husband and I were with him for many years. And he would have liked you very, very much."

"Why?" I asked.

"Because you stand so well."

I thanked her for the compliment and excused myself immediately since it was nearly time for my first entrance. But I could not resist a glimpse at the mirror before I went on. I am thirty-seven years old and, to most people, seem younger: possibly as young as thirty-one or two. John Martin Harvey made his final tour of the United States during the 1920s if not before. Nevertheless, for that dear little old woman I was apparently free from time and floated through history like the Canterville Ghost. This is far from being an ugly notion, but it is also leagues distant from reality. As for the mirror, it returned my gaze impassively. Mirrors are the only silent invention of man.

Our run-through bounded along with a fair amount of speed and grace—rather like a whippet with a sore paw: the potential is there, but we need help. Burton has power, wit, and agility, and will doubtless make a success, although many a purist will wince and chafe at the collar. Gielgud provided us rather general notes and criticism. He seems now to be concerned almost exclusively with mechanics—"Could you drift a bit to the right during that scene? It will uncover some of the others. Thank you"—as well as sound effects, entrances and exits, when swords should be strapped on and when removed, how such-and-so a light cue will be given, how light or dark the "feel" of a particular scene should be, how flooded or bright or healthy-seeming should be another. Denmark is corrupt and ruled by a characterless King. Mostly the *ambiance* is dark corridors, suspicion, and an abundance of potables: "These heavy-headed revels make us traduced and taxed of other nations. They clepe us drunkards."

But only when Gielgud speaks of mechanical exigencies does he refer to such things. Almost never does he exhort his actors to color their behavior in either one way or another. Obviously he places sublime faith in the actor's ability to work things out on his own. But *what* things will the actor work out? And in what way will they connect to what his fellow actors have worked out? Thirty people working out thirty separate notions are liable to end up by playing a queerly cacophonous symphony. Well—Sunday is a day of rest.

And Saturday calls for a drink.

Best . . .
William

23 February—Sunday
Toronto

Dear Bob . . .

The wines of Saturday evening were as fine as expected, but my Sunday rest is being threatened by adventurers. Just before noontime (I went to sleep at dawn) my room telephone beat a devil's tattoo into the porches of my ears. This unwelcome jangling was followed by the voice of Miss Jessica Levy, warm and friendly as ever but inflected with female purpose. She told me that she and Linda Marsh deeply desired to corral a nucleus of the company for a line rehearsal with Richard Burton. Grumpy and somnolent though I was, I agreed but pointed out to her that Clem Fowler, Michael Ebert, and Alfred Drake had already left town on one sort of pleasure junket or another and that they were but three examples. "Why are you planning so late?" I concluded, being a grouchy sort.

"No help for it," Jessica said. "I suggested it last night but Burton said he might be too tired. Bob Wilson called me this morning and said he'd talk to Burton as soon as he woke up. I just want to keep as many people around as possible who are willing to do it in case Richard gets energetic when the time comes."

"What time does the time come?" I grunted.

"Three o'clock or so. Linda thinks we all need it, especially the scenes with Burton. We *are* under-rehearsed, Bill, you *know* that."

I replied wittily that she was not just whistling Dixie.

"I've gotten hold of Hume, Eileen, Bob Milli, and Johnny Cullum," Jessica continued. "That just about does it. Barney Hughes can do Claudius* and I'll read Rosencrantz."

I told her I was for it—the rehearsal, that is; I wasn't so sure about her reading Rosencrantz—and asked her to get back to me as soon as she had definite news. But Jessica was not going to let me slip through her fingers. "You're not going out for lunch, are you?" she asked.

I said that I would eat lunch in the hotel. By one p.m. I was keeping my word in the main dining room of the King Edward. Philip Coolidge joined me in time for kippers and scrambled eggs as well as comfortably toasted English muffins soaked in butter and currant preserves. It was a splendid brunch made memorable by the presence of John Gielgud at the nearest neighboring table. He was dining with his young friend Martin, a most amusing Hungarian whose last name invariably escapes me but which sounds something like Zrrmk. I told Sir John that a line rehearsal with Burton was a distinct possibility.

"Mmm," he said vaguely. "Well, I'm glad he's showing a bit of conscience about it."

* Barnard Hughes plays the role of Marcellus and understudies the King.

Since this remark rather chilled the air I laughed heavily, hoping to release some puffs of warm vapor. "Don't you think," I ventured, "that he knows his lines pretty well?"

"Yes, he does," said John, "but he's not quick enough with them. These occasional lapses and misplaced nouns and verbs slow him down and make things heavier than they should be. One must be so quick, so light in Shakespeare—on top of things at all times. It hurts Richard needlessly when he must search his mind for the right word."

I was surprised by Gielgud's misgivings. It had not occurred to me that Burton could get seriously hurt in his part, aside from interpretation; I had thought only that he might hurt the rest of us—albeit unintentionally—by giving us slightly distorted feeds, unexpected rhythms, variant readings, or worst of all: the wrong *attitude* for any sort of motivational cueing. For example, one moment disturbed me especially, although I had never spoken of it during the rehearsals: directly after the Play Scene ("Bully him, Bill!") Guildenstern is sent to tell Prince Hamlet that the King is in a frenzy of rage and that the Queen wants to see her son. The lines follow:

GUILDENSTERN: Good my lord, vouchsafe me a word with you.
HAMLET: Sir, a whole history.
GUILDENSTERN: The King, sir—
HAMLET: Ay, sir, what of him?
GUILDENSTERN: Is in his retirement marvellous distempered.
HAMLET: With drink, sir?
GUILDENSTERN: No, my lord, rather with choler.
HAMLET (italics mine): *Your wisdom should show itself more richer to signify this to his doctor; for, for me to put him to his purgation would perhaps plunge him into far more choler.*
GUILDENSTERN (italics mine): *Good my lord, put your discourse into some frame, and start not so wildly from my affair.*

This short section is deceptively crucial, for it is in this scene that Hamlet rejects his old friends utterly. From this point forth,

Hamlet's duty is clear and there is no place in his world for weathercocks like R&G. From the standpoint of R&G, they have been insulted, unjustly attacked, and quite likely believe the Prince to be round the bend. Whether we think of R&G as innocent victims or men of deplorable character, there can be no dispute that from this moment forward they are the King's men, not Hamlet's.

As Gielgud has staged the scene, Burton moves away from me during the speech italicized above and I follow as I speak the subsequent speech. Obviously, I am imploring him to make more sense, please, and to behave less wildly and erratically. But not once during our rehearsals has Burton spoken this speech wildly or dangerously; not once has he moved away from me erratically or even swiftly. He all but ambles down the short staircase and he gazes at me bemusedly as though he thought me quite a silly young man not worth taking seriously. Guildenstern may well be a fool, but the text implies that Hamlet *does* take him seriously; at least at this particular moment. What is worse, however, is that Richard cannot seem to remember the proper sequence of the speech to save his soul, nor does Gielgud ever comment on his errors within it or the rather lackadaisical attitude he adopts for its utterance. Granted the speech is clumsy and difficult, it remains essential for Guildenstern and the scene itself that Hamlet become either enraged or antic or that he tread on the supplicant courtier's toes or stand suddenly upon his own head or what-you-will so long as *something* concrete is done to motivate Guildenstern's next line and, more important, keep the audience properly up to date. But what is even more important is that Hamlet's speech emerge crisp and clarified: the thought is difficult and intricate, but essential. It must be spoken quickly and with a full understanding of its meaning. Since Burton invariably stumbles over it, he makes the intuitive adjustment natural to a clever and experienced actor: he pretends that he has stumbled on purpose and he speaks the remainder of the words haltingly and contemplatively as though he were quietly making them up as he went along. Very well, but Guildenstern's next line becomes therefore senseless, the bottom drops out of the scene, and the subsequent behavior of all three characters (Hamlet, Rosey, and Guildey) must inevitably confuse the audience.

If all this is true, why have I said nothing? For several reasons, not the least of them being my reputation as an actor who talks too much, but the largest of them being that I genuinely like and admire Richard Burton quite as powerfully as I dislike the *principle* of one actor telling another what to do or begging favors from his fellow player. It is a director's job to demand the proper interpretation of a scene, not an actor's. Why has *Gielgud* said nothing? I haven't the foggiest notion.

Be all these tactics as they rightly or wrongly may, I decided to broach the subject of the messy moment at today's line rehearsal. Since my friend Jessica would be holding the book, all could be done prudently and the scene might be saved for opening night.

At ten minutes to three, Richard Burton called Jessica Levy to say that he was willing and eager to rehearse. Moments later, room telephones jangled all over the King Edward Hotel followed by Jessica crying, "Red alert!" as well as somehow producing extra fifths and pints of scotch, vodka, gin, tomato juice, soda, quinine water, and ice. By half past three, we congregated snugly in a hotel room too small for a party and too big for a chat. Mr. Burton sat in the one easy chair, looking nervously cheerful. Eileen Herlie sat demurely on one of Jessica's twin beds. I sat on the other. Linda Marsh lay supine on the floor, a habit of hers due more to nervous fatigue than sultriness. John Cullum sat hunched near the television set. Bob Milli squatted in front of a radiator. Philip Coolidge, Hume Cronyn, and a host of other favorites deployed themselves strategically. The afternoon's results turned out to be more silly than useful, but there was an entertaining atmosphere because of Burton's high spirits.

As usual, he was charming, gregarious, unpretentious, and brilliant. As for his lines, he had a surprising difficulty remembering many of the scenes completely, but I cannot help assuming that the casualness of the room, the seating, and the Sunday-afternoon plan in general made concentration difficult. All mob scenes were skipped over, as were all scenes in which Hamlet does not appear. At the conclusion of our first act, we took a break for liquid refreshment and *hors d'oeuvres*. Jessica does nothing by halves—not even a line rehearsal; I suspect her of spending at least twice her salary every week we stay in Toronto. As I sipped my way gingerly through a Bloody Mary, steeling myself for the unwelcome moment when I would ask Burton to play a key moment my way instead of his, Elizabeth Taylor unexpectedly appeared. She was lovely to look at, delightful to know, and she was again clad in quite a lot of purple. "How is it all going?" she asked us. "Does the burnt-out Welshman know his lines?"

We all shouted that he knew them perfectly, while Burton shouted even louder that he knew nothing at all. Much laughter and a few Bacchanalian cries: "Let's have another drink!" "To hell with Hamlet—let's get pissed!" "It's easier when you're smashed!"

Most theatre actors cherish nothing better than the cliché of themselves as Rabelaisian lovers of wine, women, and song who can nevertheless surprise the capacity for brilliant performances out of the lowest levels of high living. *In vino veritas* and we must both suffer and enjoy. Perhaps so, but the pretense of drunken, exhausted actors pulling up their muses by the boot straps is as amusing as it is only because it stands at such an infinite distance from the truth. It is the actor's favorite fantasy, or—as Hemingway once said—"Isn't it pretty to think so?" The boring and Spartan fact is that few actors can ingest so much as a single jigger of alcohol before a theatre performance. If they do, they trip over sandbags and forget their lines. Those who *can* drink usually limit their intake to two at the most, and even such topers as these finish their dinner, drinks and all, by five or six p.m. and sleep for as much as two hours before the evening performance. Drinking is a tension-breaker for the actor, as it is for everyone else, but drunkenness is out of the question. Actors like Richard Burton, Jason Robards, and John Barrymore—reputedly capable of consuming large amounts of strong spirits without seeming destructively high on stage—are rare articles indeed.

But on this particular occasion, with only ourselves to judge ourselves and no admission paid, few of us could refuse an extra smash of joy. What audience could we betray but ourselves? What worse could happen but that an afternoon of high purpose would transmogrify into one of low comedy? Let me serve you some details.

Jessica Levy had thoughtfully and expensively provided some Cordon Rouge for Elizabeth Taylor. As she sipped daintily at the rim of her glass, Miss Taylor scanned the room. "Who's missing?" she asked. "I want to stand in for someone."

I informed her that I thought she would make a capital Rosencrantz but that Jessica had already cast herself in the part. "Surely," said Miss Taylor, "there's something left." It was suggested that she play Osric since Dillon Evans had left for a trip to Niagara Falls that morning. "Because," Miss Taylor warned, "if you don't give me at least a tiny part to play, I'm going down the hall to read the Bible."

She laughed at our baffled expressions. "I'm not sending you up," * she said. "Three ladies in flowered hats just now approached me in the hall and asked if I would come with them to read the Bible."

"Which testament?" someone wondered.

Elizabeth smiled and said she didn't know but that she could guess. "They're in room 951, they said. Do you think I should go?"

Several of us speculated on what lay behind the invitation. Film stars, especially females, receive many curious propositions, but being requested to read the Bible in a cosmopolitan hotel room is more than uncommon; it is unique.

"I believe they think," Miss Taylor said, "that I'm a fallen woman who stands much in need of Scripture. They're probably right."

Richard Burton suddenly snapped his fingers. "It's a bloody

* English expression meaning "pulling your leg" or "putting you on."

good notion at that," he said. "Let's *all* go read the Bible. I can't seem to remember my Shakespeare. Perhaps I'll be more useful reading the Bible."

Several supported his scheme by raising their hands and shouting "Hear! Hear!" We were gradually becoming as clubby-English as the House of Lords. And Burton was our Beaverbrook.

"But first . . ." he cried, "let's have another drink!"

We obeyed.

———•—•—•———

Into the second act we plunged, a few moments later, and I again began to gather my resources for the important challenge of the afternoon. Burton floundered somewhat during the Advice to the Players, but Jessica decided to let it pass, apparently, for she did not correct him. During the difficult Play Scene all went well, and when I re-entered Richard shot the first few lines at me like bullets, getting things off to a crackling start. But when the speech in question came due, he stopped cold for a moment and then began to ad-lib his way through the thoughts like a foot soldier in a mine field. Good! I thought. Here's my chance! And I began to quote the speech to him slowly and exactly. He looked at me and seemed about to say that it was indeed a sticky moment for him, when Jessica surprised both of us by speaking up sharply. "Oh, don't bother him with that—it's silly. He always gets that right. Let's go on to something important."

I was momentarily speechless but must have gazed at Jessica as though I thought her absolutely mad. "But it's true," she continued. "He *knows* that speech. He's never said it wrong before."

I began to say, "He *always* said it wrong before," but Burton went on to his next line and the issue was lost. Moments later, during the brief exchange between Polonius and Gertrude which precedes the Closet Scene, Hume Cronyn—who knows his lines all but flawlessly—erred trivially by saying, "Tell him his pranks have been too great to bear with," at which point Jessica cried loudly "No, Hume. No!" which startled all present by its ferocity. "As long as we're here," Jessica continued, "let's get it right. The line is: 'His pranks have been too *broad* to bear with.' "

Hume nodded. "All right, Jessica," he said patiently. "Whatever you say."

Jessica smiled. "Nothing personal," she said.

"Personal?" said Richard Burton. "Why, you're the one who was shouting, my dear."

Everyone laughed and had another drink.

———•••———

Evidently, Jessica was under some sort of strain. As you can see, I became angry with myself, with Jessica, and with the whole damned incompetent world. Mostly, though, I was frustrated by the status levels of the theatre which make equality of creativity so difficult. Not having fought at the right time, I could not fight at all. All I could do was have another drink and sit and stew. To reintroduce the subject of the earlier scene became less viable with every tick of my wrist watch. To bound up from the twin bed, crying, "Damn it, Richard's got to get that speech right or that scene will fall to pieces!" would cause the gathered company to think me either drunk or insane—yet that was what I wanted to do. And if I couldn't do that, I might as well have left, so I rose from Jessica's bed and went to the liquor tray for guess what.

Moments later, we took another break. Jessica is by all accounts a sensitive woman, and she knew that I was annoyed. She stood beside me as I drained off a third Bloody Mary and whispered comfortingly, "Please don't worry about that moment. He always gets it right."

"Sorry," I whispered back, "but he *never* gets it right."

"He needs to work on the soliloquies, not the scenes."

I looked at her and frowned. "Then what the hell are *we* doing here?"

"To give him confidence. He wouldn't work at all if he didn't have company."

"For God's sake, Jessica, the man has played the part in three other productions. Not only that, he eats soliloquies the way kids eat ice cream. Richard standing alone is one of the most exciting creatures who ever filled a stage. It's in relation to other actors that he can go wrong. He's not going to hurt *himself* out there. It's the rest of us and the production itself he might hurt."

"You are absolutely wrong."

Since it has always excited my rage to be told that I am absolutely wrong when I am absolutely right, the hand in which I held Bloody Mary #4 began to tremble and I spilled a portion of it on a pair of white trousers: *my* white trousers. While wiping them clean, I spoke carefully to Jessica. "I believe that my judgment in these matters is quite as good as yours. But you've won; I've lost. What is sad about that is that the loser stands on stage while the winner sits out front. Tell me this: if all that matters is his soliloquies, why didn't you work alone with him? Couldn't *you* have given him confidence?"

"You're excited about nothing. Tomorrow night, he'll say that speech word for word, you'll see." *

Since there are few people I have met in the theatre of whom I am fond as Jessica Levy, the afternoon was a disaster for me. She's a damned nice lady and nobody's fool. I knew that she genuinely believed my fears to be exaggerated. That was precisely what depressed me. Jessica's no apple-polisher. If she had thought I was right, she would have gone down the line for me. The truth is, she thought I was wrong. Even more important, she wasn't really listening.

Was this silly little moment so critical as to cause such a fuss in my nervous system? The answer is yes.

What had happened was something that happens so frequently in the theatre that we should all perhaps shrug and say: So what? But if we do so shrug and say, the moment will be lost. Lost for the actor and lost for the audience. It is a fact that the needs of each individual actor are crucial to the success of a production. No one can enter into the heart and soul of a character as does the actor who plays him. Not even the most sensitive director can genuinely comprehend the ins and outs of a part

* Author's Note: He did not once say the speech correctly throughout the run of the play.

until he has played it himself. I sometimes wonder if even play-wrights understand their individual creations as well as the actors who must live with them night and day.

At any rate, the moment could never be successful or clear from that day forward, for Burton's habit was bound to become fixed. At times such as these, actors consider hanging signs on themselves. Mine would read: I KNOW THIS MOMENT IS POOR, BUT I AM NOT SO MUCH TO BLAME AS YOU MIGHT THINK.

Caveat emptor.

William

25 February—3 a.m.
Toronto

Dear Bob . . .

It is the wee small hours of the morning, and I sit in my hotel bed, sleepless and thoughtful.

We performed our dress rehearsal earlier tonight, complete with costumes, lights, make-up, and communal anxiety. All that we lacked was an audience to boo us. For the results of our run-through were dark enough to scare the fez off a brass monkey. Our lighting seemed appropriate to nothing other than a Grand Guignol production of *La Danse Macabre;* our set rose some fifty feet into the flies and dwarfed our actors; our sound effects came booming from the several tape machines with a volume and brio recollective of Hitler's legions shouting *"Sieg Heil!";* the O'Keefe auditorium stretched away from us like the Gobi Desert's infinite sands; and our super-star uncorked sufficient perspiration to cleanse, at last, the murdering hands of Lady Macbeth. To put it mildly, he seemed nervous.

This was no surprise. Burton is an unpretentious and candid man. He has been predicting an anxiety attack of devastating proportions for several days, and so have we. A man does not open in *Hamlet* calmly; not if he is alive. Some historians claim that David Garrick was cool as a cucumber (before, during, and after) but I would have to see it to believe it.

Two nights ago Elizabeth Taylor asked me what sort of dosage might help Richard to relax before a performance. She was at a loss to figure out so sensitive an instrument as her husband-to-be. She wanted to know what kind of pill, if any, would help him most without undesirable side effects. "He *never* takes pills," she said, "not even aspirin."

I answered that a complete lack of track record in pill consumption would make any choice hazardous, but that I would suggest Dexamil because it had brought me through some tough spots now and then despite its tendency to dry out the mouth and make "icy" speech less likely.* Yes, that's exactly the way I said it.

"Do you," she whispered, "get nervous?"

I said that I did, of course.

She moved her head from side to side, despairingly. "Theatre actors," she said. "Oh, he gets *so* nervous."

Apparently, Burton played tonight's dress rehearsal without benefit of pills. But—rather than give a false impression—allow me to explore more than the black forest by pointing out some white trees: not all was catastrophe. For example, the first act played well. That is, it *would* have played well had anyone been able to *see* it past the darkling pillars and through the murky shadows. Burton was crisp and electric in these early scenes; Cronyn is in total command; and the balance of the company is weighted with able actors. But, after our first intermission, trouble arrived like a grinning skull on a rainy night. The sort of trouble which frightens even me.

Though Burton's nervousness is neither unusual nor alarming, from the Advice to the Players on ("Speak the speech, I pray you, as I pronounced it to you . . .") he seemed all at once to lose control of his lines. A brave and experienced man, he muddled along one way or another and worked his way out of most messes, but such struggling (as Gielgud has indicated) is all but disastrous in Shakespeare. Iambic pentameter is not like prose dialogue: it cannot support or even tolerate either stammering or spontaneous revision. What Chekhov permits, Shake-

* Rhetorical actors sometimes define clean, crisp speaking as "icy." Their private practice sessions will include a poem like "Jabberwocky" recited at blinding speed in order to achieve optimum dexterity of tongue and lips. Dexamil will not cooperate with such endeavors.

speare forbids. In Shakespeare, or any playwright who composes in verse, a tentative command of the words will lead even the finest actors to the edge of a precipice: rhythms become sluggish and the forward thrust of the play begins to veer widely left or right like a badly hit ball. The actor gets only a "piece" of the scene when he has learned his lines imperfectly. He keeps hitting fouls. And, in a manner of speaking, what the actor hits is what the audience catches. Actors must be in absolute command of their lines and their *cues*. It is my Theatre Rule #1 and can disguise a multitude of crimes.

Audiences—even the most naïve audiences—seem to understand the necessity for a good memory very well. Almost the first question asked of an actor by a layman (after "Do you know Ann-Margret?") is: "How on earth can you remember all those lines?" This is rather like asking a foot-racer how he can continually throw one leg in front of the other without stumbling. Theatre actors know that a man who cannot retain volumes as well as correlate words with actions cannot begin to be an actor. One interesting sidelight to this issue is that child actors almost never have trouble learning their lines. I never did, for example, and yet I do now. Why? Something to do with a sense of responsibility, I suppose, but the child actor's freedom of memory is a faculty which could profitably be studied by adult players. As for the rest—forget children. Children are almost invariably bad actors.

On the opening night of *Annie Get Your Gun* in New York, Ethel Merman stood casually in the wings of the Imperial Theatre listening to the overture and waiting for the curtain to rise. Some say that she was chewing a stick of Juicy Fruit gum, and I wouldn't be a bit surprised, since the lady's relaxation is as notorious as her performing. Nearby, a chorus girl—less than twenty years old—was busily grinding her dance slippers into a resin box and alternately bouncing up and down in second position. She was candidly terrified and apparently trying to bump and grind her fears away. Eventually she forgot her horrors long enough to notice Miss Merman: dead-pan, fist-in-hip, jaws-slowly-working-gum, and looking altogether like a well-fed policeman off-duty. "Oh, Miss Merman!" the girl cried. "You look so, so—unperturbed! Aren't you nervous?"

Miss Merman removed a wad of exhausted gum from her mouth and dropped it precisely into a trash can. "Why should I be nervous?" she said. "I know my lines."

Back to the drawing board.

William

25 February—Toronto
10 a.m.

Dear Bob . . .

The pencil fell out of my hand and I slept. Now it seems necessary that I fill in the gaps of last night's nightmarish dress rehearsal.

It took our crew all of Sunday and up to seven on Monday evening to prepare the stage for us. We did not have a technical rehearsal (one devoted exclusively to lighting, scene changes, and cues), which is most unfortunate. There was simply no time left to have a "tech" as well a "dress." We therefore combined the two: a poor idea.

In any theatrical production, a dress rehearsal is essential; a tech is merely necessary. Since we could not have both, we settled for a little of both. We ran the play without stopping, and poor Jean Rosenthal (the lighting director) had to light us as we went along. To do so is to shoot at a charging rhino with a bee-bee gun. But Jean has been around for many years and can say what Mother Goddam said in *The Shanghai Gesture:* "I survive."

A number of rumorists tell me that Alex Cohen considered a postponement. These same "insiders" add that the social lights of Toronto found such a possibility unacceptable. The rich of any city support its theatre. Therefore, we must kneel and heel. More than that, we must be grateful. All artists have patrons. Problems aside, we will play our first public performance tonight: Tuesday, February 25th.

Though this is not our official opening, but a benefit preview, it is the psychological moment of truth for the actors. The first public performance of any play will tend to fix the future in the minds of the players. One rarely comes back from a really disastrous first performance, whether there are critics in front or not. Though "roughness" is to be expected, the rhythms planned during rehearsal must begin to throb within the actor, or he will know that he has failed. Try as he may, he cannot correct his mistakes by the following night. He can only grit his teeth and take his punishment. He is polishing a worn-out pair of shoes and he knows it.

One happy note: the dressing rooms are glorious. New York actors are accustomed to the shabbiest digs imaginable. There has not been a new playhouse constructed on Broadway since 1924. The O'Keefe, being new as paint and twice as fresh, greets a company of actors as though it were a rich aunt in love with show business. My own room (and I rank a lowly fifth in this company) is as spanking and cheerful as any actor could ask. I have two make-up tables; a shower; a personal toilet; sufficient room for my portable cot; and a serviceable panel of bright, harsh lights. Actors require harsh light to make up by. The lights in front are cruel and uncompromising. It is not a Hollywood dressing room (most of those are suites), but it is all that a man devoted to interpreting good writers should demand, and I am content. Such a room does wonders for an actor's morale. Every fixture is clean and new and works efficiently. The check-in desk is staffed by private police, all of whom are courteous, intelligent, and theatre-oriented. The O'Keefe is too large for theatrical performance, but it is a tightly run ship, and any actor should be grateful to play there.

As for my performance, I would like to be a damn sight better, but no final tale can be told until Gielgud makes ultimate selections and Richard Burton gets far enough past his anxieties to make aesthetic decisions.

Our audience-less dress rehearsal featured certain highlights which deserve reporting. For example, there was Jessica Levy's visit during the first intermission. She seemed beatified and engaged. In fact, she nodded vigorously to me and winked; her complexion was roseate and smacked of springtime. "I was right," she said. "Don't you see? I was right."

I assumed she meant that the play was well cast.

There was Elizabeth Taylor's visit, too: complete with a kiss on the cheek and liquid eyes. Actors become accustomed to hearing "You're so wonderful" and all but cover their compliments with salt, but Elizabeth is a warm, affectionate woman whose praise is hard to resist. My own embrace having been traced in white sand, she moved swiftly to Richard's room, where they undoubtedly shared a cup of trembling together. As for Gielgud, he said not a word to me but beat a hasty path to where his star sat brooding. He emerged some three minutes later and entered Hume Cronyn's sanctum; a few moments there, followed by a trip to Alfred Drake, thence followed with a moment of grace for Eileen Herlie. At this point, Gielgud's duties were done. He did not visit me, or George Rose, or George Voskovec—to say nothing of Linda Marsh, John Cullum, or Robert Milli—three major players wildly unbilled. Status shatters our hearts in the theatre. The actor must have the soul of a fairy and the hide of a walrus.

Starting with Act II, Burton's difficulties with Shakespeare's words began, and he was prompted from the wings much of the time. Was he frightened? Had Elizabeth given him Dexamil? By Act III, he resembled a gibbering lunatic and all but gave up the ghost. He was not Hamlet, he was not Burton, he was not even an actor. He was no more than a fighting soldier desperately resisting death. It was a sad, terrifying spectacle. He did not seem drunk but he did seem beaten, which is worse by several leagues. At midnight, the company was dismissed. Gielgud said nothing.

Several of us went to a cafeteria, since Toronto—loveliest city of the plains—is not hospitable to night owls. Our conversation was discouraged and frightened. The set seemed so massive and so illogical. All of us are dwarfs before it. Speculation ran epidemically as to whether we might not be a financial failure after all—despite Richard Burton's draw, despite the glamour of Elizabeth Taylor. So fearfully much had been left undone; rumors flourished that Gielgud planned to leave us the moment we opened. This could mean that countless instances of muzzy staging would stand uncorrected. While Clem Fowler and I picked at our scrambled eggs and groaned mutually over dire eventualities, young Richard Sterne spoke up boldly. "What else do you expect Sir John to do?" he said. "His work is done. I check my tape recordings every night. For over ten days, he's done nothing but repeat himself. Unless he takes every member of the cast aside and gives him private speech lessons, he has nothing left to say."

Both Clem and I leaped on the defenseless novice like street fighters defending their turf. "How many productions have you been in, my clever friend?" Fowler asked, and added, "He's got *everything* to do; he hasn't even begun to direct the play."

Sterne asked what, for instance, and we explained to him that the production was as unrehearsed as any we had ever played in: entrances and exits were messy and illogical, and did not flow smoothly; scene after scene suffered from an absence of concept —they had simply not been figured out; they were little more than staged readings for a YMHA verse concert. Actors were not on top of their roles; they were submerged in confusion. Just as Actor A began to make a point, Actor B would spoil the effect out of nothing more than an ignorance as to the scene's intent. Michael Ebert added that Gielgud's intentions were a riddle, a mystery. Others joined in, pounding poor Richard Sterne into an intellectual pulp. Were we right? Of course we were right. But what difference did it make? None of us was directing the play. John Gielgud was.

Eventually, we made stupid and separate ways to our respective hotels.

Before I went to sleep, I thought about Richard Burton: had he gone too soft, too rich and self-indulgent for one of literature's most demanding roles? Were his remaining gifts too exiguous for so extravagant an assignment? Had he borrowed on his talents at too high a rate of interest? Had he accepted a challenge he simply could no longer meet? I had been proud of him for accepting the challenge, since I knew to my depths that he no longer needed such agony for the sake of either fame or fortune. As Laurence Olivier stated, Burton had become a household word.

I felt blue. I also wondered if I was flogging a dead horse. Why should anyone expect the Brandos and the Burtons to accept challenges merely for the sake of the record? America provides no viable theatre in which major acting talents can function. Some cynics even say that the American theatre exists only for actors who cannot make it in the movies. Why should anyone give up $500,000 and more per picture in order to slither into a hair shirt? The Greek word for actor is agonistes. But what have the Greeks done for us lately?

Only the thought of Laurence Olivier cheered me up. One man, one example. Who else in our era had turned his back upon the blandishments of film? What other major actor, Burton and Brando excepted, had been presented with such blandishments? People forget that the combination of *Wuthering Heights* and *Rebecca* made Olivier one of the most sought-after leading men in the history of motion pictures. They also forget that he told Samuel Goldwyn what an actor had to do and be if he was to remain an actor and that Goldwyn has never forgotten the argument.

Olivier wanted to be an actor. In order to achieve this goal, he endured—among other trials—the worst set of personal notices I have ever read for any player,* a financial deprivation which can be understood only by those who have refused millions, plus a probable awareness that he is less than the most gifted actor of his era. Ironically enough, Laurence Olivier *is* less gifted than Marlon Brando. He is even less gifted than Richard Burton, Paul Scofield, Ralph Richardson, and John Gielgud. But he is still the definitive actor of the twentieth century. Why? Because he wanted to be. His achievements are due to dedication, scholarship, practice, determination, and courage. He is the bravest actor of our time.

Brando is the greatest actor of our time. But what difference
* *Romeo and Juliet*—circa 1940—New York City.

does it make? For the sublime nature of his endowment collided with the decline of the American theatre and his artistic modesty. Therefore, the finest acting talent of the past quarter century has now become as dependable as a Brazilian *cruzeiro* and inscribed not a trace upon the pages of acting history since 1947, when he created Stanley Kowalski. This performance, I may as well say now, is the finest I have seen given by an actor in the twenty-nine years I have been going to the theatre—and I saw it seven times. To watch an actor of such precocity and power function only as a motion-picture mannequin leaves even the most light-hearted lover of the acting art considerably less than elated.

But Burton, with a bit of Olivier in him, is brave. If I can forget tonight's goblins and witches and cast my imagination over the breadth and depth of our rehearsals, I can reasonably conclude that Burton's Hamlet will be a stunning one. It will not be everyone's Hamlet; it will not even be mine—but it *will* be Burton's, which means aggressive, temperamental, witty, colorful—and brave. Notwithstanding the outcome of an under-rehearsed and over-comfortable production, Burton's gesture is everything; his courage is everything. His will to remain a major actor meeting special challenges is everything. His willingness to endure the irritations, nuisances, and even tortures, if you'll allow me, of forgetting lines, of his badly behaving nerves, of fearing that perhaps he has lost the rhythm of theatre playing, of knowing that his muscles are going slack from film work and that he must pull himself into condition again, and of the sheer stamina and discipline which *Hamlet* played eight times a week requires—such willingness connotes a magnificent gesture, a sublime obsession. Burton's energy is not only formidable; it is slightly moon-struck and oriented to new orbits.

It was nearly three o'clock in the morning when a friend in the company telephoned my room. My comforting thoughts had calmed my distress and my voice was soft with patience.

"What do you think, Bill?" asked my friend.

"I think he'll make it."

"But he kept forgetting his lines!"

"I know."

(Pause.) I heard breathing. My friend then spoke again. "I think he had a drink between acts and it turned him fuzzy."

"He probably had more than one."

"Will he do that tomorrow night?"

"No."

"How do you know?"

"I don't."

"I think he's scared. I think he's scared to death."

"Well, of course he's scared!" I all but shouted. "Wouldn't you be?"

"I guess I would."

My friend hung up and I got my patience back. Of course he'd make it. Of course he would. For some reason, I felt better.

William

PART II

The Toronto Engagement

FEBRUARY 26–MARCH 21

Dear Bob . . .

He did make it. We gave our first public performance and he made it. He was nervous, violent, and under-contemplative, but he made it because he's got muscle and nerve. He sweated, he grunted, he strained, and often he seemed like a wounded ox shaking off the bites and clawings of a bobcat, but he made it.

It was the sort of performance given by a come-back actor who knows that tomorrow counts more than tonight, but he forgot no lines and he moved from scene to scene with the shape of his performance loosely in grasp. He began strongly in the

Court Scene; he all but sailed through "Too, too solid flesh," thereafter wavering badly at times, but he arrived at the Grave-diggers' Scene with clear eyes and a determined demeanor. The rhythm was there. From that moment on, he was roughly comparable to a first-class racehorse rounding the far turn. Something about the nostrils will tell you that the well-bred creature can smell the stable.

The audience reaction was difficult to determine: they sat in front like a sea of minnows, too miniaturized and distant for belief. When the play was over, the sound of their applause recalled to me the trained seals and dolphins of Marineland. In any case, to hell with them. We are in Toronto to rehearse.

After the performance (we were dismissed with no notes) we sat about the Studio Club, drinking and talking.

"He made it."

"He's got sand."

"He's *been* there, man."

"It wasn't a *good* performance."

"He has no concept."

"But he made it, man. What are you talking about?"

"Made what?"

"*You* play Hamlet! I want to see *you* play it!"

"I'd be better than Donald Madden!"

"I sincerely hope so!"

"I'm proud of him."

"Who? Burton?"

"No. Jerry Lewis."

"Sarcasm is a weapon of the weak."

"Fuck you."

"I'm proud of him, too. He's got guts."

"So what do *you* know?"

"Are you going to buy me a drink?"

"Anytime you need me."

"Tomorrow is the big-time."

"No kidding? Did you play vaudeville?"

There was nothing left to say. Most of us got as sozzled as we wished and trundled off to bed. Sentimentality was beginning to intrude. We were a company now. We loved each other and we needed each other. That is the way it happens. Tomorrow night was the 26th of February, 1964, and we would be facing the green jungle of Canada's critics as well as the oh-so-sophisticated visitors from New York.

I did not care. I knew that Burton had laid hands on the center of himself. And I knew that from now on, the performance would be his. Bring on the critics.

27 February—3 a.m.

We did not rehearse on opening day. We waited. It is the waiting before an opening night which makes actors kindred with ballplayers, bullfighters, prize fighters, and combat soldiers huddled in a landing barge. As with all such professional masochists, the methods used to distract oneself from the task ahead are many and varied: sleeping late in the day is highly thought of by some; reading is just about impossible for most, yet there are those who are calm enough to manage the trick. Movie-going works out well for a few. Smoking twice as many cigarettes as usual is common but inadvisable; cigarettes tend to dry out the throat and rattle the nervous system. Drinking is out of the question. Staring at a blank white wall for several hours can be an effective pastime. It is depressing at the start but one goes eventually into an Ace-High trance. Worse things could happen to an adventurous man, especially the sort who is intrigued by the sight of his own life's blood.

For those who cannot practice any of the above amnesic tricks, I have an alternate suggestion: suicide. A preferable method is to drown yourself in the hotel bathtub. Another is to jump out of the hotel window. If you happen to be at home, any reasonably wide window no less than ten stories above the ground will serve the purpose. If your home is built too close to the earth, I suggest taking a taxi downtown, renting a room with a bay window, and jumping out of that. This sort of thing affords one's final moments a certain style. Slashing the wrists, on the other hand, is not recommended because it hurts too much. Any actor interested in pain might just as well go to the theatre, put on his make-up, and open in the goddam play. By the way, if your particular hotel bathtub is too shallow to drown in, I cannot recommend defenestration too highly.

On the afternoon of Wednesday, February the 26th, 1964, I decided against committing suicide only because I had decided against it so often in the past. One picks up a number of curious habits during one's lifetime, and not committing suicide is one of mine.

To my amazement, I passed several hours staring at a blank wall (it wasn't white, but you can't have everything) and contemplating self-slaughter. Unable to eat, I mixed myself a single stiffish martini and then went to sleep for an hour. I arrived at my dressing room by six-thirty p.m. in a state of profound contemplation.

But the opening-night performance went surprisingly well—assisted no end by the presence of Elizabeth Taylor backstage rather than out front. Aside from the obvious advantages of Miss Taylor's invariably cheerful countenance, I refer at this moment to the disadvantages of having her seated in the audience. Yesterday's letter neglected to tell you that having her in front at last night's performance delayed the rise of the curtain by over forty minutes. Despite the ring of friends surrounding her, as well as the ominous presence of bodyguard Bobby LaSalle, too many members of the Toronto audience found gawking at the lady an irresistible temptation. Indeed, hundreds of them simply would not take their seats, despite the protests of hundreds of others. Both Richard Burton and Miss Taylor today decided that she will not visit the front of the house again until our official opening in New York. To make an exception of New York in this regard is psychologically sound. New Yorkers are as prurient and celebrity-minded as the citizens of Omaha, Nebraska, but for a Broadway opening-night audience to mill actively around even the most lustrous of film stars would be outrageously *de trop*. In fact, it would indicate a mass loss of New York cool.

Richard Burton delivered a smoother performance tonight, as one might have expected. The applause at the end of the evening was more forceful than at our preview, although it still sounded rather like fishes calling plaintively to each other from the bottom of a lake. A party was given in the lounge of the theatre to celebrate the occasion of our opening. I suppose one could call it a Gala. An orchestra was hired and champagne flowed as freely as the O'Keefe Centre's budget would allow.

The *Hamlet* company itself sat at tables roped off from the peasants. Other tables were reserved for the subscribing members of the Toronto audience. It was a decently handled affair. Most social occasions in Toronto are well handled. But rumors began to circulate rather early on that many members of the audience were displeased with the production. I paid little attention to such scuttlebut; I have been down that road before. Instead, I confined myself to the exquisite deglutition of both pabulum and potables, supper-society style. I also danced. I also chatted. I also avoided the stares of wide-eyed, nubile girls whose Paphian hearts have led them to believe that all actors are the amorous descendants of Benvenuto Cellini.

By three a.m., I was in my own bed and I was alone.

William

27 February 1964—Toronto

Dear Bob . . .

Once my eyes were suitably open this morning, I congratulated myself on feeling no curiosity whatever regarding the prose and opinions of the Toronto reviewers. I gleefully called room service (they seemed cheery, too) and ordered coffee with cream and saccharine. When asked if I wanted a newspaper, I said no. My decision pleased me hugely, since I have so often riffled the pages of an out-of-town paper only to find that some ex-sports reporter has decided to tell me I cannot act. Worse than that, I have sometimes been told that I was the Salvini of our generation. To count on either opinion is to fall down a coal chute dressed in a white silk suit.

On many occasions I have altered my performances because of tryout-town opinions, and I have inevitably come up a loser. Broadway reviews hurt equally well, if they are negative, but whatever changes are made by the actor will not alter the case. Once a New York opening is done with, the verdict is in and the actor might just as well be changing his underwear in a dark closet. But the provincial wits and critics who attend out-of-town premieres are awesomely addicted to sophisticated judgments in front: "William Redfield is giving one of the filthiest performances I have ever seen. In a part calling for subtlety and emotional range, he reminded this department of a bellboy calling for Philip Morris. He is loud and melodramatic, lacking any sort of style." This is almost as bad as "William Redfield is brilliant," since neither opinion will properly affect the work remaining.

Words such as brilliant, loud, melodramatic, subtlety, and style mean different things to different people, and actors too often forget that the men who write such words are merely trying to sell newspapers and establish reputations. The actor who takes such pitiable scuffling seriously is dedicated to his own on-coming doom. It smarts sharply to read anything other than near ecstasy about oneself, but the actor will damage more than his ego should he take literally a news peddler's opinion concerning the most elusive of the arts. If he damages his performance, he will have surrendered his profession to an inferior, and that is the unkindest cut of all. I know, because I have done it.

A jangling telephone interrupted my orgy of self-appreciation. Naturally, I should not have picked up that telephone, but I did and was thus euchred. A gossipy, breathless voice asked hysterically if I had seen the reviews. I said that I hadn't. It then proceeded to harangue me blow-by-blow with quotes. I tried to interrupt, but succeeded only in uttering a number of unfinished sentences: "Wait a min—" "I don't read re—" "Reviews are sil—" "Don't you ever lis—?" But nothing would stop it. Of course, I could have just hung up, but I didn't because I am weak, foolish, and self-deluding, and simply could not resist the rhythmic symphony of contumely which was being hummed to me over the telephone. It (my informer) was giddy and passionate while he-she hissed: "They're horrendous, aren't they? They're the worst notices I ever read! It sounds as though we've been produced and directed by Sonny Liston!" The last reference crushed my resolution and I lit a cigarette. "Read me all of them," I said quietly, while beating idly at one leg.

For five minutes, I listened to the eldritch details. Nathan Cohen had called the production "an unmitigated disaster" and Richard Burton "artistically impotent." Ronald Evans had praised Richard Burton highly (both chaps saw the same performance) but felt nothing but contempt for the supporting company. Herbert Whittaker expressed confusion as to the *meaning* of the production. All three gentlemen were horrified by the sets and costumes.

"Thanks for the news," I said finally. "You have given me an enormous appetite."

I hung up the phone, dressed, and forcibly remanded myself to the lobby of the King Edward with a proper breakfast in mind. On arrival below, I confronted Mrs. Robert Milli, whose husband plays Horatio. She did not have breakfast in mind. In fact, she was visibly upset because her husband had been the victim of especially negative notices, along with Alfred Drake, Linda Marsh, and John Cullum. By implication, each one of us was something less than successful, excepting Hume Cronyn, George Voskovec, and George Rose. Even Rose had been painted gray with faint praise by Nathan Cohen, who called him "mildly competent." And Ronald Evans had sneered that the men in the company "one and all . . . resemble fugitives from a mens' hairdressing salon." In other words, we were fags. Such witless writing makes me laugh, but it was bringing Mrs. Milli close to tears, and I comforted her as best I could. I told her I preferred that her husband be more enraged than defensive, and I then invited her to have breakfast. "Breakfast?" she murmured. "How can you possibly eat on a morning like this?"

"With both hands," I answered, "and ravenously."

Understandably, she rejected my invitation and went upstairs to help her husband cry his eyes out. Ten years from today, Mr. Milli (a highly conscientious actor) will not give a hoot in hell what three Toronto critics say of him.

Later today, when I got to the theatre, I was both amused and chagrined to see that Michael Ebert (Fortinbras)—a spectacularly tall and romantic-looking young actor—had succumbed to the scoldings of Ronald Evans and hied himself to a catch-penny barber shop. His wavy, Edwardian locks are now sheared away so completely that he looks like an Ivy League halfback. Presumably he will no longer resemble a fugitive from anything but the darker recesses of Ronald Evans's hair-oriented mind. But will Mr. Ebert's anxious accession to the taste of a columnist truly improve his performance of Fortinbras? Will it even cause him to look more appropriate? I fear not. If anything, Mr. Ebert has damaged his appearance considerably and cut away one of his more interesting assets. It is as though he elected a Canadian reviewer to be his personal Delilah. Will Ronald Evans return to the theatre and subsequently write an approving review of Michael Ebert's hair? Hardly. And even if Ronald Evans does return, who cares?

So much for actors who take critics seriously. When are they to learn that the worst advice given in the theatre is dispensed to artists by reviewers? More importantly, when are they to understand that critics are amateurs and that *we* are supposed to be the professionals? Michael Ebert is a talented and good-looking young actor, but he will be of no value whatever to himself or the theatre until he elects to spit straight into Ronald Evans's eye.

When actors get bad notices in plays, they usually dive into the nearest Slough of Despond and wallow about for weeks at a time. In fact, anything short of hysterical praise will send even a well-established actor into an absolute frenzy of ambivalent feelings: "Goddamn that critic! He's not being fair!" followed by, "He's right. I'm no damned good. I stink!" followed by, "I wonder if I'll be fired?" followed by, "They wouldn't dare. Suppose my replacement is just as lousy as *I* am?" followed by, "This damned part is no good anyway, and it never was" followed by, "I'm being given no direction" followed by a great deal of drinking.

Out-of-town reviews are especially dangerous. Time and again, I have seen reasonably good productions and plays ruined by the "advice" of tryout-town critics; just as I have seen good

out-of-town reviews cause producers, directors, and authors to
leave a "hit" alone. But was it a hit? Broadway later said otherwise.
Besides, there are no such things as hits and flops for the artist.
That way madness lies. What really counts is the arch of one's
career. At times, success will come. At other times, it will not.
No critic I have ever read knows a tenth of what I know about
the theatre or about acting. Now if this snippet of *gasconade
verité* is honest-to-God valid, then most assuredly no critic alive
knows a *thirtieth* of what Mr. Joshua Logan knows, yet it is
common knowledge that Mr. Joshua Logan has occasionally lost
his grip on reality because of a negative review in the New
Haven Citizen-News-Clarion. Fancies aside, Mr. Logan is a director of considerable experience and talent, but he can be shaken
to his depths by an opinion from any quarter and sometimes from
any dime. If the opinion happens to be in print, Mr. Logan dives
wildly into that Slough of Despond without even removing his
clothes.

Bad scene.

———•—•—•———

Before tonight's performance we were summoned to the Green
Room, where Alex Cohen and John Gielgud addressed the company. Said Mr. Cohen, "I got a telephone call this morning from
Nathan Cohen, who is, believe me, no relation. He told me he
felt awful about his review and that he'd waited until five a.m.
to turn it in. I told him I thought any critic had a right to say
what he believed and that he needn't apologize. Then he asked
me if I could set up an interview with Elizabeth Taylor and I
hung up on him."

Richard Burton laughed a bit too loudly at this news, as did
most of us.

"But," continued Alex Cohen, "I *do* think they have a right to
say what they please and I also think it's better to get bad notices
out of town than good ones. Besides—*we* have a right to ignore
them. Some of them have suggested that we junk our sets and
costumes and revert to a traditional production. We will do

nothing of the kind. Some of what they said about us may very well be true, but most of it isn't. Now we will do what all professionals do when out of town: we go to work."

John Gielgud spoke briefly, saying that much of the staging was messy and vague and that it was all his fault. He then gave exiguous notes and informed us that the second intermission would be eliminated and that Hamlet's speech ending "my thoughts be bloody or be nothing worth" would blend immediately into Ophelia's Mad Scene. A rehearsal was called for noon the following day and we were dismissed to prepare ourselves for our second performance.

On the way to my dressing room, I noticed that some of the younger members of the company seemed dejected and distressed. Understandable, but a mistake.

While putting on my make-up, I thought of my old, distinguished acquaintance, Sir Cedric Hardwicke. Some years ago, this amusing and practiced gentleman told me a tale of his juvenile days which defines as well as anything I have heard a serviceable, all-purpose attitude toward critics of any size, shape, disposition, prejudice, or geography. Believe it or not, Sir Cedric was once a young actor whom everyone called merely Cedric, for no one dreamed he would ever be knighted, least of all himself. In fact, young Cedric Hardwicke played several seasons with a particular repertory company (Liverpool, perhaps) and appeared prominently whenever the juvenile role was prominent. Since the company was considered "first class," each new production was reviewed by as many as three local critics plus occasional visiting reviewers from other theatre centers. Invariably, Sir Cedric told me, he received the most appalling personal reviews. Critics would either ignore him entirely or set down calamitous comments such as "Mr. Cedric Hardwicke, as usual, was dreadful," or "Mr. Cedric Hardwicke misses the point of his role root and branch, from head to toe," or "Mr. Cedric Hardwicke would do well to consider another line of work," or "Mr. Cedric Hardwicke has an especially ugly face," and so on down the shadowed nightmare alley of an actor's most mortal fears. By the time Hardwicke was twenty-five years old, he owned a scrapbook of devastating pans plus the despairing conviction that no critic alive would ever write kindly of his acting.

Yet the management of the rep company rehired him for several seasons and must surely have thought him capable, and so young Hardwicke eventually decided that he was possessed of a few acceptable qualities as an actor but that all newspaper reviewers, for whatever reason, were united in a monstrous cabal against him. One late spring, however, a similar repertory company too far away to be considered competitive requested Mr. Hardwicke for an important juvenile role, and the Liverpudlian management consented. The engagement entailed one week's rehearsal followed by one week's playing, and let us say that the location was Brighton. The management rented a flat for the young actor, but there was no one in help, and on opening day Mr. Hardwicke badly slashed the index finger of his left hand with an unfamiliar kitchen utensil. The cut was so severe that a hastily summoned physician sewed up the wound with more than ten stitches. He then advised his young patient to skip that evening's performance. "Oh, no!" Mr. Hardwicke protested. "I mustn't. It's a new company, a new play, they've gone to so much trouble. I simply have to go on." The doctor disapproved, but when Hardwicke added that this was opening night, after all, finally agreed to pack the finger in cotton. "But," he cautioned, "do not let your arm hang down in a normal position for even so much as ten seconds or that finger will likely hemorrhage. It must be kept elevated consistently or I will not be responsible, do you understand?"

When the doctor departed, Hardwicke mulled over his problem. Obviously he would have to hold his left hand arbitrarily up in the air, the wounded finger pointing weirdly at the sky. How in the world could such peculiar behavior be justified for the audience? He could admit, of course, that he'd been hurt and an announcement could be made, but an injury was inappropriate to his role, and the opening-night audience might be made uncomfortable. No, Mr. Hardwicke decided that he would curl the maimed left hand just in front of his jacket lapel, with the index finger pointing more or less toward his left shoulder. Then he elected to make up the bandaged finger most carefully and, whenever possible, conceal it behind the rest of his hand through a strategic twisting and turning.

The performance was an ordeal, and Hardwicke felt particularly silly and self-conscious to be holding his hand in so fatuous and even feminine a fashion, but he had been embarrassed before, and so he endured. As for the rest, he gave his performance exactly as rehearsed, with no point made of the hand or any explanation offered.

On the following morning he was astonished to read the best personal notices he had ever received, as well as what turned out to be the best of the Brighton season. One reviewer said, "Young Mr. Hardwicke is surely the most unconventional juvenile actor this department has seen in years; a particular character gesture held me quite spellbound throughout the evening. One hand— the left, I believe—curled gracefully against his lapel; in lieu of a boutonnière, perhaps? A lovely mystery—and a most inventive performance." Other reviewers praised him in equal measure. Not one failed to mention "his interesting hand," "his odd and fascinating gestures," "his graceful deportment." For the first time in his career, he was a hit with the critics. And ever after, too.

I asked him if he made use of this apocalypse for his next performance. "Of course not," he scoffed. "How could I? Was I to shove bananas in my ears the next time I played and hope the damned fools would find that interesting too? No—what was most bitter and ironic for me was to realize that this bizarre bit of sophistication could not be used for any worthy purpose. Still, the accident may have helped me after all. Up to that time I had been hurt so consistently by critics and taken them so seriously that now I could take pleasure in the realization that they were a lot of ignorant halfwits. I do believe that my next opening was a good deal less anxious because I had developed such a healthy contempt for the wits and wise men in front."

William

29 February '64—Toronto

Dear Bob . . .

I believe it was Galen who said that all animals are sad after coitus except for the female human and the rooster. I have not found the ancient Greek medic to be correct about this, but I have found that *I* am sad after leap year and I wonder if there are a few more animals hanging around like me.

This particular 29th of February is a Saturday, which means the end of our first playing week. Yesterday afternoon, Miss Jessica Levy informed me that her services would be "no longer required" as of this Saturday evening. This depressed not only me but most of the members of the company as well. We surely thought she would be retained through the out-of-town engagement, or for as long as John Gielgud remained with us. Miss Levy told me that Gielgud took her shyly to one side and said she was the best assistant he'd ever worked with but that he simply didn't need her any more, since there was nothing left for him to do but sit out front and take notes. Jessica offered to take the notes for him, but Gielgud shook his head. "No, no," he said. "I like to take my own notes."

It seems to me that Jessica's presence has provided an essential boost in morale for this band of players. It also seems to me that her scanty salary would hardly strain the management over the next four to six weeks of pre-Broadway testing. Admittedly, I am not the fellow who meets the payroll, but Jessica Levy has been mother, sister, and friend to many members of the *Hamlet* company and we will miss having her around, for better or worse.

Anyway, a group of us got together and decided to give her a surprise party. In whose room? Mine, of course. It is the largest, after all, and I am one of the world's hammiest and most boni-faced hosts. I ordered several quarts of scotch, gin, vodka, and even a bottle of champagne for Elizabeth Taylor: not Dom Perignon, but Mumm's Cordon Rouge, anyway, and she's a pliable sort. Thirty extra glasses were brought to my room by Canadian slaves, along with canapés, sandwiches, and a few *hors d'oeuvres*. I all but drove the assistant manager mad. Since I was lucky enough to have a refrigerator in my room, I could even serve beer to those of proletarian persuasion. Linda Marsh accepted the tricky detail of shanghaiing Miss Levy after the Saturday performance and maneuvering her toward my room for a quiet nightcap. Meanwhile, I stole back to my room, like some Elizabethan clown, to check out all the preparations, which included twenty folding chairs provided by the King Edward management, as well as five extra end tables. My room was as crowded as a subdeb's bureau. I didn't really know if Burton and Taylor would show up, since moving through the hotel hallways is more than a casual excursion for them, but I was prepared for their presence, at any rate. Five minutes after my arrival, Clem Fowler and another cast member named Alex Giannini demanded entrance and proceeded to help me with anything and all. I had bought a birthday cake for the occasion and planned to bring it out at a nice, dark moment—complete with candles, rosettes, and greeting card. For the moment, the cake sat wistfully in my bathtub, along with several extra bags of ice.

When Jessica arrived, everyone cheered and stamped and shouted, and I do believe that she was genuinely surprised. Clem Fowler turned the lights out and Linda Marsh emerged with the cake. The tiny card which sat propped between the candles was badly charred by flame before Jessica picked it up for reading. On it were inscribed the following words: "Hamlet loves Jessica. Maybe *that's* his problem."

Jessica read these words aloud and blubbed a bit, which was a fitting reaction, for we would have felt lousy if she had done any less. Then we all got down to some serious drinking, eating, and conversation. Michael Ebert and I engaged ourselves in a raging argument about critics, Michael claiming that it was the height of egotism to ignore critical reaction, and I claiming that it was the height of folly to do otherwise. Many present were positive that we would have a fist fight, but they were wrong. I like Michael Ebert. I like him very much. Not only that, he's bigger than I am. Besides, Philip Coolidge interrupted the argument. "Don't you get it, Michael?" he said. "Redfield doesn't *read* reviews. But he can quote them for you any time you ask."

Richard and Elizabeth arrived shortly after the cake-cutting. Bobby LaSalle and Bob Wilson had hustled them through the hallways like a two-man Coast Guard. There was hardly room enough for the crowd of actors and crew to accommodate themselves, sitting or standing, but the party was, on the whole, successful. Once things got wet enough, Phil Coolidge (the Yankee snipper) took me into sufficient confidence to admit a curious conviction. "Jessica," he crooned, "is for it because of production-team politics." When I asked for further information, Coolidge shook his head. "I will tell you nothing more because you are a spy."

He was right about that, but I still maintain that Jessica's contribution to the production was considerable and that she deserved to be retained. We didn't want to miss her. We wanted her with us.

Blow out your candles, Jessica—but no good-bys.

W.

3 March—Tuesday—Toronto

Dear Bob . . .

But business is simply smashing. The crowds outside the O'Keefe stage door grow larger and more pervasive with every passing performance; yet they are polite crowds, too, and show little interest in the comings and goings of such as myself. The crowds in front are also polite but becoming gradually more voluble and enthusiastic. This was especially true of our first matinee last Saturday. The young people in the audience (were they drama students?) began cheering Richard's soliloquies rather early on. At the final curtain, there was a good deal of bravoing for many of the players.

A few individuals have stopped me on the street to express outrage at the reviews and praise for the production. There is little doubt in my mind that the show will be successful in New York, not only financially but critically, but there is also *no* doubt in *anyone's* mind that the staging is messy, the lighting unfinished, the set puzzling, and John's direction of the actors more kindly than insistent. Then, too, much of the company is disturbed by constant rumors of Gielgud's impending departure. A backstage conversation between two whispering players went something like this:

"I hear it's true."

"What's true?"

"That he's leaving."

"Who's leaving?"

"Gielgud, Mr. Quick—*John* Gielgud. Do you remember him?"

"Not very well. He hasn't spoken to me since the third day of rehearsal."

"His best friend died."

"Who was that?"

"A man named Bernie. He died suddenly in London and Gielgud feels bad that he wasn't there."

"Oh, I get it. I've noticed him crying a few times."

"That doesn't prove anything. He cries all the time. I think he'd cry if his worst enemy had hay fever."

"Yeah—he sure does like to cry."

"I hope to hell he doesn't leave us."

"Why would he want to?"

"He thinks his work is done and that Richard won't listen to him any more."

"Do you think it's true?"

"That's the rumor."

A lengthy pause, during which both parties adjust their sword belts around their modern jackets and stare blankly at the floor. Finally, one speaks.

"Do you think Gielgud has a concept of this play?"

"Of course he does, but he's keeping it to himself."

"He knows more about this play than anyone living."

"And probably more than anyone dead."

"Including Shakespeare?"

"I think so."

"Why doesn't he tell *us?*"

"He's letting us find our own way."

"Are we finding our own way?"

"We are finding our own *ways*."

"Our own *separate* ways."

"That's right."

"Well, that means there is no concept."

"Socko, baby; you're right again."

"Oh, I'm an awfully smart fellow."

"You're not only smart; you're hard of hearing."

"Why do you say that?"

"Because the last line spoken on stage was our cue."

After each evening performance, we are assembled for Sir John's notes in the Green Room. I have never known why the rooms reserved for speaking to actors are called Green Rooms, but they have been so called since the days of Edmund Kean and probably long before. Perhaps it is because the post-performance complexion of an actor, once he has removed his make-up, tends toward a mild chartreuse. In any case, the Green Room of the O'Keefe Centre is sublimely well appointed and also large enough to accommodate a Board Meeting of Kaiser Aluminum. Moreover, it is comfortable and even rather warm in feeling. We actors sit about in leather chairs, some of us still in costume, some of us in robes, most of us still half in make-up. It is a bizarre and special group which should someday be photographed by a lensman who digs distortion.

Gielgud is basically a simple, humble man. At any rate, he is a man who has learned to value simple behavior. He is neither wordy nor pretentious, though he is surely possessed of a grand manner. That manner is a part of his psychic machinery as surely as a carburetor is part of a motor car. Without his grandeur, Gielgud would not be able to turn a simple corner. But all else is plain—all else is humble, philosophic, and even resigned. Some of his comments follow:

To Guildenstern: "Stand a bit straighter, dear boy. You're crouching rather, which I don't understand; especially when you use your sword. Tighten it up a bit. Everything else is quite good."

To Polonius (Hume Cronyn): "It's a bit spry, Hume. Younger

than springtime. Try using a cane tomorrow night. I know you'll loathe it, but it might work out well, there's a good fellow. Otherwise, it's beautiful. Truly."

To Laertes (John Cullum): "John, dear—you must not scurry about in the first Court Scene that way. You're the son of a Prime Minister, a personage at court. You must never scurry— you must *stride*."

Cullum explained that he had to negotiate a swift path all the way from extreme stage left to extreme stage right in order to arrive in his final position before the entrance of the King and the Queen. In other words, as he put it, "I have a long way to go." To which Gielgud replied, "Of course, darling—we *all* do."

To the Captain (Philip Coolidge): "Coolidge, it's a charming performance, but get yourself a hat. I couldn't tell you why, but you're nothing without a hat."

To Hamlet (Richard Burton): "Really splendid tonight, Richard—I must tell you that. The entire section we spoke of from 'To be or not to be' through the Nunnery Scene was excellent, excellent—I almost liked it."

It has been said more than once that Sir John's attitude toward the role of Hamlet inclines to be possessive. One anecdote gossips that when Laurence Olivier first played the role in 1937, Gielgud went backstage after the opening night and said, "Larry, it's one of the finest performances I have ever seen, but it's still my part."

To First Gravedigger (George Rose): "George, dear, it was frightfully bad tonight. Can't bear you chuckling at your own jokes and all that early music-hall biz. Wind in the puss and high fatuity. Do change it."

George Rose is surely one of Gielgud's favorite actors, and the two have worked together often, most notably in *Much Ado about Nothing*, but Rose once said plaintively, "John doesn't like the clowns, you know—neither the parts themselves nor the actors who play them. Once he went so far as to tell me that he didn't understand my acting at all because it was too common for him but that he would try to stop me when he thought I was *not* being amusing! When John trusts an actor, he can be horribly cruel."

I wished privately that Gielgud would begin to trust Redfield enough to be horribly cruel, since I wearied of being told how good I was when I knew I wasn't good at all. My posture? Could he think of nothing to help me with but my posture? More of it later.

To all Extras, Walk-Ons, Ladies-in-Waiting, and Courtiers who appear in the crucial first Court Scene: "You must all have something specific in mind. You must mutually create the atmosphere of the Danish Court which—under Claudius—is corrupt and drunken. No matter how dignified you choose to be, you must remember that if the King or Queen were to crack wise, or even Polonius, you would all fall about the place with laughter. You are sycophants and you are afraid. There is gaiety here but there is also cynicism and intrigue. Denmark *is* rotten. It is rotten to the core, like Maude in Bea Lillie's song. And there is a fearsome tension, too. Is the King in a good mood today? Is he cheerful? Is he drunk? And Gertrude, too. What is she thinking about? She's not the brightest woman in the world, but she is the Queen and it's best to stay on the good side of her. Above all, there's young Hamlet over there—clad all in black and squatting on a stool and looking thoroughly disagreeable."

To Ophelia (Linda Marsh): "At the beginning of your Mad Scene, as you pace idly along the parapet's edge humming your woebegone song, I would like you to lose your footing and drop into Horatio's arms. Once free of him, you should slink about the stage doing something serpentine and altogether gorgeous."

All these suggestions beguile and disarm us, for Gielgud is a witty and tender man—more sly than sinister even at his most frivolous—but where are the specifics and where the rock-bottom demands? A few nights later, some of the notes went as follows:

To Guildenstern: "Excellent tonight, but you're standing awfully straight and rigid—especially when you use your sword. Try to relax a bit."

I replied that I was trying to correct my slouching posture, and Gielgud said, "Yes, of course, and you have been fearfully successful. Loosen yourself now."

To the Captain (Philip Coolidge): "Charming performance, Coolidge, but the hat doesn't suit you. Get rid of it."

To First Gravedigger (George Rose): "Superb, truly. I don't understand what you do at all, but you do it awfully well."

To Laertes (John Cullum): "Can you possibly get to your position faster during the first Court Scene? We're all waiting for you after the King enters."

Cullum explained that he was trying to seem more dignified as per Gielgud's suggestion. "Of course you were," Gielgud replied. "Be dignified faster."

To Ophelia (Linda Marsh): "As you broke away from Horatio tonight, you went slinking about the stage doing a number of interesting movements. They were adequately serpentine but not altogether gorgeous."

All of these notes have value, despite the Piccadilly-on-Wry, but few go to the heart of crucial matters. How nice it would be to know if the intended period is Holbein or Elizabethan or even the time of the cuckoo. Gielgud seldom speaks to us in terms of a concept: a dramatic movement representing a moment in history and seen from the vantage of a particular mind. This definition is nowhere near so pompous as it may sound, for things really do not happen by accident in the theatre, despite its disquieting resemblance to horse racing. Good things happen in the theatre when talented people are led into the gardens of agreement and bend their respective wills to a common purpose. The theatre is teamwork just as playing basketball is teamwork.

Are there accidents? Yes, there are—and some of them turn out to be fortunate. But a production built on accidents will be easily borne away when the high winds come. The foundation of any production reposes on a thought; the more complete the thought, the more satisfying the production. Such a thought must be the director's. I am speaking ideally, no doubt, just as there is many a slip between the brewing of the tea and the drinking of it, but when Gielgud speaks of *Hamlet*'s opening scene (the Battlements) he touches poignantly on the sort of direction I admire. Since the scene is possibly his favorite in the play, he has worked tirelessly on it. Whether such labors will prove fruitful is not the point, and I mean that literally, for Gielgud's thoughts on this first scene are good thoughts regardless of the outcome. This afternoon, he referred keenly to one of his preferred productions of the play which starred one of history's actors (Alexander Moissi) and was spoken in German. It is faintly comical to watch oh-so-English Sir John Gielgud rhapsodize over a German production of oh-so-Elizabethan William Shakespeare's play, yet Gielgud's monologue touched me more than it amused me, and some of his words are worth quoting.

"Both Marcellus and Bernardo were played by men over fifty years of age. What a peculiar difference it made! Two old soldiers baffled by the mystery of a ghost who will not speak to them. I don't mean to alarm Barney and Bob,* but I would like to capture some of the same feeling. It is not a matter of being old in *years*, you see, but being old in *ignorance*, in *superstition*, in *fear*. These men are loyal, brave, and experienced—but they are completely without education, and anything supernatural simply terrifies them. They would fight bears with their fists but run from a falling star. In those days, no one of their class could read or write, but there was a new movement of literacy among the young—represented by such unusual intellects as Horatio and Hamlet himself. Because Horatio, though a poor man and a commoner, has been to Wittenberg, Marcellus and Bernardo stand in complete awe of him. They think of him as well read and therefore godlike. Who was it said that knowledge is power? True, of course, but ironic in this scene because there are more things in heaven and earth than are dreamed of in Horatio's philosophy. But all of these subtle gradations—these fear-filled steps from ignorance to learning to Horatio's skepticism to an impotence shared by the lettered and the unlettered alike—are so very sad and so very beautiful. If we can capture the mood of

* Barnard Hughes and Robert Burr, playing Marcellus and Bernardo, are both younger than middle-aged.

these good, gray geese, painfully aware of their ignorance, imploring the young and studious Horatio for guidance and explanation—asking first that he believe their horrific tale and second that he explain away their terror—we could drive home the early mood of the play so directly that the audience would be ours from the first. The two men should all but clasp their hands together and petition Horatio for wisdom: 'What think you on't? . . . Mark it Horatio! . . . Looks it not like the King?' What is the key to this black miracle? Surely the *younger* man, the man who can read books, will know the answer. Try for some of that feeling, please. It could be wonderful."

Not exactly chopped liver, is it? If only he'd do it more often. Some of our actors believe that Sir John is so worried about Burton's performance that he cannot function efficiently. Others feel that a company largely staffed by American players inhibits him, since his approach to the work is more rhetorical than emotional. All such reasons surmise more than they prove, but no professional company—be it American, English, or Vietnamese—is so paranoid as to feel itself commonly adrift without cause. Gielgud is a fine thoroughbred refusing his jump. His reasons are his secret.

Yet it is only fair to re-emphasize the hideous group effect caused by naïve players who take their personal notices seriously. Gielgud is suffering bitterly from the hangdog behavior of a few panned actors. Such discouragement cannot help dampening his constructive efforts. John himself is too experienced and too gifted to take such tommyrot seriously, but he is surely depressed by the daily sight of wounded faces and bleeding hearts. Even Alfred Drake demonstrated an almost pathetic vulnerability one late afternoon, and Mr. Drake is neither a pathetic nor vulnerable man. When Gielgud was endeavoring to make the King's rage at Hamlet's mousetrap play a more vivid bit of staging, Mr. Drake explained his objections thusly: "Please, John—remember that Nathan Cohen has already said I looked as though I'd been caught cheating at cards!"

Gielgud turned on his heels and stepped briefly toward the wings. At once, he stopped himself, turning back to stare at Alfred Drake, the painfully begotten wisdom of numberless productions in his eyes. He then struck softly at his thighs with two clenched fists and spoke as though his comments deserved to be delivered rather than merely spoken, like the ringing lines of a great author: "Why, oh, why do you *read* them, you silly man?"

On occasions such as these, my admiration for the gentleman is nearly boundless, yet it is impossible to ignore the foot of clay which periodically surprises us from below his trouser cuff. Now that our production is open and "in trouble," being directed by Gielgud is like being directed by Lewis Carroll's White Rabbit: he is late, he is late, and he is always on his way.

All of our daily rehearsals, which are called to clean up "Messy bits and pieces," end up exchanging frying pans for fires more often than not. In other words, we jettison one piece of unnecessary cargo only to replace it with another by helicopter. How can such things happen? Easily, because one of the most common clichés of the theatre is the assumption that one way of staging is per se better than another, which is true only when the "new" way is more easily justified *in acting terms* by the players or on that rare occasion when a moment of pageantry all but brings the audience to its feet with excitement. Staging—believe me—need not always be pretty or even striking, but it absolutely must be actable, and many an impressive stage pattern is simply not actable in terms of the author's text. To use an example less ludicrous than you might imagine, an actor cannot very well shout to his fellow player, "I am going to kill you!" and then run away from him—unless he is trying to get a laugh. If the moment is to be taken seriously, the man who threatens must advance on the man threatened. One of the secrets of comedy direction is to reverse matters; to stage things in opposition to their stated meaning and to have the actors play *against* what they are saying. Mike Nichols, for example, is simply masterful at it.

Serious plays, too, can be directed with "opposite colors," but it's a neat trick, I think, and deuced difficult in Shakespeare, where the primary job is to make matters clear, vigorous, and straightforward. In a very profound sense, Gielgud auditions for an improper audience reaction by forcing actors to justify staging which does not clearly feed the meaning of the scenes.

Patterns are less important than impulses. The personal conviction of the individual actor is what finally persuades an audience. No amount of pretty pictures will ever substitute for what has been called the actor's faith in the theatrical event. At the moment, however, Gielgud is trying to clean up so many untidy moments so quickly that he is not allowing his players to re-think the scenes in a more definite and convincing way. When John Cullum complains that he has "a long way to go" and Gielgud replies "Of course, darling, we *all* do," Cullum's problem remains unsolved despite Gielgud's wit. A problem wittily unsolved remains a problem and brings to my mind an image of jocose ruins. A smashed statue may be either funny or sad, but it is still Ozymandias: two vast and trunkless legs of stone interred in sand, or—as Shelley had it—a colossal wreck. This production needs to clean up its ruins and cart away its flotsam.

Our so-called clean-up rehearsals don't seem to clean anything up; we merely move our mounds of dust from one side of the stage to the other. And so quickly, too. "Try it this way, deah boy!" Gielgud will cry to me. "*You* enter first and allow the King and Queen to follow!" I am tempted to say it makes no sense for Guildenstern to precede his rulers, but I keep silent, because actors who refuse to "try" things are thought of as intractable by directors. I therefore "try" it. Gielgud quickly decides that it "looks better" and so we will "try" it in front of the audience, even though we will surely change it again because no amount of "trying" it will make it any better than it is right now. Why? Because it is wrong; because it doesn't make sense; because it is hard to play; because it can convince neither me nor the audience; and because what we should *really* be trying is something simple and actable which will communicate a clear thought to the audience.

On another occasion Gielgud worked for the better part of an hour on a small but important moment of staging. Finally he threw up his hands and cried out to us from his mid-orchestra position, "Oh, it's not improving, you see—not at all. It's Billy who's spoiling it and I don't even know why!" He then hurried down the center aisle and spoke passionately to me from just below the stage: "Dear boy, you're so graceful and clevah but you're doing lumpy, clumsy things with this entrance, and it's not like you at all. Please be inventive and amusing, the way you always are. It's tiresome to move you from spot to spot like a chess piece."

Not being the most secure actor on God's green stages, I defended myself. "But I have no lines!" I cried.

Gielgud sighed and touched at his brow. "Perhaps," he murmured, "it's just as well."

Do not think I resented this—not really—for it was a gibe born more of despair than malice, and I laughed along with everyone else. Gielgud's shimmering irony is never employed cruelly, for he is a gentleman to his bones, but perhaps you will begin to see that the very wit and charm I so admire at times combine to make our director a dangerous man. He vaporizes his responsibility with a puff of humor. He disappears in a comical cloud. That is dangerous, I think, for the wind sown by such a wit is reaping a whirlwind on stage, and we actors bob about in the currents like so many dolls in a cyclone.

Recently, Eileen Herlie—a model of good spirits and ladylike deportment—left a rehearsal session in less than equable temper. Her dudgeon was far from being high, but it was on the rise, and no wonder, for Gielgud had given short shrift to one of her demands. "Terribly sorry you're miserable," he said, "but time is fleeting and I simply cannot please everyone." The fact that Eileen's back was to the audience during one of her more important speeches seemed not to disturb him.

When I spoke to the lady in her dressing room, she sighed and examined the backs of her hands. "He's such a wonderful artist, really he is, but this hurry-hurry business is false economy. If we are going to restage things to make them better, then let us not fool ourselves. Let us either improve them or let them be. One cannot play critical scenes in a bad position. It would take a genius to dominate a stage this size where I am standing. Shakespeare is difficult material for the modern audience to absorb and each of us must be helped to our effects by the staging. No doubt I look charming and attractive with my back to the public, but what happens to the image of Gertrude?"

Eileen is well aware that Gielgud thinks of her as a fuss-pot and a worrier. Doubtless he thinks the same of me. Much has been said against worrying. Hemingway wrote that it never helped. Gertrude Stein said that to try was to die.

I am not so sure. Smugness seems more harmful to me than worrying. According to two celebrated works of fiction, Rebecca of Sunnybrook Farm never worried, no more did Tiny Tim. Neither figure seems capable of forming great events. I have the sneaky feeling that Beethoven worried a good deal and a similar feeling that Shakespeare tried his damnedest. Mindless optimism surely comforts the pawns in the game, but Richard Wagner's checkmate of nineteenth-century music was likely fed by his fevers. Wagner was not exactly the calm sort. He employed the temperament of a hungry terrier to accomplish unusual ends.

As for me, and do forgive the jolting descent, if I do not worry at least a little, I do not think. Not long ago Gielgud placed a comforting hand on my shoulder and said, "Please don't *worry*, dear boy. Everything improves despite us and you're such a good actor." My demeanor must have been less than grateful for he continued: "Must you look so glum? These are petty little changes. Can't you *do* them?"

All directors use this ploy at moments of crisis. The idea is to challenge the actor's courage as well as his talent. "Can't you do it?" is an explosive question expressly designed to induce shame. The trick is as transparent as a confidence man's shell game, but it continues to work on unsuspecting actors because it is ego-oriented. Actors are the saints of the theatre, just as directors are the devils of the theatre, and any damned fool can tell you that the devil beats the saint at every confrontation in every walk of life.

Happily for me, I am long past the effects of this particular technique and I hereby bequeath my secret thoughts to the inexperienced actor. Whenever a director says to me, "Can't you do it?" I engage myself in the following series of facts and fantasies: *Can I do it? Of course I can do it. Having worked in the theatre for thirty years, I can do about anything. Having been a live human I can do a number of other things, too. For example, I can pick my nose. I can also remember a number of Beatrice Lillie's songs. I can tap dance reasonably well and I do a fair imitation of Peter Lorre. I can clean and jerk nearly two hundred pounds because I used to go to Sigmund Klein's weightlifting gymnasium. I can remember Richard the Third's opening soliloquy as well as Deanna Durbin's best song from* Three Smart Girls. *I can speak passable French because I went to Paris once and passable Portuguese because I made a movie in Brazil. I play serviceable squash and terrible tennis. I know more English verse by heart than anyone except Richard Burton because I have a compulsive memory. I can stand on my head when I'm drunk because George Abbott made me do it in a play when I was seventeen and sober. Why, I can do a lot of things, my friend, but my being able to do something doesn't make the something good. Should I do them? Are they pertinent to the occasion? Does the audience give a damn? Are they worth doing? Who the hell cares what I can do? Lots of people can do lots of things. To all directors and for all time, I shout the following: Of course I can* do it. *I can* do *more damned things than you ever dreamed of on your wildest nights. But my being able to do something doesn't make it* good, *do you hear me? The question is not whether I* can *do something but whether I* should. *Are you asking me to show off or are you asking me to do the play? Make up your mind. Then, perhaps, we will find out what* you *can do. So far, it looks to be nothing.*

Some years ago, a friend of mine was picked up by the New York police on a narcotics charge. Released as a first offender, he was nevertheless rather battered-looking when I saw him the following day. "What happened?" I asked him, and he shook his head sadly. "I got wasted," he replied.

I am beginning to understand what he meant.

———•—•—•———

More and more, I worry and waste myself over the dark suspicion that my role in this production will grow no more than I can make it grow alone. Such a growth will be stunted at best because, like a one-armed man who has taken up rope climbing, I need help. But Richard Burton has told me privately that Gielgud will be leaving us for several days. "It's a good idea, love. I know the old boy and he tends to change things only because he's bored watching them. Some of them should not be changed. Some of them are good and I don't want him to get his itches going. After a bit of a rest and breather, he'll come back to us with a fresher eye."

Momentarily blowing my cool, I asked Burton what would happen to yours truly of the not-so-hot performance. After all, I needed direction *now*, not two weeks from now, but Burton interrupted me with widened eyes and a rising voice. "Lord, man, are you mad? How many times must I tell you that you and Clem are giving the best performances I've ever seen in these parts? *I've* told you; *Elizabeth* has told you; *John* has told you. If you dare change a spot of what you're doing I'll have you sent down to third level."

Burton's charm is like Gielgud's wit: dangerous. Gratified as I am by his faith in me, I know better than to take his compliments to heart. Good is good and bad is bad and I am cranky enough to know the difference. Nevertheless, Gielgud would be leaving and now I could understand the root of the black-crepe rumors. He was not being dismissed, nor was he dismissing himself, as so many of the company had feared. He was merely taking a sabbatical in order to allow the actors to "mature in their performance."

Oy-yoy-yoy. Yoy-yoy.

Sabbaticals can be a good idea, but only when the groundwork of a production has been meticulously laid. For the *Hamlet* company to fructify on no foundation we would need a visitation from De Lawd. One cannot expect turnips from stones merely because the stones have been left to themselves.

Once I had absorbed the hard fact of Gielgud's impending departure, I embarked upon a cagey plan. I would not wait for him to come to me. I would not approach him in front of others. I would be sneaky and desperate. I would get my direction by hook or crook.

From that day forward, I lay in wait for him like a cutpurse, poised to seduce a penny's-worth of wisdom from his carmine lips. Let him take an unfamiliar route through the catacombs of the O'Keefe and I am there—curled and lurking. Out of my shadows I burst with a cheerful and cogent question, ignoring his horrified shudder. "Good evening, John!" I cry. "Did you like the white sweater I wore tonight? And what about the first scene with Richard? I played it differently. It's better, I think!"

The agony of St. Bartholomew comes into his eyes and he answers me like an actor in a passion play. "White is a blinding color. I could not see your face. The acting was splendid."

He moves on to someone else's dressing room, but I am after him swiftly. "What about my posture? Is it improving, John?"

He does not break his stride but there is a timeless sadness in his voice. "You have a fine, straight back. Most refreshing. Try not to overuse it."

He places a hand on a doorknob and I all but claw at his fingers. "Listen to this, John! I'd like to wear an ascot scarf in my opening scene. Some mad little thing to give it a flair!"

His attention is finally arrested. He turns in place and there is a suggestion of tears in his eyes. "Please," he croons to me, "no mad little things. We suffer cruelly from mad little things. Let us have fewer mad little things. Don't worry. I beg you not to worry. You need no ascot scarf. You're such a good actor."

He is gone and I have no further questions. Still, I am less than gruntled. I go to my dressing room, muttering lost imprecations, and I mix myself a drink. I down the drink and I hope for a moment of pride. I tell myself that I am a star and that Gielgud does not understand my worrying because he thinks I'm brilliant. I try to reassure myself with echoes of praise from Burton, Gielgud, fans at the stage door, Elizabeth Taylor, and my wife. Yes, I try, I try, I try, and I fail, I fail, I fail. For no amount of alcohol or fantasy will extinguish the flame of my frustration: I am giving a less than dazzling performance and my mediocrity all but sends me hopping.

The certainty of this self-judgment obliterates my efforts at self-esteem. Stardom? I could not draw ten cents at the box office, and my name above a title is a form of gratitude for past performance. My popularity with the public? Yes, but their majority cannot put my face together with my name. Why won't Gielgud direct me? Doesn't he like me any more? Or has he simply run out of ideas for a part so half-written as Guildenstern?

Feeling as hangdog as a man who hangs dogs, I set out grimly for the dressing room of Hume Cronyn. I have in mind swallowing my pride and asking him to help me with my performance. Cronyn is not only a canny man of the theatre, he once saw fit to employ me when I was *persona non grata* with every major network and advertising agency in the United States. It will be a severely cold Thursday when I forget his continuing consideration and encouragement.

As usual, Hume tenders me valuable advice. I then ask him what he thinks of John Gielgud and what the old boy is up to. Hume mixes drinks for both of us and shakes his head. "He's a wonderful man, a wonderful artist, and a fine director. He's got it all, Bill, and I'm sure you know that. What went wrong this time is that he had a notion. It's a good notion, I think, but he never matured it into a concept. He just let it happen so that now it's shapeless and out of hand. He's shot his bolt, I'm afraid, and we will get nothing but editing and reshaping from here on in. Nobody can create a concept overnight. That sort of work has to be thought through before rehearsals ever begin. If it isn't built into the first three or four days with the actors, it can't be built in later without tearing the walls down. From now until the New York opening, John will be tasteful and considerate and he will polish up some rough spots, but don't expect any more. You're on your own now and you must stop being disappointed."

"Damn it, Hume, why did he tell me I was brilliant, brilliant in this bloody play, and why does Richard continue to say so? I'm not even good, good in the part, let alone brilliant, brilliant. What the hell are they *doing* to me? They're killing me with kindness, that's what."

Hume smiled and mixed two more smashes under the heart. "Tell me something, old sock—how many productions have you been in?"

"Around thirty."

"Mmm-hm—and how many television shows have you done?"

"Maybe a thousand."

"Yes, of course—and maybe two thousand radio shows and a few Actors Studio projects and how many motion pictures?"

"Six or seven."

"How old are you?"

"Thirty-seven."

"Do you ever think of yourself as naïve?"

"No."

"What do your friends say?"

"Yes."

"Are you like this in your personal relationships?"

"Like what?"

We had another drink. "Listen, Bill," he said, "*they* think you're good even if you don't. God knows they've seen more productions of these plays than both of us put together. I played Hamlet once, believe it or not, but I can't match Richard's experience in playing Shakespeare and I'm fifteen years older than he is. No actor living has played more Shakespeare than John. He's seen more Guildensterns marjorie around than you could shake Max Factor at. He thinks you're *good* in the part, don't you see? He also doesn't know how to make you any better or how to comfort you. He's drenched with problems and fears and you are the least of them. He'll throw you to the wolves as soon as look at you. Do you think he *owes* you anything? What if you were directing this production? Wouldn't you do exactly the same?"

I took another pull at my drink. I was cold sober, by God, and could not understand why my left foot had fallen asleep. "Hume," I whispered, "do you think I'm good in this part?"

I had not underrated my man. "No," he said, "you're not. Not for you. You're too good for this part and the part's not good enough for you. You've complicated the whole business, just as you've complicated your costume, because you are a complicated man and a naïve man. You should work for a single effect instead of lots of little effects. The part is neither large enough nor well-written enough to do more than make a single, vivid impression. You can do it, if you want to, but you've got to be less greedy. You always want to make an American flag. I think I'll call you Betsy Ross. Instead, you should make blue or red or white and stick to your guns and drive that single color home. You know what I'd do? I'd play Guildenstern like John Gielgud. I'd walk and talk and dress like him and pattern every gesture after him and put John on stage in the part of Guildenstern. Do you want another drink?"

I shook my head and hauled my ashes. I stumbled soberly as I got up from my chair, but that was because my foot was asleep. Something went wrong with Hume's dressing-room door as I tried to leave. The doorknob seemed to be broken. Hume opened the door for me and smiled. I guess he was a little bit drunk.

Anyway, I thought about what he'd said and I decided to take what I could of his advice. What the hell, it was the only direction I'd been given for three weeks. But there was something in Cronyn's realistic appraisal which depressed me: my unimportance to the over-all scheme of things left me feeling less than exhilarated. Was my contribution utterly inconsequential? Was my success or failure purely a personal matter?

As I reached my very own dressing room and my very own scotch, there popped suddenly into my mind the owlish image of Teddy Hart and the fractured ad lib. This latter form of speech was invented by Mr. Hart, so far as I know, but to define it further would be to reveal the end of my tale. Let me merely say that Mr. Teddy Hart, brother of the late, great lyricist Lorenz Hart, and famous in his own right during the 1930s for a wild, lisping performance in *Three Men on a Horse*, once appeared in a play the title of which I am too charitable to mention. Not only that, I couldn't *really* remember the title if I were tortured by Tallulah Bankhead and the whole Turkish army. Anyway, Hart was in rehearsal one day when his director endeavored to pin down a crowd ad lib involving several of the principal players. The actual printed text did not call for any ad lib at all but merely a line of Teddy Hart's which read, "I think that's one of the craziest things I've ever heard!" which is the sort of line Teddy could make a fellow remember for many a day. But the director was a nervous sort and found Teddy's delivery of the line over-vigorous. So vigorous, in fact, that Teddy managed to be heard above all the other ad-libbers. The director protested, "Please, Teddy, don't make so darned much of that line. Just throw it into the crowd ad lib. It doesn't matter what you say here."

The last remark nettled Teddy a bit and he picked up his script. He looked at his line and then he looked at the director. "In the thcript here," he said, "it only thez my line. It duthn't thay anything about any ad lib."

The director nodded impatiently. "I know, I know, but I want an ad lib here and you're so loud with that line, I can't hear anybody else. I want you to throw that line away because it doesn't matter what you say here."

"I thee," Teddy said.

At a subsequent rehearsal, the moment again arrived for the crowd ad lib. Teddy's fellow players improvised remarks going anywhere from "What do you mean, I'm a pervert?" to "I'm voting for Alf Landon!" but Teddy Hart's original printed line rang out clearly above all competitors. The director shouted, "Stop!" and ran angrily to the footlights. "Dammit, Teddy, I asked you not to make so much of that line. It's an ad-lib effect I want here. Will you throw that damned line away? I've told you it doesn't matter what you say here!"

"I thee," Teddy said.

During several further rehearsals, Teddy managed to make his line heard over the best efforts of his fellow actors and the distracted director finally lost his temper entirely. "Goddammit, Teddy!" he shouted. "I've asked you for three weeks to throw that goddamn line away. I don't want to hear those words, for Christ's sake. Say something else, if you have to. Say Alf Landon's a pervert, if you want, but I'm telling you for the last time: it doesn't matter what you say here!"

"I thee," Teddy said.

At the dress rehearsal, the moment for the great ad lib arrived, and conscientious actors said everything from "Alf Landon happens to be my sister" to "Who the hell is Alf Landon?" but Teddy Hart said—and loudly enough to be heard at the Gaiety Delicatessen—"Zollman the Wise is my permanent klender beyond any shadow of fench. Kindly remember my pleezman on Tuesday before you rollop his garn."

The director halted the dress rehearsal with an apoplectic popping of shirt buttons and a frantic waving of hands. "For God's sake, Teddy Hart!" he cried. "What in the hell was all that?"

Teddy showed his palms and smiled modestly. "What differenth duth it make?" he said. "It duthn't matter what *I* thay!"

A fond farewell to Teddy but does it really matter what I say either? Does it matter, in other words, if I am good or bad as Guildenstern? Let us even go beyond the importance to me, my wife, my children, or the scant number of humans who love me and wish me well—*does it really matter?* Ironically enough, I believe that it does because I believe that putting on a play is rather like putting together a jigsaw puzzle. Truly fine productions have nearly every piece in a convincing place. Since living actors are not oddly shaped sections of painted cardboard, no production can hope to be neat as a nun's refectory, nor is it realistic to expect each role to be given optimum care; but I do believe with whatever is in me that the *degree* of participation and conviction which emerges from each actor in a play will finally measure the degree of that play's artistic achievement.

Oh, well—tomorrow will be better. . . .

William

5 March–20 March

Dear Bob . . .

I was wrong. Tomorrow is here and it is not better. In fact, I seem to have lost my sense of humor overnight. My guru would be ashamed of me. All day long I am muttering to myself: What's to be done what's to be done what's?

We have played nine public performances and nothing is being changed but our clothes. Over the past eight days, I have worn the following costumes on stage: a brown sports jacket with olive-green slacks; a red blazer with black trousers; a white tweed jacket with brown twill slacks (no tie; I tried an ascot scarf); a powder-blue sports jacket with white duck trousers; six different neckties, three types of shoes (ox-blood moccasins, brown loafers, and black Edwardian half-boots); a white sweater with brown slacks followed by a black sweater with brown slacks. I won't go into the shirts—they are too difficult to describe. Anyway, the black sweater is by far the best costume for me, but Burton is all in black and it is disconcerting to see someone in black next to him. Not only disconcerting but also invisible. One of the really dreary things about this production is that Richard's clothes look like a conventional Hamlet costume. This makes the rest of us seem halfwits. Or awfully careless. If *he* is in costume why aren't the rest of us in costume?

Of course, Richard is not guilty of cheating or even sneaky pool. I believe that he honestly tried to concoct "rehearsal clothes" for himself but quickly discovered that Hamlet simply cannot wear ordinary clothing of any kind. Moreover, it is the better part of valor for any actor playing the part to be clad entirely in black. Colin-Keith Johnston once played Hamlet in what used to be called golfing togs: plus fours and a tweed jacket. The still photographs from this production would bring on fainting spells for any but the coolest observers.

In the meantime, Alfred Drake spends most of his afternoons at the tailor trying to evolve a fitting look. He began the engagement wearing a reddish sports coat which was supposed to suggest something satanic. Instead, he emerged looking like a nightclub master of ceremonies, and a rather underpaid one to boot. Not Alfred's fault, but still discouraging. He is now wearing a monogrammed navy-blue blazer. It is a decided improvement but hardly ideal. One expects him to make at least one entrance wearing a yachting cap.

The women are having trouble, too. Both Eileen Herlie and Linda Marsh use rehearsal skirts, which should suggest palace wear because they are long. But the linen is gray and looks cheap, for some reason. Eileen is also wearing a sweater. Since she is one of the best-endowed ladies on two continents, the sweater overemphasizes what could not be concealed by a suit of mail. I honestly cannot say what any of us are going to wear without looking like bloody fools. Clem Fowler goes absolutely ape whenever I appear at his dressing room with a sweater or a club shirt. "For God's sake, man!" he cries. "We're supposed to be on the *qui vive*. Let the rest of the people wear their crappy sports outfits. Let's you and I be Madison Avenue guys: sharp and cagey."

He's right in a way, although his real objection has more to do with his figure, which is slender and small-boned and not flattered by sweaters. Hume Cronyn has solved *his* costume problem rather handily. Polonius is dressed as a businessman: conservative pin-striped suit, complete with vest and watch chain; pince-nez spectacles suspended from his neck. Since Gielgud has added the cane to connote a bit of infirmity, Cronyn looks in character but still rehearsal-clothed.

Very well, then—what else is there to say? Are we at least exploring deeper meanings in the play? By no means. Will my own performance improve? Not on your life. Will Richard Burton get better? No doubt of it. Has Gielgud retired from the arena? Yes.

On the heartwarming side, there is Elizabeth Taylor, who visited my dressing room two nights ago for a chat (read that "pep talk"). She told me that Richard was distressed about the critical reception for Clem Fowler and myself and that she wanted me to know what *she* thought. "I am not an actor," she said. "I am a movie star, and there's a difference. I think that all of you in this play are *really* actors and I wish I were one, too. But I'd like to think I understand what it's like to deliver a performance without retakes and to go on stage every night at eight o'clock and repeat, repeat, repeat. Does it make you nervous?"

I said that it did.

"Does it discourage you that your personal notices aren't better?"

I said that I was discouraged and worried but that I had been around too long to take anything too seriously—even myself.

"Do you think you're good in this part?"

I told her I thought I was so-so.

"I think you're a marvelous actor. Richard says you give him more support and quicksilver than he would have thought possible in such a silly part. He thinks you're a brilliant actor."

"Words like brilliant should be reserved for actors like Richard and stars like you. I'm a good actor and there's an end of it."

Miss Taylor smiled, which she does very well. "And where would us brilliances be without good actors like you?"

I smiled too. "At the top of the heap," I said.

"Don't you think Richard will make a great success in New York?"

I said that he would and I meant it.

"I think he's the definitive Hamlet. He's the courtier, the scholar, the soldier. Most people who play the part miss out on one or the other. He has all of John's sensitivity and music, but his virility is special. Don't you think so?"

"I wish I had his voice."

"You have a wonderful voice."

"It will serve but it's not like his."

She smiled again. "You're very modest. It makes me suspicious."

She had me there. I asked her if Richard had asked that she visit me.

"No. I did it on my own. I do most things on my own."

Several days thereafter she told me that various legal problems would prevent her marriage to Richard until the termination of our engagement in New York. I expressed sympathy and she shrugged. "I'm used to frustration," she said. On the following week end she married Richard Burton in Montreal, the legal snags having been smoothed over by Mr. Hume Cronyn, who is deeply fond of both bride and groom. Moreover, Mr. Cronyn owns Canada. Hip-hip hoorah.

From that Sunday forward, Richard Burton ceased referring to *h-e-r* as "Miss Elizabeth Taylor," a formality I had found discreet but nervous-making. His only remark to me concerning the marriage was uttered on the Tuesday which followed their week-end honeymoon. "And you see, old man," he said, "they said it wouldn't last."

So much for romance and happy endings.

Yet, the work-to-be-done remains like a nagging backache. Perhaps it would be fitting at this moment for me to explore the many issues which have been ignored in our production. Namely, what is the play *Hamlet* really about? Is the Prince homosexual? (No.) Is he in love with his mother? (I hope so.) Does he really want the throne? (I doubt it.) Why doesn't he kill Claudius sooner? (Read Ernest Jones.) Are hockey pucks edible? (If they have been boiled for a month.) Should Polonius be played as a fool? (Yes, if you are a bad actor.) Is Gertrude a halfwit? (Yes, if you are a good actress.) Has Laertes the intellectual equipment of a paramecium? (No.) Did Ophelia sleep with Hamlet before the beginning of the play? (It's up to you, darling.) Are Rosencrantz and Guildenstern Jewish? (Yes, if you are from Düsseldorf.) Can Shakespeare write? (Frightfully well.) Is John Houseman a great producer? (Of course.)

It would be fitting, indeed, but you've come to the wrong tailor. Somehow, I'd prefer to explore a bit of life around us, since the Gielgud-Burton *Hamlet* is hardly the only significant effort going on in the civilized world. Elizabeth Taylor's modest apposition of "movie star" to "actor," for example, sharply re-minded me of your frequent requests for further enucleation of this ticklish and hilarious issue.

We leave for Boston on Sunday and will, therefore, be pack-ing our bags tomorrow, but I shall somehow scavenge the time to locate some crusty convictions on the subject of motion pic-tures. I hope you realize, though, that a middle-class actor like myself does not precisely insure his financial future by shooting his mouth off about the richest aunt in show business. It is one thing to mumble gritty remarks about Hollywood *gelt* and dirty old Louis B. Mayer (everybody does) and quite another to pub-lish provocative pamphlets on the clichés within the clichés. *That* sort of thing can get a fellow banished from court.

But, as my sainted mother once said, "Speak your mind and let the devil take the hindmost."

A few years later, she said, "The trouble with *you* is that you learned to read when you were four and never learned to count."

Mother is not what I would call consistent.

Best wishes . . .
William

P.S.: On the 17th of March (St. Patrick's Day, which I entirely ignored because of my unjust expulsion from Sinn Fein) I played Guildenstern dressed in a sharply cut blue suit with a faint red pinstripe, a white shirt, a black tie, and silk socks with clocks. After the performance, Sir John Gielgud said, "A beauti-ful ensemble, Beau Brummel, but it didn't work out."

21 March 1964

Dear Bob . . .

With the wisdom of my mother in mind, let me here and now announce a special twist to my convictions: I would rather act in a movie than watch one, just as I would rather watch a play than be in one. To act in a movie is fun. To act in a play is work.

Marlon Brando was recently quoted by Sidney Skolsky as saying, "Movies are not an art and probably never will be. Pic-tures are a craft, a business. Making movies is no different than

manufacturing any other item. They are an economic investment."

Small wonder, then, that we hear so much about the The Film
Industry. Yet we also hear that motion pictures are *the* twentieth-
century Art, and to say otherwise is to incur not only the wrath
of the men who pay the bills, but of many an intellectual *co-
gnoscenti*. Strange bedfellows.

Let's face it: Movies are the swellest way to make money that
ever happened in the history of the world. The oldest profession is much harder work and wears a body out a good deal
faster. Why be snobbish about the movies? Why be hard-nosed?
Be reachable, instead. It is important to be reachable. Mozart
once cried out rhapsodically, "Is there anything in life finer
than a good scarlet coat?"

I cannot answer the question with any degree of certainty, but
it *reaches* me. And so do the movies. They are fun. They are a
lollipop. They are something to suck. They are also *Citizen
Kane, Dr. Strangelove*, Jean Renoir, Carl Dreyer, and D. W.
Griffith. By and large, however, they are a pastime, and it is *truly*
snobbish to try to scold the medium into a conformity with fine
arts. Movies are *pop* art, and they are at their most artistic when
the pop is abrupt and unpretentious.

I have made more money from the six films in which I have
appeared than from half of the Broadway productions in which
I have played. Financially speaking, there can be no argument—
but it is important to concede that genuine success in motion
pictures has not so much to do with talent as with bone structure,
personality, and what is called "career management." This last
element demands the sort of know-how and application which
could dream up the Hula Hoop, and I wish I had done so, but
acting is quite another matter.

I once got drunk enough to tell Marlon Brando that being a
good or bad actor had nothing to do with success in motion pictures. He stared at me in silence for so long a time that I finally
became embarrassed. After all, I was in *his* house and it is a very
expensive house. I was also drinking *his* scotch.

"Stardom in the movies," I eventually coughed, "has to do

with chemistry and personality. A frightfully bad actor can be a star and a good actor can be thrown out with the cuts." Brando's silence continued until I asked him why he didn't say something. He turned to me and said, "Because I'm appalled."

He later insisted that to act in films was "harder" than to act on the stage. I replied that it was certainly harder for a *good* actor to work in films because a good actor concerned himself with character, text, the shape and weight of words, profound emotions, and the plastic skill of voice and body necessary for reaching the upper tiers of the balcony without splitting the ears of the groundlings below. "Movies are confusing for the good actor," I added, "and paradise for the bad. But solving the problem hasn't so much to do with talent as with shrewdness."

Brando disappeared into his study but emerged a few moments later to say that movies were harder because everything was performed in short pieces, which made concentration difficult. "Short scenes?" I said. "All that means is that you don't have to study your lines." He disappeared again and returned an hour later to say that the camera crew stands within inches of the actor, staring blankly at him while he tries to conjure up a true feeling. "Yes," I replied, "and they are kept absolutely silent and still by the assistant director, while a Broadway backstage crew never stops talking, never stands still, and the audience out front is coughing, moving, shifting, whispering, and must normally be shouted into submission because they think they're watching a movie." Brando then cited the tasteless producers and studio executives who make any sort of genuine creativity impossible, and I was honor bound to concede that only Hollywood had placed limitless power in the hands of men who would sell fish for a living if it proved more profitable than motion pictures. "And I'm sure," I added, "that this makes life a living hell for John Wayne."

I have not yet been banned from Brando's house, but the day may come. Consistency, after all, is the hobgoblin of little minds. And Brando, carp though you may, qualifies in my eyes as a very large mind indeed.

Back to specifics: I have been in the habit, though the years, of composing letters to *The New York Times* which I do not finally post. They are usually too long for newspaper publication, anyway, and I am weary of having my most cherished thoughts placed in the ink-stained hands of men who are paid more to compress than to clarify. The following two letters, however, express the heart of my feelings as to motion pictures and motion picture acting. A pair of short preambles explain what prompted both.

Not too long ago, the ineffable Bosley Crowther published a Sunday piece on the deaths of Clark Gable and Gary Cooper. Mr. Crowther regretted that both men continued to play romantic roles after passing middle age. He even wondered if Mr. Gable's exertions during the making of *The Misfits* did not hasten his demise. He also questioned why these two twenty-four-karat film stars did not retire to train their successors. He ended up convincing us that they were very great artists indeed and should have put themselves to pasture earlier on, like a pair of fine studs. They certainly were fine studs, but the pasture looks like smilax to me.*

The Editors
New York Times Theatre Section
New York Sunday Times

Gentlemen:
    May a professional actor speak up re: Bosley Crowther's latest Sunday piece? As usual, Mr. Crowther is temperate, friendly, and his heart rests in precisely the proper area. But he is more sentimental than he is accurate and I question whether eulogies for two impressive men will not cause many to confuse their personalities with their abilities. If this seems stuffy of me, let me hasten to explain: (A) Mr. Cooper and Mr. Gable were both exceptionally effective movie stars. (B) Being a movie star has nothing at all to do with being an actor. (C) Mr. Crowther is the motion-picture critic for *The New York Times*. (D) It is a position of large responsibility and influence. (E) There is a principle involved, and that principle

* Smilax is an artificial greenery used in motion pictures.

vitally concerns the art of acting. (F) Back to the grindstone.

For the most part, Mr. Crowther says true and unchallengeable things: Yes, it is true that the two deceased gentlemen were bigger and better movie stars than Ronald Colman, Wallace Beery, Humphrey Bogart (a bit of stirring in the gallery—restless natives), and Slim Summerville. But no—they were not particularly good actors, not the longest day either one of them lived, and is it really going to help their deservedly sacrosanct memories or even the future of the movies to pretend that they were? At the risk of seeming cruel, I suggest that the future of the movies is more important. Were these two fine gentlemen skilled technicians? Yes indeed—and so is William Holden. No better and no worse. So are Tony Curtis, Dean Martin, or even Jack LaRue, God save the mark, and I intend neither an equation of gifts nor malicious animal magnetism. In equalizing all these men, I speak only in terms of acting ability, of acting technique. The personalities of all these performers are vastly different, in both size and quality.

The late Gary Cooper and the late Clark Gable were both enormously attractive personalities, both of whom made so many pictures that they finally learned how to act. A little. More important (where movie-making is concerned), they learned a great, *great* deal about how to get light on their faces, how to lean forward while keeping the chin level, and how to look straight into a camera without blinking. These are not small accomplishments, truly, since they involve a good many personal relationships which can be difficult and a great deal of physical discipline as well, but none of these accomplishments has anything to do with acting. Instead, they have a great deal to do with being a Hollywood movie star. It would not be unfair, I think, to compare Norman Rockwell's remarkable draftsmanship ability to the skills of these late and understandably lamented film performers. But if we were to call Mr. Rockwell's magazine covers great painting, we would call ourselves fools. All we can truly say is that the work of all three men is enormously popular. And it would be best to leave it at that. Mr. Crowther, however, has all but spirited the ghosts of Cooper and Gable into the zenith regions of great acting artists. This is tommyrot. And Tommy Rot, I venture to say, is as good a name for a film star as Slip Covers and/or Tab Hunter.

Mr. Crowther's argument parallels that of a friend of mine who expressed the opinion that Burt Lancaster indeed deserved an Academy Award for *Elmer Gantry* because he was a "true movie star," whereas Trevor Howard (a rival for the award) merely gave "a brilliant performance" in *Sons and Lovers*. The argument amused me tremendously, since it cuts to the heart of my feeling about films as a medium, but I must demur at least this far: If my friend's argument be sound, I cannot then be expected to take the Oscar seriously when it reads: For Best Performance. Let us consider alternatives. It *could* read: For Best Movie Star. Or: For Most Popular Box-Office Star. Or: For Best Personality. Or: Whatever. For I am prepared to admit that exercising the full potential of one's acting gifts before a camera is usually a sure way to diminish one's success as a film star—and for a variety of predictable reasons. I do not for a moment impugn the integrity of any film star who separates the professional exigencies of stardom from the creative demands of acting. In films, "Give 'em what they want" is sound practice, both financially and aesthetically, and many film stars who are capable of acting refuse to do so because they know better than to risk being drummed from the ranks of the rich. But I do not expect my hypothetical film star (or anyone else) to call what he is doing "acting," any more than I expect a man selling candied apples to advertise them as a healthy product of nature.

As for Mr. Crowther's regret concerning Mr. Gable's overextension of his energies during the filming of *The Misfits* and his reports of Mr. Cooper's face-lifting, what else would he expect of two realistic men who surely knew that they were nothing more than highly paid symbols of American manhood? They were skilled mannequins, comparable to those in the rotogravure, who knew perfectly well that if they posed themselves this way and that the public would pay lots of money to see them. As for Crowther's suggested alternative: to retire and encourage the young. Why? Neither gentleman was equipped to educate. A man cannot educate the *personality* of another. As for the technical skill, only a series of movies can teach one how to butter up the lighting man or how to deal with one's own face. Each face is different. One must either possess a face that cannot be harmed from any angle, or one must learn what part of one's face looks best. It is said that Miss Claudette Colbert went through the entire filming of *Cleopatra* (1934) without ever showing the left side of her face to the camera. If she did (and many knowledgeable film workers insist that it is so), several factors are involved. First, Miss Colbert would have to know through incontrovertible experience that her left side was a disadvantage; second, she would have to be either brave enough or powerful enough to insist that the film be shot in such a manner, which could easily distress Henry Wilcoxon, C. Aubrey Smith, Cecil B. de Mille, and the front office of Paramount Pictures; third, she would have to be so far past any notion of "acting" her role that she could spend all her off-camera time arguing with the technicians.

Is it conceivable that Mr. Cooper or Mr. Gable could take Mr. Troy Donahue aside and say, "Now, look—here's how to get the camera operator and the lighting man on your side. Here's how to get make-up tests before the film begins. Here's how to talk to Lolly Parsons. Here's how to hold your head when the camera is below you, and here's how to hold it when the camera is above." These experiences are empiric; they can no more be *taught* than fighting a grizzly bear can be taught. For Mr. Crowther to expect wealthy men such as Gable and Cooper to teach young people how to steal camera time from fellow actors; or how to back the descendants of Harry Cohn and Louis B. Mayer into a corner; or how to get on the right side of Hedda Hopper; or how to persuade technicians and directors to show them off to best advantage, is an incredible request. Besides, most of the young male stars already *know* these things. What they lack is the personality and front-office muscle of the older stars.

As for acting, the younger stars are either incapable of any such thing (as both Gable and Cooper were incapable for years) or they know perfectly well that such aesthetic fluff is the least of their concerns. If these two gentlemen had indeed undertaken to teach younger actors how to be carbon copies of themselves, they would have been leading them straight down a path of self-destruction. No one wants to see a carbon copy of Cooper or Gable. What matters to a film star is to be unique—as a personality. And uniqueness as a personality is entirely unrelated to acting, for acting has to do with the sublimation of one's personality into a character. As for replacements, the major film companies are already breaking themselves in half endeavoring to produce carbon copies of the old stars, both in television and in what is left of theatrical films. We already have James Garner, Steve McQueen, Troy Donahue, George Peppard, and so forth. Whether Mr. Crowther cares to believe it or not, these young men—*mutatis mutandis*—are the heirs apparent to recently vacated thrones. What Gary Cooper or Clark Gable could have taught these young gentlemen about acting, the young gentlemen themselves are trying very hard to forget.

But more important than this inexplicable theme of "Where are the new Coopers and Gables and Grants?" as well as "Why don't they train their replacements?" is the changing nature of the industry in which these old-timers functioned. A new atmosphere has been created (wrongly, I think, but nevertheless it is there) and it has been encouraged by Mr. Crowther himself, which is why his argument leaves me confused. This new atmosphere would be quite unsympathetic to a young Gary Cooper or a young Clark Gable, for it is devoted not to the movies, but to *the cinema;* it is derived from the French, Italian, and British movements—which de-emphasize the "movie star" and re-emphasize the director. It is as pervasive an *ambiance* as is the lack of interest in Broadway and the thriving of Off Broadway. It works against the standard Hollywood development of the young movie star, for I maintain that George Peppard is quite as good an actor as Cooper and Gable were when they were young men. But the day of the "movie star" stands at relative sunset, for the moment, and many moviegoers are more interested in the film than they are in the star. For this very reason Mr. Crowther's implied contempt for Brando, Lancaster, Douglas, et cetera, as would-be "tycoons" is misplaced. Leaving aside the worth of the films produced by these men, their wish to do more with their energies than merely to be movie stars is not only understandable, it will likely save them from trying to have their faces lifted at age sixty or roping an unbroken mustang when the flesh has turned weak and the bones brittle. Brando, for one example, is indubitably twice the actor most film performers are, but he shows sad understanding that he is long since withdrawn as an actor and he apparently does not wish to survive as a mere poseur, and a poseur is what a movie star is. In other words, unwilling to pursue the art of acting, which pays poorly, and equally unwilling to be a highly paid mannequin, he endeavors to influence the quality of the product in which he appears. It is a neat trick, for he must also retain his mannequin position lest he lose the power over the public which will make his quality product salable. It is doubtful that such a choice ever occurred to Messrs. Cooper and Gable, for I do not believe they considered themselves actors at all. But whether I be wrong or right in this particular, no such complex considerations could be shared with the young. Both gentlemen were doomed to die with their boots on—face-lifting, mustang-roping, and all. To think of either one of them as a teacher is to miss the point of being a film star entirely.

During the shooting of *Vera Cruz*, Gary Cooper was trapped in a desolate area of the Southwest and could not be contacted by telephone, telegram, or *pneumatique*. Shortly before nine a.m. one magic morning, an expressman rode up to Cooper's camp chair with a significant message. His horse was bubbly-white around the bit and he himself was breathing harder than a modern man should breathe. "Coop!" he shouted. "I just rode in from Flagstaff and you've done it again!"

Cooper's five-gallon hat was tilted over his eyes and he appeared to be asleep.

"Coop!" the breathless rider shouted. "Wake up, for God's sake! You've done it again!"

But there was nothing but silence from the sublimely relaxed Cooper.

The rider dismounted and shook a piece of paper under Cooper's eyes. "You've won the Academy Award for *High Noon*!" the man shouted.

Cooper did not disturb his hat, nor did he move a muscle, but he finally spoke. "Yup," he said. "I sure am a great actor."

There are but two kinds of young people going into film-making today: either they are the young Coopers and Gables, who will probably find the going rougher and rougher, or they are would-be *film-makers*—they are combinations of acting, writing, photography, and film-directing. In other words, they are talents, not male models. Mr. Cooper and Mr. Gable, with no disrespect intended, *were* male models. They were the *best* male models who ever stood before a camera, but any resemblance between either one of them and an actor is the sheerest sentiment. The George Peppards and Tony Curtises have already learned all they need to know from the old-time movie stars . . . the job before them is to decide which movement will last—the Neo-European movement, with which I utterly disagree, or a Renaissance of the peppermint-candy Hollywood film devoted ˚to wit and fun and adventure, with which I agree entirely—and no one on earth can give them the answer to that one. But, in either direction, none of them has anything to learn from Cooper and Gable beyond what they have already learned from the day-to-day business of making motion pictures. In the meantime, better-established stars are endeavoring to control both the purse strings and the art of their films. I cannot blame them, but these are business decisions rather than artistic decisions, and Mr. Crowther should not be so naïve in the open air. The new stars, if there are any, have nothing to learn from the old stars except what not to do. Motion pictures *are* a business, just as Brando says, and nothing results in losses so quickly as yesterday's mousetrap.

Very truly yours,
William Redfield

Two years ago, Messrs. Carl Foreman and Tyrone Guthrie engaged in a debate in the Sunday magazine section of *The Times* and had it out in fine, forensic style on the subject of Movies vs. the Theatre. Foreman took the movies and Guthrie took the theatre, but no one else got taken except the sublimely naïve. Mr. Foreman maintained that movie acting was better and the theatre old-fashioned. Dr. Guthrie insisted that motion pictures were shallow and superficial and that true works of passion and literature belonged in the theatre. I add my own notions to the argument in the interest of atomic research.

The Editors
New York Times Magazine
New York Sunday Times

Gentlemen:

Concerning movies versus theatre (Carl Foreman–Tyrone Guthrie, 29 April) may I present the following notions:

He who has seen Laurence Olivier only on film has not seen Laurence Olivier.

Marlon Brando's screen portrayal of Stanley Kowalski was but a fuzzy outline of his original stage creation.

No film performance ever recorded can seriously challenge Laurette Taylor in *The Glass Menagerie* on stage.

The film versions of *The Glass Menagerie, Death of a Salesman, Golden Boy, Oklahoma!, South Pacific,* and even *A Streetcar Named Desire* are, one and all, faint echoes of vigorous stage work.

Shakespeare, Shaw, O'Casey, O'Neill, Strindberg, Ibsen, Chekhov, and Anouilh are rarely to never produced on film and a damned good thing, too, for in nearly every instance the results have been absurd.

No significant playwright I know of has ever, repeat ever, done better work for the films than he has done for the stage.

If all this be so, why is it so? Dr. Guthrie says why: Artistically speaking, a motion picture belongs to its director. Films are fundamentally graphic while the theatre is fundamentally poetic. The only poetry conceivable in a motion picture is a poetry of movement. A pet theory of mine is that all films should be either very slow or very fast. Slow—as in the great silent films (*Passion of Joan of Arc,* etc.)—or fast, as in the magnificent nonsense films of the Hollywood thirties (Preston Sturges, the Marx Brothers, many more); but theories aside, motion pictures are not literary, not rhetorical—not even, strictly speaking, *emotional*. They are a mechanical product produced by a committee and stand in no need of the *individual human soul*, without which the theatre simply cannot function. In other words, films are basically dead (canned, not fresh, not alive—"in the can"), while the theatre is fundamentally électric. As for creativity, and despite these limitations, a director and his cameramen (or a writer-director) can express themselves very well in that their shot planning, cutting, and sequence of footage *force* a reaction from the audience in much the same way a card sharp forces a given card on his victim. This celluloid sleight-of-hand is the most creative activity in film-making—as well as the most fun. It is a fascinating skill and takes a lot of practice, but I doubt that it is an art. Even if it is, the playwright (*qua* playwright) and the actor have no artistic connection with such business. All they can do is surrender their carefully nurtured talents to the mechanics of the medium and bend to the camera's will. Lest a writer be half a painter (or cartoonist, as Alain Resnais has hinted) there is no *creative* place for him in films at all.

As for acting, it is doubtful that any experienced or conscientious actor will support Mr. Foreman's contention that "Movie acting is better." Primarily, movie acting is based upon the manipulation of personality. At best, the film medium assists a certain ease of manner in the actor and enables him to achieve an unforced conversational reality. These two qualities are indeed difficult to evoke in the theatre without boring the audience to tears, although they are available in abundance on television. In this specific, relaxed sense, movie acting is indeed "better," if you call that acting. To exchange such ease of behavior for theatre acting at its heightened and passionate best is, I suggest, to exchange Perry Como for Pericles.

Very truly yours,
William Redfield

P.S. I hope you're satisfied.

W.

PART III

The Boston Engagement

MARCH 22–APRIL 4

22 March '64
Toronto and Boston

Dear Bob . . .

We are leaving Toronto in a blaze of publicity and wassail.
The O'Keefe management can barely keep its fingers from
trembling. The Burton-Gielgud *Hamlet* grossed $104,000 for its
first week and roughly the same for its second and third. The
extra-added fourth week grossed $96,000, all of which totals up to
more than $400,000. Since Burton has been receiving 15 per cent
of the gross for the out-of-town engagement, his personal pockets
are fatter by some $60,000 so far, which is quite a respectable
salary for an actor on the wicked-stingy stage.

209

As to the grosses, one member of the O'Keefe management delivered himself of the following astonished pronouncement: "I don't understand it at all. Believe me, there isn't $400,000 worth of business in Toronto for *any* production—not for Harry Belafonte, Sammy Davis, or even Frank Sinatra. Any one of the three could rack up $100,000 for one or two weeks, but *four* weeks is out of the question. We just plain don't have the money or the population."

An explanation arrived just before we left. Literally thousands of Toronto theatregoers came to see Burton's *Hamlet* as many as four and five times. College and drama students were especially taken with the production and especially fascinated by the modern-dress approach. Apparently they were not so offended as their more traditional fellows by our poetic failures. Anyway, we have gratified the money men of Canada, and though that may be a less than aesthetic thing to do it is certainly anti-Communist.

We are now on our way to Boston, where critics Elliot Norton, Elinor Hughes, and Kevin Kelly (among others) will have a go at us. Alex Cohen has chartered a plane from Toronto, and a good ninety per cent of the company are passengers, including Mr. and Mrs. Richard Burton. Among high-ranking members of our group, only John Gielgud and Hume Cronyn are missing because of other responsibilities. It is a gay and chatty flight, and I believe that most of us are eager to endure another opening. It will be fascinating to see how well or ill we are received. There is nervousness, yes, but there is something about a *second* pre-New York opening which always gets my blood to running.

When we land at Logan Airport in Boston, we quickly discover that we cannot disembark the plane. At least five hundred screaming fans have broken through the barriers and are shouting for the Burtons. There are no more than ten or fifteen policemen to control them. The police are losing. Burton begins to curse. "We told them, we told them," he mutters, but there is nothing for it now. We sit in the plane for twenty minutes without moving while acne-faced adolescents jump up and down outside the portholes. They are deaf to the pleas of hostesses, pilots, and airline officials. Time and again we can either lip read or hear the words of the jumpers and the shouters. "Who's that? That's not Elizabeth!" . . . "Where's Burton?" . . . "Kiss me, Dick!" . . . "Liz is a ba-a-d girl!" . . . "They're married! They're married!"

When one of them mistakes Linda Marsh for Elizabeth Burton, a cluster of young and old sycophants and insulters gathers by Linda's window seat. They scream insults and flattery at her until one shouts, "That's not Liz! Liz is fatter!" and Linda slowly pushes her body into her seat so as to be invisible. A moment later, a bouncing boy with blond hair shouts to his companion, "I see someone!" and points at my porthole. His companion is a pretty brunette girl with a mad look in her eye, rather like La Belle Dame Sans Merci. "Who is it! Who?" she shouts, as frantic as a kitten with a thorn. "That's William Redfield!" the boy cries. "He's a terrific TV actor!" The girl stops bouncing and seems disappointed. I see the couple arguing below but can hear no more. Since I had fully expected to be identified as either Sterling Holloway or Tom Poston, I am gratified by the boy's accuracy. It occurs to me that he is the only deserving lad in the lot. Perhaps I will ask Richard to give him an autograph.

A few moments later, two tow ropes are attached to the front of the plane and we begin to move. The fans run along beside us, shouting with displeasure. One cast member (Linda Seff) quietly requests that the wheels run over them. Unkind of her, perhaps, but the spectacle makes the final scene of *The Day of the Locust* seem an apology for human behavior. The strategy of the airline personnel seems to be to tow us to an empty hangar. Several of the cast show signs of claustrophobia and Burton becomes more and more enraged by Boston's lack of preparation. Bobby LaSalle prepares himself for combat.

It is a full hour after the landing before we begin to get off the plane. We have been towed inside a hangar; the few police present have stationed themselves at the exit doors and all avenues of entrance have been closed. Still, there is a good representation from the press, and there are flash bulbs and newsreel cameras. The Burtons leave the plane first but their limousine has not been able to get into the hangar. This means that Elizabeth Burton spends several minutes at the foot of the gangway answering impertinent questions and smiling for the television cameras. In the meantime, Jim Benton (Burton's secretary) exhorts and pleads with airline officials to "get the damned limousine in here!"

When the limousine finally comes through, it is followed by a mob of running fans, who use it as a shield. A few police try to stop them, but there are not enough cops in the hangar to handle the unannounced arrival of Nick Adams. The Burtons refuse to sign autographs, but the fans gather thickly around the car and very nearly make departure impossible. Since the mob outside will be even more unmanageable, a second limousine is allowed to enter. Two or three members of the Burton's entourage get inside and pull up their coat collars. This limousine leaves first, as a decoy. A few seconds later, the limousine carrying the Burtons leaves in the opposite direction. Within three minutes the hangar and its surrounding area is all but deserted. The doors are opened and the rest of us stand about in clusters waiting for our baggage to be taken from the plane. Alex Cohen's effort to save time for his company has backfired. We might as well have taken the train.

Ah, well, it is Sunday, at any rate, and the weather is clear and crisp. I am staying at the Touraine Hotel, which has been one of my favorite homes-away-from-home ever since I got rich and famous. Ah, the beautiful, brown Touraine! Where the bathrooms are larger than the bedrooms and the bellhops never grow old! One of my bellhop friends (I have known the man for eighteen years and he hasn't changed by so much as a new wrinkle) is deeply hurt by the Burtons' absence. It seems to him both demonstrable and just that the Touraine should receive the famous Burton patronage and when I mentioned that the entourage required a total of three rooms in addition to the Royal Couple's quarters, all of which had to be contained in a unified but private compound, he took me forcibly to just such an area: an eight-room suite with more separate exits, entrances, and semi-secret passageways than would have been required by Richard the Third. Though the furnishings were tatterdemalionish as well as largely done in the fiendish color I call Hotel Red, my friend proved to me that the Touraine could indeed provide a Palace Suite for V.I.P.s. Perhaps he read my mind about the *look* of the place: "We could put up-to-date stuff in here, too, if we knew people like the Burtons were coming. We wouldn't mind a little extra expense."

I suggested that the publicity value of the visit had not gone unnoticed by the management, and my old friend nodded patriotically. "Look, Mr. Redfield, we've got the space, that's all. We're not as swank as the Ritz or as new as the Statler, but *we've got the space!*"

There was a light in his eyes and I realized that I was in the presence of a dedicated man.

Nevertheless, the Burtons were to stay at the Copley-Plaza and so I placed a comforting hand on my old friend's shoulder. "Wait till next year," I said.

Rumors were already flying about the lobby and corridors of the Touraine that the Burtons had been manhandled as they departed their limousine at the Copley-Plaza and that Elizabeth's hair had been pulled in the lobby. Richard Burton, Bobby La-Salle, and Bob Wilson ran interference for her and she eventually managed to reach a private elevator but not before she had been scratched on the face and begun to cry. Bobby LaSalle's fisticuffery had been inhibited by the mob.

We will rehearse at the Shubert on Monday the 23rd, late in the afternoon, but our time is our own for the next twenty-four hours. Several of us have decided to see the Jean-Louis Barrault production of *The Marriage of Figaro* without music. Though Mozart wrote what some buffs have called "the best musical comedy score of all time," the original Beaumarchais text was always a success, and Barrault has evidently decided to show American audiences why. His company is also playing at the Shubert Theatre, and it is sometimes valuable to see another production in the house where one is to play. Boston's Shubert is one of the warmest and most comfortable large theatres in the country.

Barrault's company includes his wife (Madeleine Renaud), Jean-Claude Dessaily, Pierre Bertin, and Simone Valère. I recall Barrault's *Hamlet* with Dessaily as Horatio and Bertin as Polonius. Mme. Renaud did not play Gertrude nor can I remember who did, but I vividly recall Simone Valère's Ophelia—her face the color of ivory, her eyes wide and unblinking—one of the few truly stirring performances of the role I have seen. She will be tonight's Susanna.

When Messrs. Fowler, Harz, Giannini, Culkin, and Ragni meet with me in the Shubert lobby, we are taken to a side box as guests of the management. Makes a fellow feel warm all over. This sort of professional courtesy no longer obtains in New York. It is not that fabled Gotham's theatre managers are less friendly (they are, but that is not the point at issue); it is merely that the economics of The Apple forbid such nice old-fashioned customs as "Say, fella—you're an actor, eh? Well, come right into my theatre and sit yourself down for free! We're showing Sidney Blackmer in *White Cargo*. Be sure to go backstage afterwards and say hello to Sid! It's the first time he's played Tondelayo!" Boston can still afford such avuncular cheeriness; New York cannot.

It is worth while, even piquant, to see the play without music. It is also boring. I keep telling myself: *This is good for you. Don't be grouchy. If nothing else, it's good for your French.* My fellow actors are much taken with the production. They think Mme. Renaud very fine.

After the performance, Clem Fowler and I go backstage. We have in mind congratulating Barrault, but the stagehands are already striking and moving the set and Barrault is out of make-up, dressed in his street clothes, and supervising matters. He is a surprisingly small man with an enormous head. He is furious with someone or other and seems to believe that matters are proceeding much too slowly. Clem Fowler and I, quite inadvertently, are standing on the groundcloth. Barrault doesn't like it and gestures impatiently toward us. "*Cochons!*" he mutters forcefully to no one in particular. "What did he call us?" Clem asks me. "Pigs," I reply.

Barrault's hands are clasped behind his back, a walking stick clutched among the interlaced fingers. As he paces fore and aft, the stick traces a path on the stage. He reminds me of photographs and drawings I have seen of Edwin Forrest, Henry Irving, Richard Mansfield, David Belasco. He is more impresario than actor. He is part of a vanishing breed. He is an actor-manager. Under such men, the theatre—in every country—has achieved its highest goals. Why, I do not know, though the point is hopelessly academic since current economics make such men anachronisms—especially in the United States. No longer are there funds or space for the likes of Arnold Daly, Henry Irving, Richard Bennett, or even Katharine Cornell. Today's theatre sits snugly in the hands of real-estate operators and theatre-party coordinators. No one can be called a villain; nor are there any heroes. Even of Robert Whitehead we can say no more than "He tries," since current conditions would defeat ten of him.

Fowler and I leave the Shubert backstage feeling somewhat chastened.

"What do you think of him?"

"I'm not mad about his acting."

"Mmm—but he has a life in art."

"What do you mean by that?"

"*His* company, *his* ideas—even his groundcloth. He's not a salesman. He has a life in art."

"That's funny. I remember meeting a man on a train who said to me 'And what do *you* sell?' That was his way of asking me what I did for a living."

"What did you tell him?"

"Nothing right away. I resented the question. But I couldn't get myself to say, 'I don't sell anything, mister. I'm an actor. That means I'm an artist' and blah-blah-blah because if he turned out to be at all clever, he could make mincemeat out of me."

"Could he?"

"I think so. Obviously everybody sells something, according to him, and if you're an actor, you sell *yourself* and you scuffle and scramble and lie and cheat and steal like everyone else. Maybe even more so."

"And yet there's a difference."

"There's supposed to be. I finally told him I was a draftsman."

"I know an actress who whenever anybody asks her what she does for a living says, 'Nothing. I'm rich.' "

"Good for her. But still—we've got to bring in the people."

When I arrived in my room and mixed myself a nightcap, I thought of tomorrow night's opening. No matter what the critics said or what the word of mouth was, we would bring in the people like sheaves. Richard Burton was a classically trained actor but he had become Pop Art. He was as well known as Dick Tracy. Would he get good reviews this time out? It would be fascinating to see.

More tomorrow . . .

William

23 March—Monday—Boston

Dear Bob . . .

It is a so-so performance we are giving, and I write this to you from my dressing room between the first and second acts. The house is a beautiful one to play and perfectly suited to our production; the audience is warm and friendly and has already interrupted Hume Cronyn's speeches twice for applause (yep, he's hot tonight); but I have just come from an intermission spot of grog with Richard Burton and he said, "My friend, I cannot act. Pack it in, I say. I can't act. Not at all. I told Elizabeth tonight was it. I'd either be good tonight or I'd pack it in. Well, I'm *not* good and there's an end to it. How are *you* doing?"

I told him I was as rigid as a pikestaff.

"Are you nervous?"

"No. Not nervous so much. Just embarrassed."

"And as rigid as a pikestaff."

"Yes."

He poured a small drink for himself while Bob Wilson looked skeptical. One does not often see Richard Burton looking thoughtful. He conceals his unconscious most effectively, but he looked thoughtful at this moment and he stopped moving as completely as though he were caught in a candid photo. "I am out of breath," he said. "I cannot get my breath, which means I can't be still. Stillness is so important. When I am not still, I am poor."

———•—•—•———

At the end of tonight's performance, the bravos began early. All the audience applauded vigorously, many of them stood up for Richard, and we seem to have had a success. Still, let us wait and see. Experienced actors learn not to take audience enthusiasm literally. Cold receptions can be followed by warm reviews and vice versa.

All of us are invited to a supper party after the performance. When we emerge from the theatre, a mob of autograph seekers awaits us, the front line of which does not recognize myself, John Cullum, George Voskovec, and George Rose.

"Who are these four?" one hydrocephalic young man asks his neighbor.

The woman next to him all but snarls her reply. "One-X, Two-X, Three-X, and Four-X."

This burns me up a bit, but my feelings are somewhat placated a few steps later when an elderly man whose hands are shaking with the cold presents me with a Daniel Blum album and asks that I sign a picture of myself. "I saw you," the man says, "in *Barefoot Boy with Cheek* right here in Boston," which is like saying, "I've enjoyed you ever since I was in school," but I am gratified nonetheless and secretly wish for the insulting woman to see me signing my name. The fantasy goes even further. I think of saying: "You see, madam, my name is not Four-X at all. Four-X is the name of a condom, though I realize you do not move in such lively circles."

Seymour Herscher (our business manager) passes by with his arm around Eileen Herlie. He is telling her how especially full and emotional she has been. "But I was so frightfully nervous," Eileen protests. Seymour is obviously delighted with the way the opening has gone. He is a good soul, Herscher. "You were wonderful," he says. "Wonderful, wonderful."

Yes, all of us are wonderful. Good night, William Shakespeare, wherever you are.

24 March

My spies have called this morning to tell me that Burton's reviews are superb and that the production has been well received on the whole. I spend the day looking for "just the right sports jacket" in Boston's men's stores. I find nothing new. When I arrive at the theatre, I am summoned to Burton's dressing room. "You remember what I told you last night? Well, I didn't stop until four in the morning. I told myself and I told Elizabeth over and again that I was through as an actor, could not cut the mustard, and must surely pack it in. I still think so, by the way, but she read me a few choice passages from the reviews to calm me down so that I'd shut up and go to sleep. Then I asked about you and Clem. All right then, I said, what about my two boys? Were they better received?"

This was the first I knew that our personal notices had amounted to nothing special. One or two reviewers have mentioned me as "one of the stars" because of my billing but with no discussion of my performance, whereas Kevin Kelly has said that R&G are "poorly played" by Clem and myself. Bob Wilson grips his lips together sympathetically and shakes his head. Burton interlaces his fingers and then unlaces them again. Finally he slaps the heels of his hands against his knees. "They know nothing," he says. "Unbelievable. The best Rosencrantz and Guildenstern I have ever seen. They simply know nothing."

I leave the dressing room just as Elizabeth arrives. "I don't understand it, love," she says. "You were never better than last night and they still don't seem to understand." I tell her that I don't care especially but the words are beginning to taste dry. Maybe I *do* care after all.

25 March

Just before half-hour of our first matinee on Wednesday, Clem Fowler arrives at the theatre with several copies of the Harvard *Crimson*. The critic implies that Rosencrantz and Guildenstern have never been so strongly played and says specifically that Hamlet's cold-blooded dispatch of such snarling toadies is finally justified. Though his words are carefully chosen and coolly set down, he quite obviously likes us. "For God's sake," I say to Fowler, "let's show the damned thing to Richard."

We do so, and Burton is mightily pleased. "I am going to write that man a fan letter," he says. Right handsome of him, since the evaluation of *his* performance is more ambiguous than enthusiastic. I do not know whether he will write to the man or not, but I find myself beginning to see Guildenstern a bit differently. Not quite so cheerful nor so foolish. Not quite so anxious to please. He is royalty, after all—what if he were to be more certain of himself? I have always thought of him as an Establishment figure —loyal to the King; my country, right or wrong. What I must decide is the degree of his hypocrisy. Until now, I have played him as a man who curries favor, complete with bowing, scraping, and smiling. He could be the same without bowing and scraping so much. He could, in fact, be a bit sinister, a bit cool. Slowly, I begin to intrude this new notion into the performance. Slowly, things begin to feel more comfortable; less strained.

We shall see.

26 March–4 April

During the past ten days, our costumes have been "finalized." I am wearing a pale-blue tweed jacket with olive-brown trousers, an off-white shirt, and fairly bright necktie. Clem is wearing light-blue slacks with a brown sports jacket. Odd combinations, I know, but that is how it finally worked out. No longer can Gielgud call me "Beau Brummell." I have spent over $500 buying clothes for this production and ended up wearing the working clothes of a shoe clerk.

Our business is sellout, of course, and the audiences are enthusiastic. Gielgud seems pleased with the show's progress and I am gratified by the way my performance is going.

At the beginning of the second week, Linda Marsh comes to my dressing room with some encouraging news. "Please don't tell anyone, but Rita is here and loves your performance." She referred to a member of the Actors Studio who had come to Boston to help Linda with some private coaching. This is not hugger-mugger, by the way; such extracurricular arrangements are sometimes a flat necessity, and it is entirely possible that Gielgud knows all about it. But for the coach in question to advertise her presence or appear backstage would be less than yar. Hence Linda's caution. "She's worried about some of the show," Linda continued, "but she asked me please to tell you how good you were. She says that you're sinister in the part, but sinister in a very modern way, and that she couldn't take her eyes off you even when you were just standing around."

This makes me feel good, since I trust this particular person's opinion enormously, but I am all but positive that I will not be allowed to give my current performance on opening night in New York. In the first place, Eileen Herlie is already complaining to me about "the sinister quality." She claims that I must be "charming" in the part or that Gertrude would see through me at once. "Old Gert may not be the brightest girl in the world but she is surely devoted to Hamlet. If Guildenstern looked at all untrustworthy, she would run to Hamlet at once and say: Look out for that chap. He seems a bit slippery. Do you see what I mean, darling?"

I saw very clearly. What I saw mostly was that I would be asked to change my performance back again, no matter how happy and comfortable I had become with it. Nevertheless, I did not change until I was asked and asked I was. On April 1st—the perfect date—I was told by Gielgud, "You're becoming a bit too much of a thug—a bit dangerous. It's frightfully interesting but also cold-blooded, and I'm not sure I approve of that. Make him more cheerful and charming and ingratiating and all that. I've told Clem about this, too. Let's toddle on back to what we had, shall we?"

At this point, I fully realize that what I have gained I must surrender. It is not in my personality to say to my director (or even to Eileen Herlie), "Look, darlings, I'm happy with this performance and I'm damned if I'll change. I was miserable up till now and now I'm at least comfortable. Right or wrong, this is what I want to do, and if you don't like it you'll simply have to lump it."

Perhaps I *should* be able to say such things, outside the privacy of my hotel bathroom, but I *don't* say them, at any rate, and there's an end of the matter. Some people ask incredulously why an actor in such a spot doesn't merely say okay (and give the performance everyone wants) until opening night in New York and *then* just come out and do as he pleases. If he is right, his reviews will be good and no one will dare gainsay him thereafter. If he is wrong, the reviews will ignore him, and he may as well go back to his old performance and explain his erratic opening night any way he chooses. It is a cute and canny plan suggested mostly by agents. Agents are all cute and canny but don't know much about acting. The suggestion is unrealistic because a stage performance is fleshed out and fulfilled only by constant repetition. A genuine concept firms up only when the part is played over and again in pretty much the same way. If there is too much dispute about the concept and the interpretation, the actor is bound to lose out, because original ideas only germinate properly in a peaceful atmosphere. To expect an actor to play his part one way for several weeks and then open it playing another way is to expect him to be not an actor but a crap-shooter.

Moreover, I always feel obliged to do what will make my fellow actors comfortable, just as I believe in the director's right to dictate the choice of interpretation. If you sense an undertone of gall and vinegar in the sentences above, your senses are working very efficiently indeed, but that is the way I am and nothing seems to change me. This is by way of clarifying why I am not a star. Do not think me guilty of sour grapes. I am in absolute earnest and I am also absolutely correct. Anyone destined to be a box-office star, irrespective of his or her talent, will be exclusively dedicated to personal self-advancement and will defy everyone in sight in order to achieve particular goals. There will be no reason involved nor rationalization either. Stars do not care about what is good for plays, directors, or fellow actors. They care about what is good for stars. Sometimes I wonder if I can blame them. After all, if one is playing in a game one might as well play it to win.

Years ago an actor friend of mine saw me play the leading role in a play called *Snafu*, in which I had been more than normally well received. He told me I was giving one of the three or four best performances he had ever seen but that I would never be a star. When I asked him what he meant, he said, "You do not have a star's temperament. You are not a killer. A star must be a killer. You will be one of the best actors in the country but you will never be a star no matter how many times you are billed above the title."

I was only seventeen at the time, and I decided it would be better *not* to be a star since all I really wanted to be was a good actor anyway. What I later discovered, to my horror, was that only stars were cast in good parts and that an actor who did *not* become a star would end up frustrated and bitter if not downright unemployed.

Ah, well—one hardly expects a performance as Guildenstern to make him the toast of the town, any more than one expects his image of dignity and strength to be enhanced by whining and complaining. All that I can see from where I stand is that I might as well have been allowed to give a performance which made me feel good. But—that's show business and *c'est la vie* to say nothing of Never Volunteer, Ora Pro Nobis, and Pax Vobiscum.

We leave for New York City on the 5th of April. Our two weeks in Boston will have grossed some $140,000, which is utter capacity with all standing room sold out at every performance. We will play two previews at the Lunt-Fontanne on the nights of April 6th and 7th. We will rest on Wednesday, April 8th, at the request of Richard Burton. We will open officially on Thursday, April 9th, to what will doubtless be the posh audience of the year.

See you then . . .

William

PART IV

The New York Opening

APRIL 6–APRIL 9

7 April—Tuesday
New York City

Dear Bob . . .

We played the first of our two New York previews at the Lunt-Fontanne last night, and I would call the results inconclusive. Gielgud gathered the company on stage afterwards and told us that we were a good company doing well. "I've done all I can for you now. You must forget about me. The play is yours. From now on, everything is up to you, the audience, and Uncle Will." Several of the actors had questions for him, all of which he answered with grace and gentleness. He is a dear man, truly. Thursday night will be in the hands of history, luck, and the prevalence of witches. Gielgud will leave us after that. But actors never say good-by.

When I reached my dressing room, I found my old friends John and Dorinde Ryan waiting for me. They are theatre fans of the first persuasion as well as "in" enough to feel that seeing a preview is more exciting than seeing a New York opening. They say the production is a good one and Burton their favorite Hamlet. I mention my performance dilemma to Dorinde, who replies that she enjoyed my cheerfulness and cannot imagine my playing the part in a sinister fashion. Good old DeeDee. She is not only loyal, she is a positive thinker.

The psychology of an opening night is, for most actors, suicidal. I know of few serious players who look forward to a Broadway opening as anything other than an ordeal, but this particular opening is doubly special because of Burton's decision to eliminate tomorrow night's performance and rest the entire company for nearly forty-eight hours. Part of an actor's pre-opening edginess has to do with time lying heavily on the hands, but Burton is convinced that *Camelot* suffered from a bad New York opening largely because the players were overtired. According to him, the final preview played the night before the opening reached a pinnacle of energy and precision which the performance for the New York critics lacked. He is likely correct, but taking a holiday guarantees nothing, since having the time to rest does not mean that a fellow really rests. As I see it, actors never rest. They merely chew their nails. An opening night can go any number of ways, nor have I the slightest idea how a player can insure being at his best. Burton's plan is probably as good as any, at least for himself, and, since he is about to perform one of the most exacting roles ever written, so be it. Happily for him, he is an actor who can force an entire company to his own conceit. Such a man is free. In a very profound sense, Richard Burton is free and I wish him luck on Thursday.

In the meantime, I am left with myself.

W.

9 April—Thursday—
The Opening

Today is the day and tonight the night. I decided to go to the theatre this afternoon and familiarize myself with the colors. This may sound strange, but the fact is that each theatre is different, and the smallest discrepancy can throw the actor for a loop. To have "surprises" on opening night is like being accidentally shot by the starting gun. It's a discrepancy, all right, but makes it harder to win the race. As far as I am concerned, a pox on surprises.

I arrived at four p.m. Moments later, I realized that I had given the cab driver a ten-dollar bill and received thirty-five cents in change. I might as well have hired a limousine. Before passing through the stage door, I decided to get a container of coffee. As I emerged from the little diner, a rotund and red-faced man grasped me by my free hand and complimented me on my face. "You've got one of the best faces in this business, you know that? Terrific eyes. What are you doing these days?" I told him that I was in the play next door and he brightened up considerably. "With Dick Burton? Terrific guy. What a face he's got!" The man had not released my hand and I could feel the bottom of the bag which held my coffee growing damp. "Listen, pal," the man said, "I've fallen on hard times, you know, and I could use some help. I used to be the best juggler in Barnum's circus but there's not much call for that these days. I'm your biggest fan, you know that."

I gave the man a dollar because I began to feel superstitious about my misfortunes. "Give my best to Dick!" he requested, and I assured him that I would.

I entered the theatre and drank my appallingly cold coffee. As I did so, I noticed four or five police who were padding about the backstage area like so many second-story men. A police captain asked me who I was. I told him I was one of the actors. "Watch your step around here," he said gravely. "Someone has planted a bomb." I left to get some more coffee. On my way back to the theatre, a panhandler stopped me and asked me for a quarter. I reached into my pocket and found only a half dollar. I gave it to him, figuring that God would pay me back with a good performance.

After finishing my coffee, I headed straight for the set, ignoring the policemen who hunted beneath the platform for Leon Trotsky's Revenge, and I jogged up and down the staircase a few times. I also shouted a few of my lines to the empty seats out front. Some of the policemen looked up at me as though they thought me mad. As I looked down at *them*, they seemed rather mad to *me*.

I left the stage and bid my *adieux* to the cops. Once I was in the street, I remembered that there was no club soda in my dressing room. Since I knew there would be many visitors, I went to the corner grocery and bought a carton. On the way back, another panhandler accosted me and asked for a dime for a cup of coffee. "Coffee?" I said. "You want a drink is what you want or my name isn't David Belasco." The beggar's eyes blinked twice and he shifted his feet. "That's right, Dave," he said. I gave him a half dollar.

Once I had deposited my mixers next to my booze, I left the theatre again and was immediately confronted by the *first* panhandler. "Look, buddy," I said, "you already cadged half a rock out of me and you can go to hell." He did not wait to hear all of this sentence, but crossed the street as soon as my tone became ominous. I pursued him, however, and gave him another half dollar. As he glanced at the coin and back to my face, I could tell he thought me eccentric. But I knew what I was doing. I was behaving masochistically in order to guarantee an appropriate aggression when the bell for the gladiators rang.

Just before getting into a taxi for home and a nap, I called a press agent I know named Phil Leshin who is too nice a man to be a press agent, even though he is a brilliant press agent. "Phil," I said, "I've given away almost fifteen dollars trying to buy a good performance. Cab driver, panhandlers, and repeaters. What do you think?"

He told me that it wasn't over. "When you go home, there'll

be a beggar in front of your house. When you leave for the theatre again, the same beggar will get another half dollar out of you. When you arrive at the stage door, the same beggar who hit you twice will hit you again. Believe me, friend, it's not over. It won't be over until eleven o'clock."

"Phil," I said, "eleven o'clock always comes."

"And so does seven."

He had me there. I went home and lay down for half an hour. I couldn't sleep but I went through the motions. I left for the theatre at six. As I bade farewell to my wife, who was tactful enough to postpone donning her finery until I had left, my five-year-old son, Adam, asked me where I was going. "I am going downtown," I replied, "to kill some bears." The boy looked at me skeptically. "Not really," he said.

He had me, too. Apparently, everyone had me. I fully expected a troop of Leshin's Beggars to accost me while I tried to hail a taxi. They didn't, though. Sometimes there is God so quickly.

The performance went moderately well and was received in a sophisticated manner by an audience too overdressed to watch *You Can't Take It With You* in comfort. For the benefit of history, I can say only that Richard Burton was vocally strong and emotionally insistent; that Hume Cronyn pleased the crowd; that many of our performers did well; and that I myself was relaxed. Since "relaxed" is one of the most confusing words in the actor's lexicon, let me add that I may merely have been paralyzed. It is said that Katharine Cornell has been all but dragged on stage for an opening night, so terrified was she; that Ruth Gordon has announced for over twenty-five years that she would never again endure an opening night; that Edmund Kean, on the occasion of his "contest" with William Macready, had to be forced onto the stage where he proceeded to "hammer Macready into the ground until only his head showed"; and that to be relaxed on such an occasion is to be half dead. In any case, I decided to be pleased by my "relaxation."

Afterwards, there was a gigantic party at the Rainbow Room, which has but recently become "in." I had hired a limousine for my group and we appeared, dressed to the nines, to face the professional audience, which is a good deal more professional than it is an audience. Immediately upon our entrance, my wife was asked who had made her dress. She replied, "Anne Fogarty," which was a bald-faced lie. My wife was wearing a copy of Jacques Fath by Bloomingdale's, but Anne Fogarty is a personal friend and why not let the *Daily News* print a white lie along with its black ones?

The first familiar face I saw was that of Nancy Berg, who was on the left arm of Sam Spiegel. Miss Berg said to me, "I *saw* you, Billy," and flashed her expert model's smile. Mr. Spiegel looked through me as though I were a script clerk, and the two of them passed on to respective grandeurs. I ran into Lee and Paula Strasberg. Lee looked as though he were reluctantly attending a meeting of the League of Women Voters. Paula was warm and *hamish*, which is her specialty. She said, "I love a good actor," and I decided to accept the remark as a compliment. "I was relaxed tonight, Paula," I said, and she agreed with me. I then told both of them that I was glad to see them there and was, in a way, surprised. "Oh," said Paula gently, "we would never miss a Hamlet." Now *there* is a lady in love. Lee then spoke to me of recent Hamlets, including Donald Madden and George Grizzard.

Peggy Cass quoted Ernest Martin to me: "No direction for this show. Everyone was left to strike out on his own. Hume Cronyn got a triple." Miss Cass then added, "But *you* were good. Cool and greasy. I hated you and I think that's the way it should be."

Bob Fosse came by and asked if I could sing as well as I used to. "Better," I said, fully aware that he had not enjoyed tonight's performance. Much dancing and much drinking followed, to celebrate Shakespeare's birth year. Around 1 a.m., rumors began to circulate about the reviews. All of them were good, said the spies, and some of them sensational. A well-known actor approached me and gripped one of my shoulders. "I've got to tell you something," he said. "When we got the reports down here from Toronto, I thought you'd close out of town. I never heard such black prophecies in my life. It turns out you're the hit of the year. *Hello, Dolly* in blank verse. What do you think of that?"

"There's nothing like a hit," I said.

"Shakespeare's got it, hasn't he?"

"He certainly has."

I downed another glass of champagne as fast as possible. Clem Fowler approached me and said, "Taubman says you were good, but he doesn't mention me." I shrugged and said, "That's because of my billing. No matter what you do in the future, Clem, try to get billed above the title."

Hamlet has opened. Long live *Hamlet*.

William

Epilogue

THE NEW YORK ENGAGEMENT

Dear Bob . . .

It has lived four months in New York and six weeks on the road. A total of 185 "official" performances, setting a new record. We are still playing to absolute capacity at the Lunt-Fontanne and could continue to do so through the coming fall season, but Richard Burton has had enough, and I can't say as I blame him. Edwin Booth played Hamlet for 100 performances. Barrymore stopped at 101, for which some members of the Players' Club never forgave him. Not because he *stopped* but because he didn't stop at 99, out of respect for Booth.

Burton has changed all that. It will be many a moon before

another actor can support so lengthy a run in so demanding a role. Richard will now return to motion pictures, where he earns $500,000 per performance, and where his wife is the highest-paid star in the world.

As for me, I leave within two weeks to begin a 20th Century-Fox film called *Morituri*. My role is small, my dignity minuscule, but my salary is very good indeed. Much have I traveled in the realms of gold, and it's time to take some of it home.

These letters have endeavored to explore what life is all about for the working actor. His problem remains duplex: how to act well, hinged with how to make a living. Motion pictures and filmed television have become the final goal for most actors, since making a consistent living from the New York theatre is plainly impossible. Nor does the gradually improving repertory situation really solve the problem, since most rep engagements are good for no more than two or three seasons—which is just enough time to lower the actor's reputation to freezing in all other cities but the one where he has been playing. The non-theatrical money which New York actors once earned in radio and live television no longer grows on the advertising tree.

Though many things occurred during the New York run of *Hamlet* which could be reasonably set down for posterity, most such events are a matter of public knowledge. But the crowds of two thousand or more which gathered nightly outside the theatre astonished us all, including the Burtons. This was star-gazing at its most intense, as well as patience at its most compulsive. The rubbernecks began gathering around ten p.m. and remained convened until as late as midnight. I never saw one of them desert the vigil until Burton's departure, with or without Elizabeth Taylor. It was as though they were democratically agreed to keep the watch—like those hardy citizens who wait for the electric ball above Times Square to descend on New Year's Eve. They were mule-stubborn and giddy with forbearance. Put to other uses, such mass determination could rule the world.

There was also the Man Who Booed. On the night of Wednesday, May 6, in the year of our Lord 1964, a man seated somewhere in the balcony of the Lunt-Fontanne Theatre loudly booed one of Richard Burton's soliloquies. The sound of a boo is seldom heard in a contemporary Broadway playhouse—not even at curtain calls, let alone in the midst of performance. I once played the leading male role in a play called *Bruno and Sidney*, which both audience and critics loathed with a passion past describing, yet no one booed. They merely stared.

But this uncensored fellow expressed his disapproval in a truly Elizabethan manner. He had both the audacity and the lungs to make himself heard above the applause which followed Richard Burton's whispering fiercely, "The play's the thing wherein I'll catch the conscience of the King!" Mr. Burton exits at this point, all the while pointing an accusative finger at Alfred Drake, who is entering. Alfred is followed by Eileen Herlie, Clem Fowler, and myself. All four of us distinctly heard the boo and my own blood ran truly cold. Several members of the audience shouted "Bravo!" as if to hush the mad obtruder but he straightaway booed again—more loudly than before. By this time, I had picked up a book which is used as a prop in our production. At the sound of the second "Boo!" I dropped the book to the floor, which should prove for all time that I am not a mechanical actor.

Through the remainder of the performance, the man was silent and I assumed he had left the premises. I was mistaken. Richard Burton refused to believe that it was a boo. He maintained that one of the stagehands had hooted at a television program, momentarily forgetting that the curtain was up. Burton was also mistaken. Though it is true that stagehands are sometimes noisy, it is also true that Richard, in the fever of his peak moments, is not likely to hear things so accurately as a man less passionately engaged.

At the conclusion of our play, the principal performers take individual curtain calls. Clem Fowler and I appeared without especial approbation, but there were no boos. Linda Marsh and Robert Milli entered and received their customary applause. John Cullum appeared and was suddenly booed by the same horrific voice that we had heard before. The audience gasped. John laughed. Eileen Herlie strode boldly to her position and bowed. No untoward demonstration. Apparently the fellow in question (he was either alone or his companion had fainted) did not intend to embarrass ladies or secondary players. Alfred Drake appeared to a loud solo boo as well as vigorous applause. Alfred laughed out loud. Brave fellows, Alfred and John—laughing at life's misadventures, like Victor McLaglen and Edmund Lowe. I wouldn't have laughed. Hume Cronyn entered and received his usual sizable hand. No boos.

Richard Burton then lumbered on stage and received an ovation, sliced suddenly through by a boo loud enough to summon cattle. Burton's head trembled and he went pale. As the curtain came down, he ordered the stage manager to leave the curtain up following the next call. He then stepped forward and said, "We have been playing this production in public for over eighty performances. Some have liked it, some have not. But I can assure you—we have never before been booed."

The audience as a whole applauded him wildly but the dauntless chap in the balcony booed even louder than before. Taken altogether, he had delivered himself of six unholy boos, each being more stentorian than the last.

Now a booer, rare though he be, can be evaluated in a number of ways. (1) He is probably drunk, (2) if he isn't drunk, he is likely a frustrated actor, (3) if he is neither, he is certainly a minority, for booing is not a custom among American audiences, (4) he may very well be wrong.

We can only hope that he was wrong, but since the audience as a whole obviously disagreed with him, why explore the matter? For several possible reasons but one in particular. Following the performance, as we were later informed, Richard Burton returned to his Regency Hotel suite and told Mrs. Burton that he had been booed. Mrs. Burton was watching television at the time and said, "So what?" Mr. Burton became agitated and asked her to turn off the television. "Do you understand, my darling, that I have been booed? I played Hamlet tonight and I was *booed!*" Mrs. Burton—being a woman who does not take an individual opinion seriously unless she knows the individual—could not understand her husband's arousal and was reluctant to turn off the program. Mr. Burton then kicked at the screen of the set with sufficient force to shatter the picture tube. Since he was not wearing shoes, he wounded his foot so badly that a physician had to be summoned. A number of stitches were inserted between the first two toes.

Burton arrived at the theatre on the following evening with a decided limp. He insisted on playing the performance with the limp and said, "Some critics have said I play Hamlet like Richard the Third anyway, so what the hell is the difference?" Burton is not only a plucky boyo, he is often very funny indeed. He limped his way through the performance—growling, snarling, and crooning and (in many ways) giving one of the finest performances of the engagement.

During the intermission, a special-delivery letter was presented at his dressing room. Since Burton had earlier asked me to discuss a proposed film version of our production with him that night, Bob Wilson arrived with the letter in the midst of our conversation. Burton looked at Wilson balefully. "Give it to *him*," he said, indicating me with a nod of his head. Wilson smiled and obeyed. "What do you want *me* to do with it?" I asked, auditioning for a scatological reply. "Whatever you wish," Burton said, touching up his make-up. "Throw it away or take it home. Read it to yourself or burn it before my eyes. I don't like special-delivery letters. It is undoubtedly from the booer."

I momentarily felt like Dr. Watson. "How can you possibly assume that?" I asked. "It could be from anybody."

Burton grunted. "It's from the booer," he said.

"Do you really want me to open it?"

"If you wish."

After a short hesitation, I opened the letter. It was from the booer. After reading a few sentences, I was too embarrassed to continue. "It's not right to read any more," I said. "This is for you."

"Then tear it up," Burton said.

I did and that was the end of the matter.

A few days later, I broke two bones in my right hand while trying to knock down one of my dressing room walls. Never mind why, but a remark of Rod Steiger's deserves repeating.

Since I was forced to play Guildenstern with a plaster cast which could be only partially concealed by the sleeve of my jacket, more than one playgoer commented on my injury, which embarrassed me no end. But it remained for Steiger to put a fine point on the matter. He told me that he had no objection to the injury, since Hamlet's contemporaries were all duelists and competitors, but that I could at least have asked my orthopedist to make me a 14th-century cast!

During July, we consigned our production to film, courtesy of a new process called Electronovision. The film version played four performances in a thousand theatres and has grossed (to date) a total of $4,000,000. The financial details of this venture involved a mass screwing of the acting company so excruciatingly delicious that only a separate letter could do the tale justice. Another day. Another diary.

The fundamental question remains: Do actors wish to remain actors? If so—where are they going to act and how? If I have handled the era's most important actors with an unbecoming roughness, it has been necessary to my explorations.

Brando, Lunt, Olivier, Scofield, Burton, Richardson, and Gielgud are all powerful and graceful men who deserve respect and attention. But all actors—as actors—seem to be members of a moribund species. Aztec civilization has nothing on us. The theatre of today is rife with pitfalls while the world of international film is a gigantic flea market in which talents of any dimension are bought and sold like so many cylinders of salami. The money rolls in but the talent rolls out. We are dominated by money men of no talent whatever and we are betrayed by an indolent public.

I am reminded of my original riddle: If a man, in fury, hacking at a piece of wood, constructs thereby the image of a cow, is that beautiful? If not, why not? I still don't know the answer and probably never will, but the question continues to amuse me —through many a restless midnight and many a noon's repose. Joyce maintained that the object of the artist was the creation of something beautiful. Actors don't go in much for beauty these days. They cannot afford to. But beauty is on their minds if they are truly actors, and don't think that it isn't. Otherwise, why become an actor? Why become any sort of artist at all?

As for the technique of how to act well, the late Cedric Hardwicke maintained that actors were born, not made; a few years' experience might transform a so-so player into a fine one, but if the talent did not emerge in full power rather early on, best forget the whole thing. Lee Strasberg, I believe, would disagree, saying that a difference in talent was up to God and nature but that a proper working process could cause anything to happen to any actor. I stand with Strasberg, while also persuaded that a proper working process on a conscious level is, to say the least, elusive.

Having endeavored to summarize the creative and professional situation for the working actor, I am duty-bound to mention that some theatricians question whether there is any use at all in these examinations and probings—these wonderings about technique and the self—as well as the plain, old-fashioned business of getting ahead. Though I am far from proving my case, I obviously believe the effort worth while. Besides, actors may as well ponder life and love and themselves these days, since most of them have more than a little time on their hands. At times I wonder whether acting is not more of a personal psychology than anything else—a system of impulses controlled partly by intuition and partly by will, shaped by the experience of the individual player. Since there seem to be no rules to acting, while there are decided rules to other arts, whether they be broken or bent, and since acting is undeniably intertwined with the personality of the individual, perhaps it would be best to leave all to chance and allow the more natural talents to rise above their less endowed contemporaries as cream rises to the top of the milk bottle.

Perhaps, but I don't think so. I would have to commit philosophical suicide if I did not believe that almost anyone who genuinely wants to act possesses the capacity to be "good" if he makes proper use of his personal resources. The technique of acting has never been defined—not even by Stanislavski—and I believe it to be definable. At any rate, I believe that it should be continually explored. Acting is the most accidental of the arts and contains a mystery which deserves daily examination. If a naturalist can wonder forever at the transformation of caterpillar into moth and the sheer silk left behind, is it surprising that the caterpillar himself should wonder? To say nothing of the moth?

What all actors want, of course, is to move the audience. Does that mean to tears? By no means; tears indicate nothing. To move means to change the position, to alter, to refresh. Though the current production of *Hamlet* offended many while it pleased others, Robert Preston (a splendid actor) was quoted as saying that the production was lacking because the audience didn't cry at the final curtain. "When we did it as a bunch of kids in Pasadena, the audience cried. They cried!" As for me I have cried only once in a theatre; that was at a Palace Theatre screening of *Now, Voyager* starring Bette Davis. When that formidable lady turned to Paul Henreid at the end of the film and said, "Let's not ask for the moon. We have the stars," and the camera pulled back to make both humans small against the sky, I cried my damned eyes out. But if my crying is the proof of great art, I'll eat the handkerchief I used. As director Robert Lewis once said, "If crying were acting, my Aunt Rivke would be Duse." I would add that audience crying is no more indicative of artistic work than Bobby's aunt. Crying is for Bette Davis and Joan Crawford movies. If a large number of people cry at the end of *Hamlet*, I'd venture a guess that the performance was sentimental punk.

Hopefully, I have saved the best for last. Mrs. Alfred Drake, who is an alert and responsible woman, recently watched a performance of *Hamlet* from the fifth row of the divan section. Before her sat two well-dressed ladies in their middle years who were inclined to whisper secrets from the beginning to end of the play. Just before the dueling scene, which comes no more than ten minutes before the end of the nearly four-hour performance, one lady leaned to the other and pointed to Mr. Drake. "Who's that?" she asked. The other replied, "That's Alfred Drake." After a short pause, she added, "He was in *Oklahoma*, you know." Her friend nodded.

Moments later, two young men appeared pushing a wardrobe rack into position. They were clad in mohair sweaters and stood at attention. "Look at *them!*" one lady whispered loudly. "That's Rosencrantz and Frankenstein!"

Since both Clem Fowler and myself had "died" no less than forty-five minutes before, I can only wonder at the minimal impression we'd made on the two ladies. As Clem said to me last week, "I don't want to be a good actor any more. Just a successful one."

Or, as the old actor said to the young, Sic Transit Gloria Mundi, which—freely translated—means: Why don't we get into some other line of work?

Best wishes . . .

William

Afterword

ADAM REDFIELD

"Good my lord, will you see the players well bestowed? Do you hear, let them be well used; for they are the abstract and brief chronicles of the time."—*Hamlet*, Act II, scene ii

Hamlet here is speaking of actors, but *Letters from an Actor* itself is both abstract and brief chronicle. As an actor's timeless "abstract" the book continues to prove its relevance. Since its publication in 1967, *Letters from an Actor* has spent more time out of print than in and yet, year after year, devotees search for copies for themselves and to give as gifts. In our pre-internet days, actors would scour bookstores searching for used copies.

Over the decades, first my father, then my mother, and finally I would get requests for a copy, "any copy you could spare, please." It was not uncommon for performers to tell me that a random chance reading of the book is what made them become actors. About thirty years ago a working actor told me that when he was a young Marine, unsure of what to do after he was discharged, the book was recommended to him by his drill instructor, of all people, in a latrine, of all places. More often than I could have anticipated, people have told me *Letters from an Actor* changed their lives; some read it every year. And now, so many years after its first publication, *Letters from an Actor* has been used as source material for Jack Thorne's play *The Motive and the Cue*.

In *Letters*, my father took acting riddles, predicaments, successes, and failures, and abstracted them timelessly. The actors of 1964, who populate the book, are faced with the same challenges as those of our time and those of Thespis's. If a man in fury accidently creates great art, does that mean technique is irrelevant? Surely technique matters, but then what to make of the accidental work of genius done with no conscious technique? And just what exactly does "technique" mean anyway? Is an exciting theatrical effect worth marring the integrity of a performance? Is the character subordinate to the actor or the actor the character? What if it is both? If so, how can an actor make that balance work? And what effect do the answers to these questions have on the choices the actor must make? What is the proper relationship between actor and director?

Abstract yes, but *Letters from an Actor* is also a brief chronicle. It is a window into the state of American theater two-thirds of the way through the twentieth century: a chronicle of a passing moment, a timebound brief. The time period in which it was written is far in the past. The media landscape in which actors work today is radically different from that of the 1960s. We twenty-first-century readers may reflect on these issues, if we choose: Were English actors really better than American actors? It was a widely held view in 1964 that my father disputed vociferously. Is movie acting really as vapid as is described in *Letters*? My father's opinions about film acting seem almost fanatical now, but a look at what Hollywood was producing in the era makes the opinion seem more measured.

My father's disdain for theater critics is probably still shared by most actors and maybe by the average reader. "The trouble with 99 percent of critics is that they know nothing about the theater. . . . Before disgorging themselves of so many top-hatted judgements, shouldn't our more pretentious young critics learn how to dress a dancer? Or speak one line of dialog before an audience?" So he wrote in a letter to the *New York Times* that accurately reflects his opinion while writing *Letters*. Note, he didn't opine that the critic dress the dancer competently or that the single line of dialog be well-acted, only that the critic actually work in a professional production in a professional capacity.

I know my father would want me to mention three people in particular. My father's editor was Corlies "Cork" Smith. Every word of the book was written by William Redfield, but Cork Smith was a master at distillation and much of the efficiency of the text is due to his mastery. Bob Mills was my father's literary agent and, more importantly, the man to whom all the letters were addressed. Without so receptive a recipient, I'm not sure *Letters* would have held up so well.

Most important of all was my mother. Even after their divorce, my father was enthusiastically inclined to praise her guidance throughout the process. He'd even say, "Your mother wrote the book." At hearing this, my mother would roll her eyes, and correctly so. She wrote none of the book but while my father was exaggerating, he wasn't exactly lying either. My mother had an uncanny ability to keep him focused on the next right point that needed making and picking out the finest parts of his writing and making sure those parts stayed in the final product. An incident occurred at the eleventh hour before publication that demonstrated this perfectly. One last cut was needed, but no one could find anything left to excise, not my father, not Bob Mills, not Cork Smith. But she found it, revealing an elite level of editorial sophistication.

One sad casualty of the publication of *Letters from an Actor* is it seemed to have ended my father's close, decades-long friendship with Marlon Brando. I write "seemed to have ended" because Marlon never gave an explanation either directly or through channels of why he iced my father out of his life. But the timeline suggests it must have been due to the book. After its publication, their only interaction was a brief conversation, six years later, at the wake of their mutual friend Wally Cox. "I'm not going to throw away twenty-five years of friendship," Marlon said. Given that he had already done exactly that, I've always found the remark cryptic. Was Brando gaslighting my father? Had Brando compartmentalized his world so thoroughly he was oblivious to the obvious untruth of his remark? Was he implying that it was my father, not he, who had thrown away twenty-five years of friendship by writing *Letters from an Actor*?

If the last option is correct, then Marlon Brando never read a word my father wrote about him, though he had had opportunities to do so stretching back two and a half years. An advance reader's copy of *Letters* was sent to him. Prior to that, it was sent to him in galley form. And prior to that, my father either sent or handed off personally every page on which Marlon or his career was mentioned. Marlon never said a word, let alone raised an objection. Had he read the book, he'd see no confidences were betrayed and, apart from acknowledging their friendship, nothing personal published.

There are two points worth making here: *Letters from an Actor* is about the state of American acting in the post–World War II era. One can no more write on that topic and leave out Brando's career than one can write about the state of baseball in the 1920s and leave out Babe Ruth's. Moreover, my father's opinions about Brando's career were the consensus in the New York theater community of the 1960s and opinions exactly like those in *Letters from an Actor* were expressed frequently, in print and otherwise, including by Marlon Brando himself! There was nothing unexpected about my father's take. Being abandoned by so close a friend broke my father's heart. It did Marlon no good either. And it was all for nothing.

The motive and the cue for this afterword of mine is the reissue of *Letters from an Actor* and the motive and the cue for that is Jack Thorne's play, *The Motive and the Cue.* (In addition to my father's book, *The Motive and the Cue* drew on material from another book: Richard Sterne's invaluable *John Gielgud Directs Richard Burton in* Hamlet: *A Journal of Rehearsals*.)

The play's title is taken from Hamlet's "rogue and peasant slave" soliloquy. Hamlet has just seen an actor burst into sobs while performing a monologue, an actor acting from a script. Hamlet, on the other hand, has a real-life problem so grave it involves a visit from the dead and the murder of a king. Hamlet wonders how much more emotional this actor would get if he had a real-life problem as bad as Hamlet's own. "What would he do had he the motive and the cue for passion that I have?"

Letters from an Actor ponders this exact question: "The spine of a role is the motive (the intellect, the reason); the juice is the cue for passion—the inner switch which ignites the heart. Though we color ourselves with limps and canes, with green umbrellas and purple suits, we cannot escape the motive and the cue."

To live up to its title, *The Motive and the Cue* needs a central conflict. This conflict is found in the interplay among the characters of John Gielgud, Richard Burton, and Elizabeth Taylor. The motive in Mr. Thorne's mind (intellect, reason) must place the action within that trio and those characters must provide the cue (the juice, the passion). Nothing must distract from the motive and the cue.

Ah, but many of the play's themes come from Redfield's riddles found in *Letters*. So, a secondary character, William Redfield, must be on hand to serve up the riddles. And this leads me to the question I am most often asked about *The Motive and the Cue*: "What do you think of the William Redfield character?"

The *real* William Redfield can be found in *Letters from an Actor* and he's complicated, clever, explosive, funny, even at times outrageous. For Jack Thorne's play to work, the complex character of the author of *Letters from an Actor* needed to be tamed. For Mr. Thorne to have attempted to write so complicated a Redfield as Redfield wrote himself would draw focus from the play's center: Gielgud/Burton/Taylor.

So, I believe, Jack Thorne faced a dilemma. How to retain Redfield's riddles while keeping him under control? (I speak only as a member of the audience with no actual connection to the play.) I believe Thorne solved this by creating a Redfield who is the world's most eager acting student. The William Redfield character of *The Motive and the Cue* is a lot like the real-life William Redfield of 1947, a twenty-year-old charter member of the Actors Studio. Yet, he is nothing like the thirty-seven-year-old Redfield of 1964. And that gets it exactly right. Jack Thorne wrote a multilayered, entirely realized secondary character who serves the play precisely as he must. And, it just so happens, the playwright named the character William Redfield.

For me, there is a lovely coincidence on this point that occurred to me as I watched the play. When addressed by his first name in *The Motive and the Cue*, the Redfield character is always called "William." Yet in life, my father was never called William. Oddly, it was the only version of his name no one ever used. Most of the time he was "Billy," though many called him "Bill." There was the occasional "Will" or even "Willy." But no one, absolutely no one ever, called him "William."

I know my father would be delighted by *The Motive and the Cue*. It is an intelligent, exciting play, a wondrous love letter to theater and art in general. Sam Mendes's incisive direction of the actors leads to fascinating and poignant performances, and he moves the play from scene to scene and moment to moment seamlessly.

It would be presumptuous of me to suggest any changes to *Letters*. Then again, if a fellow can't be presumptuous towards his dad, whom can he be presumptuous towards? There are four or five minor changes I would make and I suppose I'm entitled to point out that one of those is that my father got my age wrong in one anecdote. I was four years old at the time, not five. And, if I could have softened one remark in the book, it would be a crack about another actor (a fine actor not in the Gielgud/Burton production) who had recently played Hamlet in New York. But the rest is silence.